OLD TIES, NEW ATTACHMENTS
Italian-American Folklife in the West

OLD TIES,

Italian-

NEW ATTACHMENTS

American Folklife in the West

edited by **David A. Taylor**

and **John Alexander Williams**

LIBRARY OF CONGRESS

WASHINGTON 1992

STUDIES IN AMERICAN FOLKLIFE NO. 5

Library of Congress Cataloging in Publication Data

Old ties, new attachments : Italian-American Folklife in the West / edited by David
  A. Taylor and John Alexander Williams.
      p.   cm.—(Studies in American folklife; no. 5)
  Includes bibliographical references.
  ISBN 0-8444-0753-4
    1. Italian Americans—West (U.S.)—History.2. Italian Americans—
West (U.S.)—Social life and customs.   3. West (U.S.)—History.
4. West (U.S.)—Social life and customs.   I. Taylor, David Alan,
1951–   II. Williams, John Alexander, 1938–   III. Series.
F596.3.I8T54   1992
978′.00451—dc20   92-11572
                                                  CIP

For sale by the American Folklife Center
Library of Congress
Washington, D.C. 20540-8100

Design: Adrianne Onderdonk Dudden

Old Ties, New Attachments: Italian-American Folklife in the West
accompanies an exhibition of the same name that opens in Santa Clara,
California, October 12, 1992, and travels to four other sites:

   de Saisset Museum, Santa Clara University, Santa Clara, California
   The Nevada Museum of Art, Reno, Nevada
   The Gene Autry Western Heritage Museum, Los Angeles, California
   The Museums at Stony Brook, Stony Brook, New York
   The Library of Congress, Washington, D.C.

Women arrange dishes of food on the Saint Joseph's Day table at the Shrine of St. Therese church, Pueblo, Colorado, March 19, 1990. Photograph by Myron Wood, IAW-MW-B002-25

CONTENTS

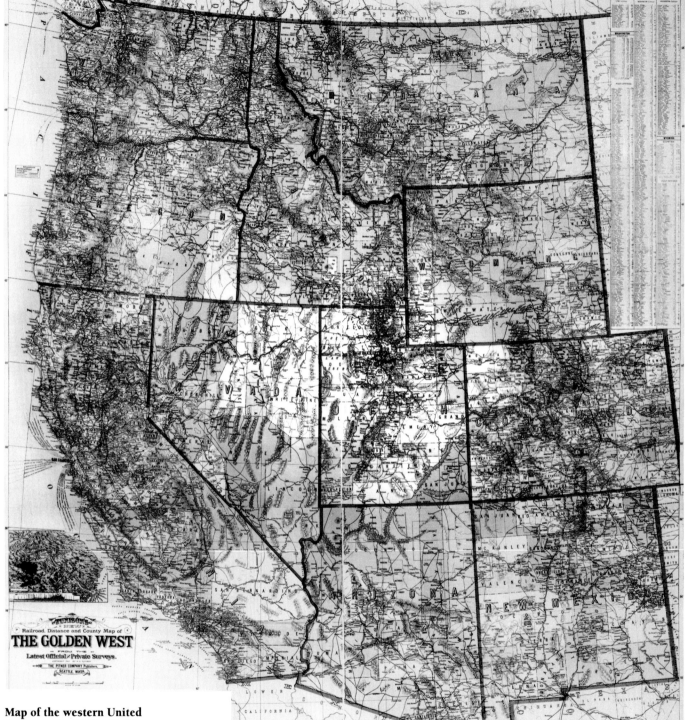

Map of the western United States, early 1900s. Field research for the Italian-Americans in the West Project was conducted in five states: California, Colorado, Nevada, Utah, and Washington. Geography and Map Division, Library of Congress

PREFACE

Most Americans associate Italian-American life, history, and culture with the urban East, but an important and much less understood aspect of Italian-American history is to be found in the American West. In the mid-nineteenth century, large numbers of Italian immigrants settled in California and other Western states. They brought with them a number of cultural skills and arts—agricultural techniques, wine culture, stone masonry, and many others. More than most people realize, these Italian-Americans helped shape the cultural landscape of the modern West.

The story of Italian-Americans in the West, particularly their impact on the cultural landscape of the western United States, was the focus of a major project undertaken by the American Folklife Center, the federal agency created by act of Congress in 1976 to preserve and present American folklife, the traditional expressive culture shared by the various groups in the United States. Titled "Italian-Americans in the West," the Center's project envisioned an exhibition that would open in October 1992 and travel to various sites around the country, and the publication of a collection of essays. The project, which began in 1989, was undertaken in order to commemorate the 500th anniversary of the voyage of Christopher Columbus and is part of a larger program on the Quincentenary sponsored by the Library of Congress.

Why focus on Italian-Americans in the West? To answer this question one must go back to 1980 when the American Folklife Center, in keeping with its mission to preserve and present folk cultural traditions, undertook a field project to document the ranching culture of Paradise Valley, Nevada.

The conceptual framework of the project focused on the ethnic components of a well-known occupational culture, that of the American cowboy, or, to use the Nevada version of the Spanish word *vaquero,* the "buckaroo." The fieldwork team expected to find Hispanic buckaroos in Paradise Valley, both of Mexican cultural background and also of the Basque ethnic group that represents the West's largest immigration direct from Iberia since Spanish colonial times. They also expected to find Anglo ranchers and cowhands, primarily representing a cul-

Map of Italy showing its contemporary administrative divisions. Geography and Map Division, Library of Congress

Loui Cerri moving cattle at his ranch in Paradise Valley, Nevada, 1978. Photograph by William Wilson, NV-30-19354-30A

tural background that has its roots in the ranching country of Texas, as well as Native American cowhands largely descended from the Paiute people. To their surprise, the team found one other group: Italian-Americans. These Paradise Valley Italian-Americans were ranching families as well as townspeople in Paradise and the nearby trading town of Winnemucca. They were third- and fourth-generation descendants of immigrants who had come from a cluster of neighboring valleys in the Piedmontese Alps of Northern Italy. They have left a significant mark on the Paradise Valley landscape in the form of stone buildings derived from the vernacular architecture of the Italian Alps, adapted to the uses of the ranching culture of the western United States.

In the 1980 book and exhibition that resulted from this project, both titled *Buckaroos in Paradise,* the emphasis was on occupational culture. But these represented only a small fraction of the materials generated by this and similar field projects conducted by the Folklife Center. An enormous corpus of data was produced in the form of tape-recorded interviews, fieldnotes, still photo-graphs, and motion pictures, and, in the long run, these materials are of great importance since they became part of the Library of Congress collections, available for researchers in the future. And so, after the Paradise Valley project ended and the exhibition was dismantled, there remained a wealth of information on the region's Italian-Americans.

Thus, when it came time for the Folklife Center, along with other departments within the Library, to devise a project for its contribution to the commemoration of the Quincentenary, the Center's director, Alan Jabbour, decided to build on these holdings. Instead of choosing a single location for additional field research (an approach that characterizes most of the Center's previous projects), he determined that multiple research sites were appropriate, since this approach would allow researchers to map the cultural intersections of ethnic and regional history more successfully.

But which sites, among the multitude of western communities where Italian-Americans live today, should be chosen for field research? In addressing this question, the Center's researchers realized that there is not simply one West, but several. For example, there is the West of the Great Plains and the Great Basin—the one Hollywood has taught us to think of as the "Old West." But there is also the "oasis west," which engages in intensive and highly specialized agriculture on irrigated land. There is the urban West, which, along with the West Coast, includes a complex of maritime institutions and cultures as well as the usual array of urban cultural groups. And there is the mining West that spreads eastward from California in its hard-rock manifestations and westward from Pennsylvania and Appalachia in its coal mining phase. Clearly, these subregions are based on an economic definition of the West. The West can also be interpreted culturally on the basis of ethnic mixtures and ethnic enclaves. However, the critical fact is that Italian-Americans are found in all Western economic and cultural subregions.

The selection of research sites was made on the basis of cultural and economic definitions of the West, choosing communities where Italian-Americans have long been associated with the distinctive economies of the regions. Field research in 1989 focused on the maritime community of San Pedro, California; the agricultural community of Gilroy, in California's Santa Clara Valley; several mining and ranching communities in central and eastern Nevada; and the agricultural valley surrounding Walla Walla, Washington. In 1990, fieldwork was conducted in the coal mining district of Carbon County, Utah, and the city of Pueblo, Colorado, where Italian-Americans have long been involved in steel production and truck gardening. Additional research, ongoing since 1989, was concerned with publications, records, photographs, and other documents, concerning Italian-Americans in the West, that are located in the collections of the Library of Congress, the National Archives, universities, and historical societies.

Although fieldworkers devoted attention to Italian-American involvement with the distinctive occupations of these regions, occupations which, in most cases, were the magnets attracting initial Italian settlement, they also documented many other aspects of contemporary Italian-American culture. More than simply recording the expressive dimensions of the daily lives of Italian-Americans in individual communities, researchers addressed over-arching questions. For example, foodways research illuminated the important role food traditions play in the assertion of Italian-American identity, with particular reference to connections between family and community traditions. Of special interest were the wide array of food-related economic activities in which Italian-American immigrants and their children specialized in Western cities and farming districts, and the creation of a recognizable set of "pan-Italian" foodways and their incorporation into the general American diet and culinary culture. The investigation of

Andy Briguglio of San Pedro, California, prepares to bake the first pizza in a *forno* he constructed in his backyard. Photograph by David A. Taylor, IAW-DT-B008-20

Girls dressed as angels ride on a float carrying a statue of Santa Rosalia, during the annual Santa Rosalia Festival at Monterey, California, September 10, 1989. Photograph by Ken Light, IAW-KL-B107-27

or has it shaped them? These are the central questions the Center's researchers were asking. More than just validating the cultural expressions growing out of the Italian experience in America, one of the primary results of the project—expressed through this book, the exhibition, and the archival collection—will be to provide present-day Italian-Americans with an enriched sense of personal connections with an authentic past.

stonework by Italian-Americans led to a better understanding of the diffusion of immigrant artisans and their integration into areas of Western life not usually perceived as being "ethnic," illustrated the continuity and modification of traditional arts and associated values brought from Italy, and showed the interrelationship of folk art and fine art within the Italian tradition. Research in coal and precious metal mining communities shed light on the role Italian immigrant labor played in building extractive industries, and revealed family and cultural connections between Italian-American settlements in the West, their counterparts in the mining areas of the East, and the home communities in Italy. And the study of community-based sacred and secular festivals disclosed continuity and change of old-world traditions, as well as the emergence of syncretic pan-Italian forms (including Columbus Day) drawn from the popular cultures of the United States and Italy.

Are the informants contacted in the project's study communities Italians or Westerners or both? Have they shaped the contemporary culture of their Western subregion,

O ne of the principal products of the American Folklife Center's Italian-Americans in the West Project is a large quantity of data collected by its field researchers during 1989 and 1990. These data, used in the development of this book and the Quincentenary exhibition, consist of over 300 hours of tape-recorded interviews with Italian-Americans and other residents of the study communities; approximately 24,000 black-and-white and color photographic images, and some 35 hours of videotape documenting many aspects of informants' lives; approximately 2,000 pages of researchers' fieldnotes, photo and tape catalogs; and assorted ephemera collected in the study communities. All these materials are housed in the Center's Archive of Folk Culture at the Library of Congress in Washington, where they are available to researchers. For more information about the contents of the collection and the policies related to its use by researchers, contact: American Folklife Center, Library of Congress, Washington, D.C. 20540-8100.

Notes and captions accompanying the essays in this volume frequently include the accession numbers for specific photographs, tape recordings, and fieldnotes in the project's collection. The prefix "IAW" in the number indicates that these items are part of the Italian-Americans in the West collection.

ACKNOWLEDGMENTS

The American Folklife Center deeply appreciates the kind cooperation of scores of Italian-Americans and other residents of the communities where field research was conducted. Although it is impossible to list the names of everyone who assisted in one way or another, a list of the names of those who provided contributions begins on page 210.

The American Folklife Center gratefully acknowledges major financial support received from:

Henry Salvatori
John Ben Snow Memorial Trust
Dell Computer
R.R. Donnelley & Sons Company
Pacific Western Bank

and special thanks for the leadership and valued financial assistance of

Murphy Sabatino Chair, Northern California Committee
Countess Angela Dandini Chair, Nevada Committee
Rollan Melton Vice Chair, Nevada Committee

Alpine Insurance Associates
Dave and Inky Amoroso
Bank of America Foundation
Philip C. Barbaccia family
Famiglia Filiberto C. Feroni de Bellavista
Bruno and Edna Benna
Leonard and Helen Isola Buck
Edward S.J. Cali
Natale A. Carasali
Earl and Wanda Casazza
Aldo and Madeleine Chiappero
El Dorado Hotel Casino
Dominic and Virginia Fanelli
Mr. and Mrs. Clarence Ferrari
Mr. and Mrs. Frank Filippi
First Interstate Bank of Nevada
Mary Ellen and Michael Fox
Famiglia Nello Gonfiantini, Jr.
Nello Gonfiantini III

Home Federal Bank of Nevada
Vincenzo and Natalina Isola Family
Arthur K. and Agnieszka Winkler Lund
In memory of Mariano and Concettina
    Lo Bue
James P. Maccora
Mr. and Mrs. Bert Mantelli
Mr. and Mrs. Henry Mantelli
Mr. and Mrs. Stanley Mountford
Nevada Bell
Pasta by Costa Macaroni
    Manufacturing, Co., Inc.
Mr. and Mr. Donald Perrucci
Rancadore and Alameda: in memory of
    Sal J. and Ignatius Rancadore
Roy J. and Jean M. Sanfilippo
Scolari's Food and Drug Company
Bruno and Frances Selmi
Elizabeth Stout

INTRODUCTION
Regionalism and Ethnicity
JOHN ALEXANDER WILLIAMS

In assessing the balance of cultural continuity and change among Italian-Americans, due regard should be paid to regional and even local variations in the Italian backgrounds of their immigrant ancestors. From late Roman times until the last third of the nineteenth century, Italy remained a territory of city-states and small duchies and kingdoms. In Metternich's contemptuous phrase, Italy was merely "a geographic expression," and Italian national unity was elusive, even after political unity was achieved under the Piedmontese royal house of Savoy and reinforced by the twenty-year fascist dictatorship of Benito Mussolini.

While standard Italian based on the Tuscan dialect emerged as a written language at the time of Dante, it was not a widely spoken language until after World War II; even educated people preferred to converse in their regional dialects. Regional differences were reinforced by the mountainous terrain of the peninsula and its adjacent islands and by the lack of a dominant metropolis such as London or Paris. Rome, Milan, Naples, Turin, Venice, Florence, Genoa, and Palermo have each played important roles in the formation of modern Italy, and even today the country's urban network more closely resembles the decentralized network of the United States than the centralized cultural regimes of other West European states.

Only since World War II, with the growth of popular democratic institutions and of national transportation and communications networks has Italian cultural unity been achieved. And yet, it is also worth noting that regionalism in Italy has not yet spawned separatism, as it has in Britain, France, and especially Spain. Apart from small linguistic enclaves along the French and Austrian borders, Italy presents a complex picture of ethnic unity amid regional diversity.

The transformation of Italian-Americans from immigrants to ethnics parallels—in time, and to some extent in character—the transformation of Italy from a geographical expression to a modern state. Only a relatively small number of experts and political refugees among the immigrants brought with them a significant sense of Italian nationalism. The *campanilismo* (suspicion of anyone born outside the village) that affected the outlooks of Italian villages was reproduced to some extent in the village-based clusters found in big American cities, notably in the form of *feste* in honor of the patron saint of an ancestral village. But except in New York City, immigrants from a particular village were not numerous enough for *campanilismo* to serve as a principle of social organization, and so the earliest forms of community organization followed regional lines.[1]

Emigration from northern Italy to France, North Africa, and South America preceded mass migration to the United States, and northern emigration generally

Winnemucca, Nevada, cattle rancher Joe Boggio with some California zinfandel grapes he uses to make wine. Photograph by Howard W. Marshall, NV-25-20656-5

Third-generation miner Joe Carpine, manager of the Twin Pines #2 mine in Rockvale, Colorado. Photograph by Ken Light, IAW-KL-B289-22A.

Italian immigrant settlers Mr. and Mrs. John Forgone at their ranch in Paradise Valley, Nevada. Courtesy of Loui Cerri, NV 23739

preceded emigration from southern Italy (where, in turn, a generation of internal migration preceded emigration abroad). Most Anglo-Americans were aware of the distinction between northern and southern Italians, and this distinction gained force from the official classification of immigrants into one or the other group upon entry to the United States. However, immigration officials usually lumped Liguria with Sicily and other southern regions, despite the fact that the Ligurian capital, Genoa, lies considerably to the north of Tuscany and other "northern" classifications. Apparently the distinction was drawn on racist lines between lighter and darker-skinned immigrants, and the Ligurians—doubtless as a result of the seafaring traditions that took them to all corners of the Mediterranean— apparently looked swarthier than the Anglo-American notion of what a northern Italian should look like allowed.

Regional organizations, mostly mutual benefit insurance organizations or devotional societies organized within larger Catholic parishes, were the first building blocks of Italian-American ethnic identity in

U.S. communities. But by the 1890s, there were Italian-American leaders who could no longer find in regional mobilization sufficient scope for their ambitions. Businessmen and politicians had the most to gain from mobilizing a sense of pan-Italian ethnicity. Promoting pan-Italian ethnic solidarity among Italian and Italian-American small proprietors and wage-workers led to the formation of interregional business institutions in San Francisco, such as the Colombo Market and the Bank of Italy (later Bank of America), and created a bigger labor force that manufacturing and agribusiness leaders such as Marco Fontana (Del Monte) and Pietro Rossi (Italian Swiss Colony) were ready to exploit. The mobilization of Italian-American voters in San Francisco increased the city-wide influence of ethnic politicians, while the entire community was galvanized by the political debate generated by the rise of fascism in Italy.[2]

The Italian language press was yet another secular promoter of ethnic identity as it evolved during the late nineteenth and early twentieth centuries from compilations of reports of regional matters to a focus on pan-Italian issues and organizations. Meanwhile, fraternal organizations, such as mutual benefit societies, organized originally along regional lines, evolved into federated membership organizations, such as the Italian Catholic Federation or the Order of the Sons of Italy in America, whose local lodges developed around the nuclei of the original regional clubs.

Judged by the success of Italian-founded California corporations and San Francisco area politicians, the efforts to promote pan-Italian sentiment among later immigrants and their children were successful, but after World War II both the corporations and Italian-American wage-earners and voters merged into the regional mainstream. By the 1980s, a well-delineated system of ethnic brokerage had evolved in the Bay Area, but only a relatively small number of people actually made their living as brokers. Chiefly the leadership of pan-Italian organizations fell in the postwar era to men, such as the owners of food-related businesses or independent professionals, who could increase their customers and clients through the continued promotion of Italian-American ethnicity.

Italian-American fishermen baiting up trawl lines at San Francisco, 1940. Prints and Photographs Division, Library of Congress, OWI LC-USW3-94 2162

Three notable aspects of expressive culture derive from the organized promotion of pan-Italian ethnicity during the first half of this century. One was the reinvention of Christopher Columbus as an ethnic hero and of Columbus Day as an amalgam of a traditional Italian saint's day festival and an Anglo-American patriotic ceremony. The second was the development of a repertoire of popular music drawn both from Italian art music and from Neapolitan vaudeville as well as from folk music. The third was the development of the pasta-and-pizza restaurant cuisine known to (and adopted by)

Chef in an Italian restaurant at San Francisco's North Beach, December 8, 1941. Farm Security Administration photograph by John Collier, Prints and Photographs Division, Library of Congress, USF34-81839-E

Anglo-Americans as "Italian food." Today these interrelated pan-Italian festival, music, and food complexes are significant components of Italian-American ethnic identity, both within and outside of the ethnic community. Further research in each of these areas may illuminate the processes of cultural construction, both as they involve negotiation between the Italian-American minority and the host culture and the fusion of folk cultural elements with elements drawn from the popular and elite segments of organized cultural life.

The "re-Italianization" of Christopher Columbus at the end of the nineteenth century is the subject of the concluding essay in this volume. Suffice it to say here that Italian-American leaders who saw a need to build bridges over the many fractures within their community found in Columbus an American national hero superbly suited to their needs. While his reinvention as an ethnic hero began in eastern cities such as New York and Philadelphia, Italian-Americans in the West made significant contributions to this process. The holiday and its associated practices and artifacts remain an important cultural landmark for

many Italians in the region. For example, when during the recent restoration of California's Gold Rush era capitol in Sacramento architects proposed eliminating an anachronistic Columbus statue that had been installed in the capitol rotunda under Anglo-American auspices in 1882, Italian-American politicians and organizations raised a storm of protest, forcing the reinstallation of the statue.

The emergence of a pan-Italian musical repertoire is more difficult to trace, but the historical record provides tantalizing clues to a process of borrowing from folk, art, military, and popular music sources. Walt Whitman's "Italian Music in Dakota," referring to strains of Verdi played by a military band the poet heard at a fort on the Missouri River in the 1880s, derives from an era when most of the bandmasters and many of the musicians posted at forts throughout the western states were drawn from the ranks of Italian experts.[3] Carla Bianco noted in *The Two Rosetos*[4] that many of the Italian-American males in Roseto, Pennsylvania, belonged to that town's brass band, which entertained at community functions and competed on a regional basis in contests with other bands from similar communities.

Local histories contain photographs of brass bands in Italian-American coal mining communities in Utah and Washington State, and they were probably widespread in other western states.[5] Sidney Robertson Cowell recorded mandolinists and other Italian folk music performers in fishing communities on San Francisco Bay during the 1930s, while commercial recordings were made of individual mandolinists and of Italian string orchestras.[6] Mandolin bands apparently remain a popular form of Italian-American music making in the Bay Area and probably elsewhere in the West. Russ Colombo, the Italian-American singer who perfected the "crooning" popular music style later made famous by Bing Crosby, Frank Sinatra, Vic Damone, and Tony Bennett, was from Washington State (as was Crosby, the only non-Italian on the list). Bianco found the belief widespread among Italian-Americans that Italians had actually "invented" music, while the typical *prominenti* accounts of Italian-American community history often emphasize associations with famous Italian operatic performers such as Enrico Caruso, Adelina Patti, and Luisa Tetrazini. Yet Louis M. Martini refers in his oral history to a "secondary opera" in San Francisco where poor Italian-Americans who could not afford to attend Caruso performances went to hear the music they loved.[7]

A historian of San Francisco Italians notes that vaudeville performers flowed from Naples to the Bay Area along the same route that linked San Francisco immigrant banks to the Bank of Naples and food importers and travel agents to their Italian trading partners.[8] While folk music and operatic traditions contributed to the pan-Italian repertoire, probably the Neapolitan music hall of the early twentieth century was the greatest single source of the music that Italian-Americans—and Anglo-Americans—today think of as uniquely Italian.

Neapolitan commerce probably also had a formative influence on what (until recently, at least) most Americans think of today as "Italian food"—pizza, pasta, red sauces, and cheap red wine. According to one source, American pizza—generically a derivative of the flat bread and *conpanatico* that has existed in some form or another in Italy since Roman times—derives from a dish specially produced in 1890 incorporating the colors of the Italian national flag (red sauce, white mozzarella cheese, and green garnishes) to celebrate the annual residence of the Piedmontese royal house in Naples as required by the kingdom's consti-

Margherita Briguglio of San Pedro, California, cooks chicken cutlets for her family in the "second kitchen" in the Briguglio's garage, July 1989. She uses this kitchen to prevent the smell of cooking oil from permeating the house when fried foods are prepared. Photograph by David A. Taylor, IAW-DT-B008-10

tution. As for pasta, the few folklorists who have investigated its Italian-American foodways disagree as to the reasons for its Americanization. Bianco found that the use of pasta in Pennsylvania differed from Italian precedents only in the more frequent use of richer sauces and the adaptation of forms, such as lasagna, which had not been part of her informants' Apulian regional repertoire.[9]

But Toni Fratto, another Pennsylvania researcher, found that her informants used pasta more frequently and more as a staple in America than had been the case in the southern Italian regions from which they or their immigrant parents had come. Fratto attributes this to the more limited availability in America of the vegetable staples that peasants had grown in Italy, an explanation that may hold true for Philadelphia and other urban or industrial communities but probably would not hold true for California and other western locations where Italian-American private and commercial gardening was established.[10] Food researchers in Utah found that some more exotic food choices persisted among Italian-Americans as a kind of "ethnic performance," especially in the use of organ meats and other animal parts that Anglo-Americans found distasteful.[11] Regional specialties, such as the Ligurian pesto sauce and the Sicilian use of anchovies, may also have served as badges of regional identity within Italian-American communities and households.

Household foodways do not tell us as much about the creation of pan-Italian restaurant cuisines. The evolution of "Italian" restaurants beyond the boarding house and neighborhood clienteles paralleled the creation of other pan-Italian institutions and cultural expressions. This evolution took the form of a simplification of food types (such as the elimination of organ meats from menus and the more central importance of pasta and tomato sauces) and the expansion of menus from a regional to a pan-Italian repertoire. Another marker was the adop-

Frankie Briguglio (Margherita's son) proudly displays the first pizza baked in his family's new *forno*, an outdoor oven built by his father. Photograph by David A. Taylor, IAW-DT-B008-27

tion of a red-white-and-green presentation aesthetic comparable to the one embodied in the Neapolitan pizza. Finally, both commercial and household Italian-American tastes became "Americanized" through the use of more meat, less garlic and other spices, and lighter oils. And like Columbus Day and "Italian" music, pan-Italian restaurant cuisine became both an internally proclaimed badge of ethnic identity and one recognized and widely admired by non-Italians as well.[12]

The transformation of the deep town lots of eastern Pennsylvania, in a place such as Roseto, for example, into Italian fruit and vegetable gardens represented a consistent marker of Italian ethnicity, found everywhere that they settled. But foodways hold a special place in Italian-American history in the West due to the stimuli to commercial truck gardening provided by the characteristic urban-oasis pattern of western settlement and by the suitability of favorite Italian foods to the complex of large-scale commercial farming institutions we know today as "agribusiness." Italian *prominenti* such as Angelo Pellegrini, an immigrant who grew up to become a literature professor and university president in Washington State, waxes poetic in his memoirs about Italian gardens, cooking, and winemaking in a benign climate, while the autobiographies of California winemakers such as Louis M. Martini and Robert Mondavi illustrate some of the ways in which immigrant-based food businesses have led to successful agribusiness careers.[13]

Italian immigrants, like many others from nineteenth-century Europe, were peasants, but unlike many, they expected to go back to the land after making money in America. Thus they clung to traditional food habits for more reasons than the usual peasant conservatism. Traditional Italian peasant food consisted chiefly of wheat in the form of bread or pasta, accompanied by as much *conpanatico* (accompaniment of bread) as family resources and the local environment could provide. When they could get or afford it, Italians ate meats, fowl, and vegetables widely known in other parts of Europe, and they had taken to American-derived foods such as tomatoes and corn-meal long before they began to migrate to the United States.

But the distinctiveness of Italian-American food consumption derived from other ingredients: flat breads (such as *foccacio*); a large and regionally ordered variety of pastas, sausages, and cheeses; an array of vegetables and spices little known outside of the Mediterranean region (such as eggplant, artichoke, broccoli, basil, and oregano); salted fish varieties such as anchovies, sardines, and cod; and, above all, the more exotic elements (to Anglo-American tastes) of the classical Mediterranean triad of wheat, grape, and olive, namely olive oil and wine.

The Anglo-American diet was richer but seemed blander to Italian immigrants, and Italian food had the advantage of being cheaper as well as more appealing to immigrant palates. Their diet may have been exotic by Anglo-American standards, but the numbers of Italian immigrants were sufficient in most American cities to ensure a profitable demand for products that had to be imported, such as olive oil, or that could be manufactured cheaply enough to supplant home manufacture, which was the case with dried pasta.

Wherever they could in the United States, Italian immigrants established kitchen gardens to grow the vegetables, fruits, and spices they could not buy in American stores; in settlements of any size, this provided opportunities for truck gardening, often on small bits of land leased cooperatively on the outskirts of cities, or, as in the California valleys north, south, and

east of San Francisco Bay, on the less productive fringes of rich agricultural districts where Italians had initially come as seasonal stoop laborers. In smaller cities, such as Denver, Italian truck gardeners peddled their produce themselves door-to-door at the turn of the century. In San Francisco, the volume of business was sufficiently large to justify an Italian produce market, the Colombo Market, organized in 1874 and run cooperatively by commission agents who had sprung up to act as middlemen between urban consumers and the gardeners and farmers who had become established in the districts surrounding the city.

In places such as California's Central Valley or the Walla Walla region of southeastern Washington, Italian immigrant growers developed specialty crop niches in emerging agribusiness districts already established by Anglo-American entrepreneurs. In Walla Walla, as Jens Lund's article in this volume relates, Italian growers specialized in onions, while in the Central Valley, they specialized in grapes and "coarser vegetables" such as cabbages, broccoli, and cauliflower. In neither area were Italians very active in the wheat and related grain or fruit production that had introduced the large-scale market-oriented rural economic order now known as agribusiness.

Italian truck gardening, though often initiated by groups of single men working leased land cooperatively, usually became a family enterprise. But the fact that most Italian immigrants were young men without families, at least in their initial migration to the United States, created other food-related business opportunities. Those men who did have families often established boarding houses; Italian boarding house keepers (nearly always women) thus became restaurateurs of sorts, but independently operated restaurants and saloons soon followed. Food service thus joined production, distribution, and manufacturing as typically Italian-American business enterprises. In San Francisco, the economies of scale were such that entrepreneurs originally confined to the Italian immigrant community, or even to a regional segment of it, eventually built their businesses into major corporations, such as the Italian Swiss Colony in wine production, Del Monte Corporation in food canning, the DiGiorgio enterprises in fruit and vegetable growing and canning, the Ghirardelli Company in candymaking, the Petri family enterprises in tobacco manufacturing and winemaking, and A. P. Giannini's Bank of America (which originated as the Bank of Italy to handle immigrant remittances but grew toward its modern scale as the financier of Italian-American agribusiness).[14]

The complicated connection between traditional Italian and modern Italian-American foodways is also evident in the history of California winemaking. Italian immigrants made wine at home everywhere in the United States where they could grow or acquire grapes. Moreover, since Italian wine drinkers were afflicted neither with the drunkenness or with the recurrent bouts of prohibitionism that periodically swept Anglo-American and other Protestant ethnic groups, Italian and Italian-American saloon-keepers (along with hotel and restaurant owners) were common in western towns and cities throughout the late nineteenth and early twentieth centuries.

California provided special scope to winemakers, but initially Italians were more important as grape growers and wine consumers than as manufacturers.[15] Before 1918, California wine was predominantly bulk wine and the industry was dominated by distributors rather than producers. Thus while the Italian Swiss Colony had been started as a cooperative venture for poor immigrants by the San Francisco banker Andrea Sbarbaro, it succeeded commercially as a private corporation whose stock was quietly acquired by a non-Italian distributor, the California Wine Association. Most Italian-American farmers and householders continued to make wine, and those who also ran boarding houses, restaurants, or saloons sometimes sold the product commercially as well. In either case, Italian-American wine was coarse, traditional peasant wine, universally known as "Dago Red," the sort of drink with which ancestors had washed down bread and its accompaniment for generations but a far cry from the fine wines for which immigrant offspring like Robert Mondavi would one day be famous.

The coming of Prohibition in 1918 changed all this. Home winemaking remained legal, but commercial winemaking did not. An unexpected result was the creation of a sudden and lucrative boom in the production of wine grapes, especially the cheaper thick-skinned (and thus more easily shipped) grapes in which the typical Italian-American grape producer specialized. The fortunes of such famous Italian-American California winemaking families such as the Martinis, the Mondavis, and the Gallos

Traditional Italian stonework continues to be a prominent feature of the architecture of California wineries. The stonework for the central building of the Robert Pepi Winery (Oakville, Napa Valley), pictured here, was executed in 1981 by stonemason Eugene Domenichelli of nearby Healdsburg. Photograph by David A. Taylor

originated with grape production and sales during Prohibition. When commercial wine production again became legal in 1933, these and other Italian-American families began making and selling wine commercially, while Giannini's Bank of America used its influence over agricultural loans to impose quality-control standards and to prevent the reemergence of a dominant marketing organization.

Italian-American winemakers remained influential in the industry and participated in its transformation from bulk-wine production to bulk and fine wine production after World War II. But while they often promote the image of a traditional family enterprise in their advertising, the actual making of commercial wine by Italian-Americans has little to do with the winemaking traditions of their ancestors. Rather the Mondavis, Gallos, and the like studied formally or informally the French-derived practices already institutionalized in the California industry, supplemented by formal study at the wine chemistry and enology programs established by the University of California campuses at Berkeley and Davis.

Noncommercial home winemaking is another matter, however, and so are many of the nonmanufacturing aspects of the commercial industry, such as family management of wineries and vintage grape production, allied skills such as equipment manufacture and cooperage, and the continued demand for Italian craftsmanship in stonemasonry in the wine districts. Winemaking may thus be characterized as a food-related enterprise with historic social but superficial folkloric connections with Italian tradition. Nevertheless, as David Taylor's article on the Conrotto family of Gilroy, California, illustrates, winemaking of both varieties is still to a significant extent a locus of traditional Italian culture in its American setting.

Edward G. Robinson (left) and Douglas Fairbanks, Jr., in the motion picture *Little Caesar* (1930), the first talking gangster film glorifying the gang wars of the twenties. Robinson won the role of Rico on the strength of his performance in the Broadway play *The Racket*, in which he played a character based on Al Capone. The movie performance made him a star. Film still copyright 1954 Warner Bros. Pictures Distributing Corporation. Motion Picture, Broadcasting, and Recorded Sound Division, Library of Congress

Three forces have shaped the construction of pan-Italian ethnic identity since World War II. One is the reaction to the widespread stereotyping of Italian criminality inspired by congressional crime investigators in the 1950s and by film and television portrayals of famous Italian-American gangsters in the 1960s and 1970s. The second is the emergence of contemporary Italy as a leader in the production of high-fashion consumer goods. The third is the ethnic revival of the 1970s, an impulse toward "neo-ethnicity" that parallels the scholarly interest in ethnic studies.

Humbert Nelli, whose scholarly study *The Business of Crime*[16] is the best available work on the subject, points out that in its origins and earliest manifestations in urban immigrant communities, Italian criminality was no different in kind or degree from the criminality of Irish, German, Jewish, or other immigrant groups. But two factors helped to emphasize Italian and Italian-American criminals, both in reality and in the popular imagination. One was the connection of criminal activity in America with traditional Italian secret societies, such as the Neapolitan *camorra* or the Sicilian mafia. Nelli's research shows that this connection was often more imaginary than real, but sensational newspaper publicity around the turn of the century generated horrified fascination among other Americans, even when the misdeeds of Italian criminals were largely confined to immigrant districts. One possible source of this fascination, although Nelli does not mention it, was an even older Anglo-American cultural tradition of associating violence and a particularly calculating type of ruthlessness with Italians. Though the tradition derived from Machiavelli, the Borgias, and assorted Shakespearean villains rather than from immigrant behavior, it probably contributed to the American readiness to believe practically anything about the cunning and ruthlessness of Italian-American crime.

A second factor elevating Italian-American criminality to a perceptual plane above that of other ethnic groups was the collision of Italian cultural values and Anglo-American sumptuary laws and moral regulations during the Progressive Era. In smaller western communities, Italian-Americans often specialized in hotel, restaurant, and saloon-keeping—legitimate commercial activities which Anglo-American ambivalence about alcohol and sex served to endow with a certain disreputable aura. This reinforced the criminal stereotype, as did the fact that some saloonkeepers and winemakers became bootleggers during Prohibition.[17]

The Volstead Act of 1920, which created the enforcement machinery of nationwide prohibition, gave Italian-American criminals their opportunity to expand the scope of organized criminal activities far beyond the confines of the immigrant communities. Organization builders—such as John Torrio and his successor, Alphonse (Al) Capone, in Chicago, and Charles (Lucky) Luci-

ano, in New York—were to the business of crime what their contemporaries Henry Ford was to manufacturing, Julius Rosenwald (of Sears Roebuck) to retailing, and A. P. Giannini to banking. Their means of reducing competition of course created more sensational headlines than did the oligopolistic behavior of legitimate businessmen, and the headlines and the myths they inspired provided fodder for future generations of novelists and scriptwriters.

A consolidation of criminal gangs across neighborhood and ethnic lines took place during the 1920s in New York, Chicago, Cleveland, Detroit, Boston, Kansas City, and Denver, thanks to the expanded criminal opportunities created by Prohibition. Nelli points out that cities with traditionally relaxed standards of enforcement of drinking, gambling, and vice laws did not experience this phenomenon. Both Italian and non-Italian criminal organizations in San Francisco and New Orleans, for example, remained small and fragmented during this period, and while Carlos Marcello later created a crime syndicate in New Orleans during the 1950s, a local civic vice and gambling clean-up movement driven by Anglo/Protestant moral values was one of the factors which gave Marcello his opportunity.

These historical circumstances help to explain why Italian-American criminals managed to capture the public imagination on a scale that Anglo-American and non-Italian ethnic gang leaders had not. But the resulting publicity tarred all Italian-Americans with the mafia stereotype. The stereotype is unfair and inaccurate, especially as it applies to the West. Historically, only San Francisco and Denver developed crime syndicates, and in both cities their size and influence were modest by the standards of the New York and Chicago mobs, according to Nelli. The postwar development of Las Vegas, Nevada, as the western capital of legitimate gambling and a place where criminal earnings could be "laundered" was the achievement of Jewish gangsters, although Italian mobsters soon cashed in on it.

The fact that *The Godfather*'s author, director, and principal male actors were Italian-Americans legitimated its reinforcement of the criminal stereotype for non-Italians, but resentment of the stereotype has been a principal motivating force for ethnic spokesmen and organizations during the postwar era.[18] Both the Sons of Italy and the National Italian American Foundation have undertaken successful antidefamation campaigns against entertainment corporations whose programming reinforced the stereotype. In relaxed circumstances, folklore about *mafiosi* seems to be as popular with Italian-Americans as it is with other Americans. The difference is that Italian-Americans, even when they take good-humored advantage of the fearful respect that mafia references evoke, are usually kidding. Other Americans, on the other hand, apparently believe what they hear, even when logic and a little historical knowledge should counsel them otherwise, and this faith in the folklore of criminality can act to the detriment of their understanding of and relations with the Italian-American community.

The reemergence of Italy as a center of contemporary art, fashion, and design during the postwar era has had an opposite but, in many respects, equally distorting effect on the image and self-perception of Italian-Americans, especially in California. The satisfaction of wearing Italian fashions, driving Italian sports cars, or collecting objects designed by famous Italian designers is of course confined to a relatively small number of well-to-do people. But middle class people can identify with such products symbolically, especially if they can afford to indulge occasionally in meals in trendy restaurants that specialize in "reinterpreting"

classic Italian regional cuisine or in purchases at the new specialty Italian food shops that supplement or compete with the traditional Italian foodstores. This appeal is particularly strong with younger Italian-Americans to whom the established pan-Italian modes of ethnic performance seem old-fashioned and trite.

This development has reinforced the tendency to define Italian-American eth-

The popularity of high-fashion items from Italy has led to a tendency to identify Italian-American ethnicity with elite elements of Italian culture. Current issues of fashion magazines regularly contain advertisements for Italian cars, watches, wines, shoes, and clothes. Collage by Ray Dockstader

nicity in terms of elite elements of Italian culture. Thus while demographic changes threaten established organizations like the Sons of Italy and declining attendance at Columbus Day rituals in many cities is a source of concern to their leaders, Italian-American "cultural centers" are offering instructional language courses in standard Italian and appreciation courses on Italian fine arts and cuisine. In California, Italian-American winemakers report declining sales and production for varietal wines made from grapes brought over by their ancestors, such as the Piedmontese *grignolino,* but others are growing newly imported Tuscan varieties to make fine Italian wines to accompany the high-style *nuova italiana* cuisine.[19] In these ways the performance of contemporary Italian-American ethnicity is moving toward a very American blend of consumerism and nostalgia, an expression of personal style rather than of group identity.

The work of sustaining the idealized family relationships that lie at the heart of nostalgic Italian-American ethnic identity falls mainly upon women. As Micaela Di Leonardo points out, Italian-American women are increasingly disinclined to assume this responsibility as they, like their non-Italian counterparts, reshape their family obligations to accommodate career and personal interests outside of the home. She finds the surviving association of ethnic brokerage and food businesses objectionable, partly because it represents the trend toward the "commoditization" of ethnic identity and also because an emphasis on ethnic performance in food preparation places a disproportionate burden on women, "sustaining an idealized patriarchal past in which women stayed home and served men and children."[20]

But there has always been a link between economic interest and the promotion of Italian-American ethnicity. The fact that this link is now manifest primarily in areas relating to food-processing and services partly reflects the importance that foodways have always had in defining Italian-American ethnicity. It also reflects the absorption of ethnic businesses into the mainstream of other sectors, such as agribusiness, banking and insurance, entertainment and journalism, leaving food-related businesses as one of the few remaining places where occupational and ethnic identities converge.

These changes have restricted the opportunity for men *or* women to sustain ethnicity through occupational cultures and work processes. In contrast to other ethnic groups such as Jewish-, Irish-, Greek-, Polish-, and Armenian-Americans, Italian-Americans lack religious or foreign policy issues that serve as ethnic rallying points, and so while the impulse toward "neo-ethnicity" is strong, the available projects which might sustain it—defensive combat against the mafia stereotype, consumption of "commoditized" ethnic food or of elite Italian culture, nostalgia for a patriarchal family structure, or the commemoration of *prominenti* ranging from Columbus to Joe DiMaggio—are each in some way unsatisfactory in that they are unable to guarantee that sense of personal connection with an authentic past that most people search out in the name of "heritage."

Such circumstances have led some sociologists to talk of "the twilight of ethnicity" among Italian-Americans, and indeed among all ethnic groups of European ancestry. Sociology has traditionally defined ethnicity as a linear process, wherein immigrants and their descendants have moved past certain demographic checkpoints in a seemingly inexorable movement toward assimilation. Measurements taken at these checkpoints today show slight differences, if any, between Italian-Americans and British-Americans in residential locations, educa-

tional attainment, family incomes, or inter-marriage with members of other ethnic groups. As a result, "core values [among Italian-Americans] have been overwhelmed by a common American culture so that even though cultural uniformity has not been the end result, the remaining differences among groups are so mild as to constitute neither a basis for group solidarity nor a barrier to intergroup contact."[21] Italian-Americans have thus become candidates for inclusion in a pan-European ethnic group that some sociologists have seen emerging among "unhyphenated whites" of northwest European descent.

But the sociological viewpoint ignores the potential connection between neo-ethnicity and cultural conservation. It embodies a static view of ethnicity, defining it almost entirely in terms of biological descent and of social behavior—segregation, conflict, and mobility—reflected in aggregate data. Scholars who give more weight to cultural studies offer alternative definitions. In *Beyond Ethnicity,*[22] for example, Werner Sollors contrasts the ethnicity of descent with that of consent, ethnicity sustained by voluntary efforts as well as by external pressures and boundaries. In this view, the desire of Italian-Americans to sustain a sense of separate identity, and the organized efforts made on behalf of this goal, are just as valid expressions of ethnicity as those that sociologists measure. In the context of American cultural history, the ethnicity of consent, like American regionalism, constitutes an ongoing search for "a wholesome provincialism," a *via media* between the extremes of cultural isolation based on the ethnicity of descent, on the one hand, and the submergence of everyone is a standardized national culture, on the other. As the essays which follow amply demonstrate, in the West—that most American of American places—Italian-American ethnicity of this type is alive and well.

Four generations of an Italian-American extended family in Pueblo, Colorado; several family members are holding cherished photographs of relatives. First row, left to right: Anthony Cuchiara, Stacey Fortino, Marianne Cuchiara Everett, Spencer Everett. Second row: Marie Cuchiara Fabian, Mary Louise Morone, Ann Cuchiara, Frances De Luca, Charles De Luca. Third row: Palma De Luca Ferraro, Anthony Ferraro, Joe Ferraro, Ann Ferraro, Susan Ferraro Cuchiara, Kenneth Cuchiara, Charles Cuchiara, Barbara Morone Fortino, Tony Fortino, Carmella Morone Cuchiara. Photograph by Ken Light, IAW-KL-B267-22

THE ROYAL FAMILY OF SAN PEDRO

An Interview conducted and edited by DOUG DeNATALE and DAVID A. TAYLOR

Every family possesses its own oral tradition, manifested in the stories of family history that are passed from generation to generation. In some families, a central theme emerges, often embodied in the tales of the exploits of one remarkable figure. The Royal family of San Pedro, California, is such a family. The figure of Achille Reali, known variously as Archie Royal and Jumbo Royal, looms over the family history, a larger-than-life hero who left an indelible mark.

During the fieldwork for the Italian-Americans in the West project in San Pedro, California, I encountered Archie Royal's son, John, the executive secretary-treasurer of the Fishermen's and Allied Workers' Union, Local 33, of the International Longshoreman's and Warehousemen's Union in San Pedro. The long afternoon that I spent in John's office yielded a series of rich family stories in which the themes of family, labor, and struggles for justice emerged. The following evening, I returned with project director David Taylor to visit John and his mother, Albina, at Albina's home. As the balmy evening darkened toward night, John and Albina recounted the family story.

The account that follows has been edited from the stories that John and Albina told on those two visits:

John: My dad's name was Achille Reali when he came over as a young boy from the old country. He was born [on January 31, 1896] in a little town called Valbona, way up in the mountains in the Province of Reggio Nell'Emilia. His dad was a stonemason and had some land up there. And he was acting as a sheepherder for his old man.

Albina: They had a lot of land, but not in one piece. Maybe a few acres here, and you travel a few miles and they got another little piece of land. It's strange how they have land back there. It's not all in one place.

John: Then he ran away and went down to work in the marble quarries in Carrara. He was just a kid. The job he got: he was scaling the cliffs by rope and knocking off the loose chips of marble so it wouldn't fall down and kill the workers. They had to communicate with him by flags. He'd swing from one cliff to the other and on the ledges and that.

The next spring, his dad found what he was doing down there, and his dad fainted! He said, "My God! You're going to kill yourself!" My dad said, "Well, I don't want to go back up in the mountains and herd sheep

Achille Reali (Archie Royal) as a young man in Italy. Courtesy of John and Albina Royal

Archie Royal's birthplace, Valbona, Italy, as seen ca. 1970. Courtesy of John and Albina Royal

and freeze in the wintertime." So his old man said, "Well, if you don't want to come back, then go to America and find your brother."

He had a brother living and working in the steel mills of Pueblo, Colorado. So he did come. In 1913, he landed in Pueblo, Colorado, and found his brother. The brother had been there for seven or eight years before my dad came over—he was older. He came over to work and send money back to help the family. After a few years the brother went back to Italy and married and never did return. So my father became the only member of the family that stayed in this country.

He told me that when he landed in New York and went through Ellis Island, they sold him a sack of food for a dollar that had oranges, apples, bread, and salami in it. And for three days he lived off that bag of food, going on the train from New York to Pueblo, Colorado.

He landed in Pueblo, Colorado, on July Fourth. The fact he landed here on that day always seemed to have significance for him.

Albina: His brother worked in the steel mill in Pueblo. So, when my husband came from

Italy, that's where he went. But he didn't like working in the steel mill, and he heard about the coal mines. So he jumped freight trains and went to the coal camps. That's how he traveled.

[Achille Reali was seventeen years old when he arrived in Pueblo. At that young age he stood six feet, two inches, tall and weighed two-hundred-and-eleven pounds.]

John: He was as hard as a rock. He was a big man, a strong man, and he was looked up to by most of the Italian miners that he knew at the time. In fact, they nicknamed him Jumbo, because he had put the largest single piece of coal in a coal car that had ever been done. I guess because of his phenomenal strength and what he had done at that time, they kidded him and named him Jumbo. And until the day that he died, if you asked anyone if they knew Archie Royal, they didn't know who in the hell he was. But if you asked did they know who Jumbo was, oh, right away they knew who Jumbo was.

Things were very bad in the coal mines. Most of the guys at that time were bachelors. They either lived in tents or they had makeshift shacks. They worked for the companies, got paid with company money, company scrip, and had to shop at the company store. It was like slave-labor conditions. It was very, very bad.

He told me that if you got a job in the mines at that time, they would hold back thirty days of your pay, and they'd hold it over your head so you wouldn't quit and leave.

As he got more and more active in the coal mines there, they tried to form the [United] Mine Workers Union. Maybe you know it, and maybe you don't—they had a big strike and it practically ended up in a civil war for eighteen months in and around Pueblo, Ludlow, and Trinidad, Colorado. It was called the Ludlow Massacre.

[Ludlow, Colorado, is a tiny town located about 185 miles south of Denver, in the coal fields of southern Colorado. On April 20, 1914, it was the site of a battle between striking coal miners (many of them immigrants) and the Colorado militia that resulted in the deaths of twenty-four men, women, and children. This event came to be known as the Ludlow Massacre, and it is one of the most famous confrontations in the annals of American labor history.

The unrest that precipitated the Ludlow Massacre stemmed from coal miners' grievances against coal operators. In essence, the miners were the vassals of the operators. They lived in isolated camps owned by the companies, and anyone who would not do what the companies wanted was forced to leave. The miners' civil rights were routinely ignored.

In 1913, the United Mine Workers began to organize miners in Colorado's southern camps. Despite considerable opposition from the operators, as well as from law enforcement officials, union organizers made good progress. In August of 1913, the union invited the coal operators to meet with miners for the purpose of discussing the miners' grievances. This invitation and another that followed were ignored. Subsequently, workers from various southern Colorado coal mines met on September 15 and decided to strike for the following demands: (1) recognition of the union; (2) a 10 percent increase in wages; (3) an eight-hour work day; (4) payment for "deadwork" (work necessary for mining that did not immediately result in mined coal), as well as for weight of mined coal; (5) the right to elect miners who would verify the weight of

The miners' tent colony at Ludlow, Colorado, before the battle that came to be known as the "Ludlow Massacre." Courtesy of Colorado Historical Society

coal mined; (6) the right to trade in any store, board anywhere, and secure the services of any doctor; and (7) the enforcement of Colorado's mining laws and the removal of armed mine guards.

The strike began on September 23, and eight thousand miners, along with their families, moved out of the company camps and into tent colonies erected by the union. The coal companies, in turn, brought in several hundred more armed deputies and guards. The miners armed themselves as well. The largest of the mining companies was Colorado Fuel & Iron, partly owned but completely controlled by John D. Rockefeller.

The strike continued into 1914 and, on April 20, after several months during which no serious disturbances occurred, miners and militiamen began shooting at each other in the vicinity of the Ludlow tent colony. According to one account:

The gun battle raged throughout the day and reached its climax when the militia overran the colony, looted the tents, and, after dousing them with kerosene, put them to the torch. Ten men and one child were killed in the shooting. The following day, two women and eleven children who had sought refuge from the gunfire in a room dug under one of the tents, were found dead of suffocation; the burning tents over their heads had denied them oxygen . . . . When the bodies of these hapless victims were discovered, the strikers erupted in a retaliatory frenzy. Armed miners occupied the city of Trinidad. Others moved as mobs through the coalfields setting fire to mine buildings and engaging mine guards and militia men in gun battles.[1]

Order was finally restored when federal troops, ordered into the strike zone by President Wilson, arrived on April 30. The union, which had exhausted its financial resources, ended the strike on December 10, 1914. Although the strike did not lead directly to enduring reforms, it focused the

Red Cross workers view the devastated Ludlow tent colony after the battle. Courtesy of Colorado Historical Society

nation's attention on the condition of industrial workers, and served as a grim reminder to employers and employees that negotiation, not bullets, is the preferable course for the resolution of conflict.[2]]

Albina: He told us about when they were striking. That was before I knew him. See, all of the union men moved out, they had to move out of the camp because it was a company camp. And they moved into what was nothing but sagebrush and put up tents. And they sent the militia out there, and they killed women, children, and all. Set fire to the tents. He said it was terrible, what they did.

John: Pop and a lot of miners took to the hills then.

Albina: He had no shoes. He used to wrap his feet with gunny sacks. See, they were on

strike, they couldn't buy anything. They lived on wild game, whatever they could get. He could never forget it. That's why after we were married for several years he took me back there to show it to me. Took a trip down there. That's how we got pictures of the monument.

John: He went through that whole thing for about eighteen months. They burnt down the company camp and killed thirteen women and kids and all. They had the militia on them, the Pinkertons, the guards, the sheriffs, the rangers. In many cases they just shot the strikers on sight. There was cases of lynching and dragging people through town with a rope behind a horse. He told where these miners literally were forced in self-defense to take to the hills. They'd come down at night and break into stores and steal blankets and food to survive. And they were involved in a lot of stuff such as sabotage of coal cars and mines. It was just basically like a war.

He went through that whole era and it was a very, very bad time. He talked about it extensively. Till the day he died, he hated any symbol that gave recognition to authority such as a sheriff or a ranger or a Pinkerton, because he had such brutal memories of them. He became very militant for the unions. He became a totally dedicated man of labor.

[After his experiences in the Ludlow Massacre, Achille Reali searched for work with another coal company. Through the network of miners, he heard of work opening up in Mount Harris, Colorado.]

John: They'd find out if a mine was opening up and if it was going to be hiring. And they'd hop a freight and go to wherever that area was and look for work.

The mining town of Mt. Harris, Colorado, in the summer of 1918. Archie Royal met his future wife, Albina LeDonne, in Mt. Harris when he stayed at a boarding house operated by her mother. Courtesy of John and Albina Royal

Albina: When they got hungry they'd jump off the train. He had a partner, and they'd go fishing, catch fish, and they'd cook it. They'd eat a lot of wild game: rabbits, wild chickens. He said they'd always take salt with them. I don't know, he seemed to enjoy that type of life, but it was a rough life.

[In Mount Harris, Reali first met the girl who was to become his wife. Albina LeDonne Royal's family immigration history paralleled Achille's to a degree. Like Achille, Albina's father, Antonio, came to Colorado in search of a brother, and the family's process of emigration from Italy was not a straightforward, one-directional process.]

Albina: My parents came over here in the eighteen hundreds. I don't know just what year. They were from the Abruzzi province. My father came first, and he settled in Syracuse, New York, and lived there for seven years. Then he went back and married my mother. They stayed in Italy for a couple of years and then came back over here. He came out to Colorado to find an uncle of mine. He promised his parents that he would find him. Otherwise he would have settled back in New York. He came west to find my uncle. And he found him.

I was born in Newcastle, Colorado [in 1904]. It was a nice little, old-fashioned town. We had the boardwalk and just one main street. Grocery stores, and saloons, and schools, everything was on that one street. There were twenty-four saloons, and eighteen dance halls in that town at one time. It's just a little ghost town now.

Then my parents moved to Mount Harris [Colorado], and my mother took over the boarding house. She had thirty-three boarders. She used to get up at three o'clock in the morning and cook three meals a day for them. God, she worked hard. And they were just barely breaking even. So my dad got all the boarders one evening and told them, "We're going to have to raise the board bill, because we're not making it." And they all agreed. He showed them the figures and everything. And they were nice about it. They raised each one three dollars.

My mother used to make her own bread. She was a wonderful cook. She used to knead a hundred pounds of flour at a time. My dad built her an outdoor oven: an Italian *forno*. And my mother got to be an expert at it. She would build a fire out of wood, and she knew just how long to keep that fire going. She'd rake all the hot coals out, and wash it with a mop. Then she'd put her hand in there, and she could tell if it was the right temperature, just by putting her hand in. Then she'd knead this bread and make it into big round loaves. Dad made her a big paddle, and she used to put the loaf of bread on there and push it right back in the oven. She baked the nicest bread.

She also raised a big garden and never bought any vegetables at all. She always had her herb garden, always. And she used to make her own tomato paste: she'd cook her tomatoes, strain them and cook them until a certain degree, and go out and spread them on this board and dry it in the sun. Every once in a while she'd go out there and turn it. When it was about ready, she'd get a big crock. She'd put a layer of that paste in there and a layer of sweet basil leaves and olive oil. And she'd do that till she filled the crock. And we'd use that for making our spaghetti sauce.

Oh, they worked hard in those days.

I met my husband when I was twelve years old. He was one of my mother's boarders. See, I was living in Newcastle, Colorado, with a brother of mine and his wife, going to school. My parents were in Mount Harris. Then, mother needed help in the boarding house, so she sent for my sister and her husband, and my brother and his wife. And we went over there to help cook.

[Though Achille met Albina at her mother's boarding house, he did not display any immediate interest in her.]

Albina: My husband stayed there quite a while mining coal. Then he felt like he wanted to leave again. This was when he was a boarder with my mother. He left and he went traveling. He joined the circus—it was the Barnum and Bailey Circus—as a wrestler. Anybody could stay up with him ten minutes would win so much money, you know. He traveled with the circus for three years, wrestling.

John: That's an interesting story about how he became a wrestler in the circus. When he was a young man, he liked to work out at the YMCA. And, one time this circus came to the mining camp and they had a professional wrestler there that was challenging all comers. You know, if you stay in the ring ten minutes you win a hundred bucks. All the Italian miners were kidding my dad, you know: "Jumbo, why don't you go in the ring with this guy." My dad was bashful and didn't want to. They kept egging him on, so finally he went in the ring with the guy. I guess the guy started to get pretty dirty with him, and he got mad. What he did: he picked him up, slammed him down, broke a collarbone and all his ribs, and put the guy out of commission.

So, the next day, the guy that owned the circus got an interpreter, and they come down to the coal mines and they were looking for my old man. He thought they were coming with the sheriff to put him in jail because he hurt the wrestler. He ran and hid in the mine. And the guy told him, "No," he said, "we want you to take his place till he gets out of the hospital." My dad said, "Well, I never wrestled before." "Well," he said, "you're doing fine."

So, my uncles and the other old miners told him, "You know, you can be famous, travel all over the United States, make lots of money." And they talked him into it. He made me laugh. He said that's where he learned all of his bad habits, wrestling with the circus. Learned to smoke and drink and all that kind of stuff. He said his trainer used to stop him from smoking. And he said he'd get some kids and he'd give them money to try to sneak him cigarettes.

Albina: He was with the circus three years.

John: And then he came back to Mount Harris, and went back to the mines.

Archie Royal dressed as a cowboy, August 4, 1917. Archie donned cowboy clothing for the fun of it and had this photograph taken for Albina. Courtesy of John and Albina Royal

Archie and Albina on their wedding day, January 31, 1920. Courtesy of John and Albina Royal

Albina: That's when we got together, after he come back. [laughs] He probably had it in the back of his mind. He sent me a card and a picture when he went away, one of these places where you dress up. He dressed up like a cowboy and got a picture taken for me.

John: Oh, I remember that picture! With the chaps, and the cowboy hat, and the neckerchief, yeah.

Albina: He asked me to marry him. I told him he had to wait until I was eighteen—that would have been three more years. We went together eight months.

John: You were, what? Sixteen?

Albina: Fifteen. My dad didn't approve of it. But he was a fair, honest person, my dad was. He got a-hold of me and he said, "Now, look," he said, "you don't even know how to boil water." He even told him that, he said, "she's just a kid. She doesn't even know how to boil water." He told me, "I won't stop you if you want to get married, but I'm telling you, you're making a mistake. You're too young." But, we were together sixty-four years.

John: Yeah, that's a little bit of time.

Albina: My uncles convinced him to Americanize his name. He didn't know what it would be, so they told him the translation would be "Archie Royal."

[After their wedding, Achille and Albina obtained the rights to a 160-acre homestead in Wolf Creek, outside Mount Harris. They began raising vegetables to sell to the mining community, and Achille divided his time between work in the mines and on the couple's homestead.]

Albina: You should've seen the potato crop he used to get. My husband and I one year planted one sack of potatoes, and we harvested one hundred sacks out of that one sack. That was a great crop that time. And when we lived in Wolf Creek, our summers were only three months long. You'd be surprised at what you could raise in three months. We used to raise cabbage that weighed twenty-six pounds a head. Huge, big cabbage. We sold them to the people who worked in the coal mines. It was surprising what you could raise. We got some chickens, we got some ducks, and we got some pigs.

John: But in addition to working the homestead, he worked in the mines, when the mines were open.

Albina: Yeah, he worked in the mines. Dad worked every day. But it was a nice life. It was hard work, but it was a nice clean life.

[Albina and Archie were married in 1920 and enjoyed a few peaceful years on their homestead. Their peace was disturbed, however, when local feeling began to turn against foreigners.]

Albina: They were bad back then in Colorado at the time. They had it in for the Catholics and the Italians. I don't know, maybe all foreigners, I don't know. But around Mount Harris there were mostly Italians.

John: The word was out they was going to drive all the foreigners out of Wolf Creek, Colorado: all the Italians, all the Catholics. Purify the land.

They came up one night, the Ku Klux Klan, and they built a big wooden cross up on the rimrock behind the farm up there, and they sent word down that they weren't

going to tolerate having any Italian people and/or Catholics in the area, and they were going to burn him out. And if I remember correctly, the old man got the rifle and threw a lot of shots up there at them and chased them off.

A lot of the Italians, they just wouldn't move. Everybody had rifles—they lived on deer meat and buckskin and elk and that—and they'd go out and shoot at them. So, I guess the Ku Klux Klan started to back off a little.

Pop told me that he knew who most of them were, even though they wore a white sheet and they tried to hide themselves. He

Archie Royal standing atop his horse, Geney, at Mt. Harris, Colorado, 1924. Courtesy of John and Albina Royal

Archie and Albina Royal standing behind Grandpa LeDonne's house in Wolf Creek, Colorado, with their children John, Virginia, and Marian. While in Wolf Creek, Archie divided his time between work in the mines and work on the homestead. Courtesy of John and Albina Royal

said most of them were business people down in Mount Harris.

Albina: Yeah, the people you'd deal with in town. They'd treat us fine when we went to the company store. See, the stores at that time were all owned by the company. There was no place else you could shop. For some reason they didn't like Catholics and Italians.

I was scared. I was always kind of scared. But he'd always tell me not to be afraid. He said I was scared of my own shadow. They tried it a couple of times, but the people didn't scare so easy.

[Though the Realis stood up to the Klan, they could not stand up to the changing conditions in the mines. In 1928, after nine years of homesteading, they left Colorado.]

Albina: The mines all shut down. People started using oil, see. They shut down all the coal mines. And all those thousands of people were left out of work, 'cause that's what they all did—worked in the coal mines. And everybody lost jobs.

We didn't know what to do. I remember he wanted to go to Detroit to work for Ford Motor Company. He said, "I'm sure I'll find work." He wasn't afraid of nothing. But I told him I didn't want to go to Detroit.

[By that time, part of Albina's family had migrated further west, and the family decided to try their luck in California.]

John: My mother had a sister who lived in Wilmington, so she said, "Well, let's stop and visit with her." So we landed in Wilmington on Christmas Eve of 1928, my father, my mother, my three sisters and myself. I was six years old. So we stuck around for a few days, and then my old man got a job working; they were building the Don Hotel over in Wilmington, and he got a job doing some work on the breakwater out here. And then he started working on the waterfront down here. And my uncle convinced him that he ought to stay here.

Albina: I had a niece staying with me in Wilmington, and she had a boy friend. He used to come here to see her, and he told my husband, "You want to go longshoring?"

We had no idea what longshoring was. That was something new to us. He said, "I longshore on weekends so I can go to school during the week." He said, "I'll come and get you Saturday morning, and show you how to longshore."

They used to go down on the docks, and they'd walk on the docks where the ships were. And if they needed men they'd hire them right off the dock. They'd look at your hands to see if you had callouses. And he had these great, big rough hands. So, he got hired. They called it "extra," you know, whenever they needed extra help. And then he got on steady. They liked the way he worked. He was a good worker.

When he started longshoring they didn't have regular hours. They worked the men from sixteen to twenty-four hours a day without sending them home. Talk about slavery. I'll never forget: it used to pour rain, and they'd make them work in that rain. They couldn't come home until they finished that ship. That's before they organized. They talk bad about the unions but I'll tell you, there's nothing better. They finally got tired of it. So they decided to strike. And they did. And they won.

God, they had a terrible strike here in 'thirty-four. Harry Bridges was the leader. He was in San Francisco, but I guess he'd tell them what to do. My husband was Italian. They got him to talk Italian to all the Italian longshoremen and tell them not to go to work. And they got a Slav to tell all the Slavs. A lot of them still wanted to go to work because they said they had kids to feed. My husband would tell them, "I got four at home." He said, "You're not going to starve for a couple of weeks."

[The strike that Albina Royal describes is the West Coast Maritime Strike of 1934, one of the epic events in the history of American organized labor. Like the

1913–14 Colorado coalfield strike, it stemmed from workers' dissatisfaction with working conditions. After the crash of 1929, dockside employment opportunities declined, and, because jobs were scarce, longshoremen put up with harsh conditions. For example, they drove themselves to exhaustion working thirty-six- to forty-eight-hour shifts and endured the risks of dangerous cargo-handling practices. In addition, they were at the mercy of employer-operated hiring halls they called "fink halls." In San Pedro, the Marine Service Bureau was such a fink hall, and it "controlled the life and destiny of every longshoreman on the water front."[3] If a longshoreman broke any of the bureau's rules, his card could be taken away and with it any possibility of employment on the waterfront.

Because of these working conditions, the time was ripe for radicalization of waterfront workers. In 1934, leftist members of the International Longshoreman's Association (ILU) led by Harry Bridges succeeded

The violence of the 1934 West Coast maritime strike is depicted in the painting above: Fletcher Martin *Trouble in Frisco*. 1938. Oil on canvas, 30 x 36 inches (76.2 x 94.4 cm). Collection, The Museum of Modern Art, New York. Abby Aldrich Rockefeller Fund

in having their contract demands and radical political demands passed at a coast-wide rank-and-file convention. The demands adopted at the convention included: a closed shop, union-controlled hiring, a six-hour day, and a coast-wide contract. The shipowners refused to bargain, however, charging that the convention was dominated by Communists. In response, the longshoremen voted to strike all Pacific Coast ports. However, a request from President Roosevelt led to a postponement of the walkout. This did not sit well with the rank and file, and they voted to oust the local president, who had acceded to Roosevelt's request. The leadership was then assumed by a strike committee chaired by Bridges.

The walkout finally began on May 9, 1934. Violence soon broke out between strikers and police in San Francisco, and other confrontations occurred in Seattle, Portland, and San Pedro. On May 15, the San Pedro strike turned violent. According to the union's account, published twenty-five years later:

The strikers went to the Wilmington stockade to picket and tell many innocent workers who had been tricked into scabbing the facts of the situation. The strikers came from the Wilmington-San Pedro road down Neptune to peacefully picket. . . . Hundreds of police, armed guards and professional strikebreakers met the pickets with a hail of pistol and rifle fire and tear gas bombs. Machineguns were posted at the entrance to the stockade. The combined forces opened fire on the longshoremen and our dear Brothers young Dick Parker who had just become a longshoreman and John Knudson were shot. Dick Parker was killed on the spot and John Knudson died of gunshot wounds three weeks later.[4]

In addition to galvanizing San Pedro's working class population, Parker's death sparked strike actions in other ports, and violent confrontations between strikers and police and guards continued to be widespread.

Finally, the West Coast maritime strike ended in arbitration and the strikers returned to work on July 31, 1934. "During the three-month walkout, nine marine workers lost their lives, hundreds were arrested, and literally thousands clubbed or teargassed by Pinkertons, police, and national guardsmen."[5] But definite benefits for the maritime workers resulted. The arbitration board gave the union control over the hiring process. And since union members were substantially protected from employer retaliation, they were able to negotiate better working conditions. In sum, power on the waterfront shifted from the shipowners to the union.]

John: The paisans, I'm sorry to say, weren't as militant as the rest of them. You got a paisan who gets his neck bent, and gets tough, and gets militant—he'll make up for about ten of the others. See, most of these guys hadn't been through a big strike like that. But my dad got a taste of it as a kid in the marble quarries, and then he had just come out of that Ludlow Massacre and the big mine strikes when he came out here. So, a strike wasn't new to him. He had to run around and kick a few butts and put some backbone into a lot of these guys who otherwise weren't going to stand up.

A lot of the stores at that time were mainly mom-and-poppa stores, neighborhood, you know. They knew everybody and they were poor people, too. And as much as they could they extended credit to these strikers. Some made it. Some went broke. But one thing they prided themselves on. When that strike was over, they paid back all these people every dime. Which was the right thing to do.

And then, too, they got a lot of donations. The truck farmers would give them vegetables. The fishermen would give them fish. One guy, Erickson, had a fish boat, and these guys would go on his fish boat to Santa Rosa Island [one of the Channel Islands], and they would kill twenty-five or thirty head of [wild] sheep, or goats, and skin them and put them on the fish hatch and bring them back. And then at night time, pop had a 'twenty-six Chrysler with a big wooden trailer, and when the ferry stopped running at midnight, he'd back that trailer down there and they'd put the goat and sheep carcasses in the trailer and take it up to the soup kitchen on Seventh Street.

The single men, they would eat in the soup kitchens, then they'd go do their picket duty. And the married men, they'd do picket duty, and then they'd give them some vegetables and a fish or piece of meat to bring home to their families. They had a lot of sympathy in the community and a lot of support.

The employers would load up street cars with scabs up in L.A., and they'd recruit people from all over. Some knew there was a strike, some didn't. They'd say, "You want to go to work?" And they'd put them in these street cars, bring them down from L.A., and put them in these big tents, they called it the bull pen. House them there and feed them. Then under escort they'd take them to the ship and they'd work the ship. And in the night they'd escort them back. Kept guards around with search lights to protect them.

My dad and these guys would go out and they'd intercept these street cars coming down the tracks. They'd stone them and stop them and they'd beat hell out of the scabs to discourage them.

They'd find ways of camouflaging their meetings because the police and the detec-

Archie Royal's picket duty card, stamped to show his picket activity during the 1934 strike. The card shows that the date of his first picketing was May 10, 1934—one day after the start of the strike. Courtesy of John and Albina Royal

tives would come around harassing their meetings. If they'd see them in groups they'd bust them up, take them down and throw them in jail. They would have meetings downstairs in the wine cellar, or they'd meet in a park somewhere like they were having a picnic or a family gathering. I remember they used to follow my old man. You'd get up in the morning and look across the street, there'd be two of them sitting in an old touring car over there, watching the house. They always had you under surveillance.

Then this one night they decided that they had to really do something. So they got together and they planned it. They raided the bull pen at midnight. They had a big fence around it, and while they were tearing the fence down there was a young kid that lived across the alley from us—Dickie Parker. He was only sixteen or seventeen, and he was just starting in on the waterfront. My dad said that they were pulling these boards off this fence, trying to make a hole to go through, and he said Dick Parker fell down. He thought he was overcome by tear gas. So he went over to pick him up, but when he got to him he said the kid had been shot.

[The bull pen was a large stockade consisting of eight-to-ten-foot-high wooden fencing and guard towers with search lights. Tents were set up inside the fence for the scabs. The bull pen was located by the docks, near Pier 140.]

John (continues): They got inside there and they beat the holy hell out of the scabs. They set the tents on fire. They threw some of the Chinese cooks on top of the grills, and they threw some in the bay. They cut the power lines, and the firemen come with the fire hoses, and they chopped the fire hoses. And then when it was over, they scattered and went home.

Albina: I'll tell you, they really had a battle. We were living down on Mesa Street. Five o'clock that next morning, a policeman came to our house, and he knocked on the front door. My husband, well, I'll tell you because it's over with now, my husband said, "Anyone comes to get me, tell them I was here all night." So, I said, "Okay." And,

This drawing depicts the May 15, 1934, fight at Wilmington between striking longshoremen and scabs, police, and guards that John Royal remembers from his father's eyewitness account. The stockade or "bull pen" used to house scabs is shown at the upper right. Illustration from the program of the twenty-fifth anniversary of Bloody Thursday, July 5, 1959, courtesy of John and Albina Royal

sure enough, they came at five in the morning. They said, "Where's your husband?" And I said, "In bed." He *was* in bed. They said, "Was he all night?" And I said, "Yes, he was."

There were three policemen, one at each door. I told them, "He's not a murderer." I said, "What are you doing?" I got mad. He said, "Open the door and let me in." I said, "Well, wait until I get myself a robe." I let them in, and they went in and grabbed my husband and jerked him out of bed, took him to jail and for seventy-two hours we had no idea where he was. I didn't know what they did with him or where he was or anything.

John: I remember I was sleeping on a cot in the front room there and my mother went to open the door and they just knocked her down and come charging right through the house. Went in the bedroom and grabbed my old man who was in bed. They didn't even give him a chance to dress. He had long underwear on, and they just handcuffed him, and drug him out, and threw him in the touring car and away they went.

Albina: They had taken him off to Lincoln Heights Jail in Los Angeles. But I didn't know. There I sat with the kids, scared to death, didn't know what they did with him. It was awful.

After seventy-two hours, they had to turn him loose. See, they couldn't get nothing on him, they couldn't prove nothing. So, he came home. But that was a scary experience.

John: He didn't talk much about it. He never did tell me what really happened there, but I imagine that they probably worked him over pretty good for a couple days and nights. And then he finally got out. But some guys during that strike disappeared. They never did find them.

Albina: You know what he said they did to him up there to make him talk? They used sand bags to beat him, to make him confess. So they wouldn't bruise their bodies. They used sand bags. They beat them with sand bags.

[Albina keeps a framed memento of Archie's incarceration on her wall: the scrawled property receipt that was given to Archie when he was released from jail.]

Los Angeles Police Department "Prisoner's Receipt," issued upon the arrest of Archie Royal at 6:00 A.M. on May 15, 1934. The receipt notes that Archie was arrested on suspicion of arson and assault with a deadly weapon. It also notes that he was of Italian descent, was born in Italy, and was employed as a longshoreman. The document is framed and displayed proudly in Albina Royal's home. Photograph by Doug DeNatale, IAW-DD-B013-11

"Strike clearance card" issued to Archie Royal by the International Longshoremen's Association, indicating that he participated in the 1934 strike, and that his strike record is clear. According to his son, John, Archie highly valued this document and others that illustrated his role in the fight for workers' rights. Courtesy of John and Albina Royal

John: He got a good indoctrination in the labor movement and the abuses the employers could put upon working people. Today, one finds it hard to imagine some of the things that really happened did happen.

[The strong union sentiments that Archie Royal held have been passed down in his family. His son, John, a union man for over fifty years, serves today as executive secretary-treasurer of the Fishermen's and Allied Workers' Union (Local 33) of the ILWU. As John says, his own career in organized labor bears some parallels to his father's history.]

John: I never thought I'd get involved in the labor movement. I went to sea in the Merchant Marine during World War II, and then when I came back I went fishing as a navigator in a tuna boat here. I fished for sardines in the forties out of San Francisco, Monterey, Moss Landing, and down here. Then I went to Mexico fishing tuna. And I joined this union, fishermen's union, and it was primarily a Yugoslav union. We had two unions in town: one was predominantly Yugoslav and the other one was Italian fishermen. The Yugoslavs were the distant-water fishermen. I got a job on a Yugoslav boat because I was a navigator, and I got in the Yugoslav union.

I would attend the union meetings, and I didn't like some of the abuses that was taking place, and I eventually started to voice my opinion. And little by little, the members pushed me into office. I really didn't want to, it wasn't my ambition. I was looking to maybe buying into or getting a fishing boat of my own at that time. But I thought I'd try it for a year. That was 1957.

There was quite a lot of problems with the ethnic groups at that time in the fish industry. We run into the same situation all over again where the fish canners were just like the mine companies. They had heavy mortgages on the fish boats, and the owner owed the cannery a lot of money. When they'd catch fish, the cannery would deduct some of it for the payment on the boat. And the crew members were brought over from the old country and a lot of them had a pretty tough time of it. So trying to organize them into the fishermen's union was tough, because the canner told the boat owner that if the guys went into the union it was going to kill the industry, and that the union was a bunch of communists, and that they would have to foreclose on the boat and take the boat away from him, and the boatman would lose his boat and investment, and his crew and family would lose their jobs.

I worked for two years trying to organize them all into one union. Then we went before the National Labor Relations Board. The week or two before the election, all the boat owners were having their crews coming up to their houses and having barbecues and telling these guys that they had to vote against the union because if they voted for the union the cannery was going to foreclose, take the boat away from them, they'd lose their jobs. They put the fear in them, and we lost by a pretty close margin, I think it was seventy-five votes.

I was pretty disappointed, because I had two years of thirty-hour days trying to do this. I was unsuccessful in creating one fisherman's union in San Pedro. I became persona non grata. Men would tell me, "John, we need three men on the boat." I was a navigator, I could splice a rope, I could do everything. So I would go to the captain and tell him I needed a job: "I understand you need a couple of men." He'd say no. And no one would hire me. The men liked me, but the owners were scared to hire me because of the pressure behind them from the canners.

So I went over and started working

The Royal family at their home in San Pedro, California, June 14, 1947. Seated (left to right): Archie, Albina, and John. Standing: Marian, Virginia, and Betty. Courtesy of John and Albina Royal

extra as a longshoreman. I eventually got into the longshoremen's union, and got active, and I got on the executive board. Then the fishermen's union got in trouble in a big union dispute. They went to San Francisco and talked to Harry Bridges and said, "We need some help down here, we're being raided by the AFL-CIO and we've got troubles with the canneries." He told them he had no one in the International up there that was qualified to give them the assistance they needed and told them to look around.

So they came over and asked me if I wanted to come back over—this was about five or six years later. I told them about the things I had wanted to do but couldn't do, that I was blackballed now and it didn't

make any sense for me to come back. So Harry Bridges came down from Frisco and came to see me, along with other guys in both the fishermen's and longshoremen's unions, and they convinced me to come over and try to help the fishermen out. So I left the longshoremen's union and went to work for one year as an International representative to try to help the fishermen out. And I knew all the guys. And subsequently these guys put me into office. I told them I didn't want to, but they basically just drafted me, so I thought, well, I'll try it for a year and then go back to the longshoremen. But I never did go back, and I've been here all these years.

We caught the canneries stealing weight on the scales and robbing them. It was a re-

Eighty-seven year-old Archie Royal (right) with former ILWU president Harry Bridges at the dedication of the Bloody Thursday Memorial, San Pedro, California, July 7, 1983. Courtesy of John and Albina Royal

peat of the stories my dad told me happened in the coal mines. When they'd bring a car-load of coal out of the mines with four thousand pounds of coal, they would weigh it at two thousand pounds. The coal miners put a union man on the scales, and they found that they put railroad ties under the scales so the load of coal would only come down to two thousand pounds and stop. I got the idea of putting a union man on the fish scales to watch the company man from the story my old man told me. And when we did that we found that the fish boats increased their carrying capacity by anywhere from 15 to 25 percent per load.

So they took us to court and said we were a bunch of communists and it was restraint of trade and collusion. It was real bad. We went to court for years, and we finally won. Our lawyers said, "Look, if this is really hurting you, open up your books." Fi-

nally, the judge said, okay, he was going to give our union ten days in which to look at the canners' books. There was ten, twelve, fifteen canneries at that time. So they went to San Francisco and got a guy who was an economist and a pretty sharp guy, and they brought him down here. They found just on a spot check that over the years they had stole ten million dollars or better. When that came out, the canners all at once dropped all their lawsuits against the union, and said we weren't communists, we were good, God-fearing people.

[In the years that John Royal has served as a union official, he has witnessed many changes in the fishing industry. For every victory won in establishing better working conditions, a health or pension plan, there have been changes in technology that have changed the scale of fishing and disadvantaged West Coast fisheries. In response, John has turned his attention increasingly to the intricacies of the international regulations that affect the fishing industry. Today he is as likely to be found meeting with or serving on commissions on international fisheries as on the San Pedro waterfront. Though the scope and nature of his work have changed, John can trace a common thread from his father's experiences to his own.]

John: I learned about labor ever since I was old enough to sit at the kitchen table and have a bowl of soup with the old man as a kid. I was raised in a strong union home and labor house. I never thought I'd wind up in the labor movement per se, but I guess water seeks its own level somehow.

I had to laugh at Dad's funeral. [Archie Royal died on December 19, 1983.] Mom, she says to me, "Gee whiz," she says, "You know I feel bad." I said, "Why?" "Well," she said, "I don't see any of your dad's friends, all of his old life-long friends. They're not here." I told her, "Ma, they're all gone. The old man buried most of them, he out-lived most of them." I said, "That's why you don't see them here."

Albina: Well, he had a full life, I'll tell you. He wasn't a man to lay around, just sit and watch TV. He wasn't that kind. Had to be doing something all the time. It's too bad they didn't get someone to write a book about his life.

John: Well, we may do it yet.

Albina and Archie Royal in their wine cellar in 1980, celebrating their sixtieth wedding anniversary and Archie's eighty-fourth birthday. Courtesy of John and Albina Royal

THE MELTING POT WORKS
Italians in Central Nevada
BLANTON OWEN

The Italian presence on Nevada's rural landscape is hardly noticeable today. With rare exceptions, notably Paradise Valley in northern Nevada and the Delmue Ranch in southern Nevada, the visible evidence of Italians in the state is sometimes little more than a name in a phone book or on a mail box. There are many stone buildings in the central Nevada town of Eureka, for example, and the reputation that northern Italians were excellent stone masons is well-known by Eurekans today. The same is true, however, for the Irish and the Germans. In Eureka, no specific historic structures are identified as being Italian built, nor are any Italian families identified as preeminent builders. In central Nevada, by the late nineteenth century when large numbers of northern Italians were settling here, a predominantly non-Italian physical and cultural landscape was already built and in place.

Italians first came to central Nevada in large numbers during a relatively short period of time, primarily between 1870 and 1880. At that time, the Eureka Mining District was booming. Large silver deposits were discovered in 1864, but a successful smelting process to separate the silver ore from the lead with which it was mixed was not developed until 1869. This smelting process required the use of high heat produced by burning charcoal. During the first few years of the ensuing boom, most of the people who cut wood and made it into charcoal were Irish, English, and German.[1] By the late 1870s, more than 90 percent of the charcoal burners were northern Italian.[2] There were charcoal "ranches" scattered throughout central Nevada, and the hills around Eureka for a fifty mile radius were virtually denuded of timber and sagebrush.

Most charcoal in the Eureka district was made in fifteen- to twenty-foot diameter circular "pits." A spot was leveled, often requiring a low retaining wall, and cut wood, between three and four feet in length, was stacked on end in an ever-expanding circle. The final stack was approximately twelve feet high and completely covered with brush and dirt. A small draft hole was left in the center of the stack from bottom to top, and enough air allowed into the bottom to start a fire. When the fire was started, it was watched closely and only allowed to smolder. Benny Damele described the process as "baking" the wood until it was charcoal.

There is archeological evidence of large rectangular charcoal pits in the area, although they are rare. These pits were up to seventy-five feet long and twenty feet wide.

Map of Nevada. Detail, "Tunison's New Railroad Distance and County Map of the Golden West . . . ," 1913. Italian-Americans interviewed in connection with Blanton Owen's essay live in Lander and Eureka counties, in eastern Nevada. Geography and Map Division, Library of Congress

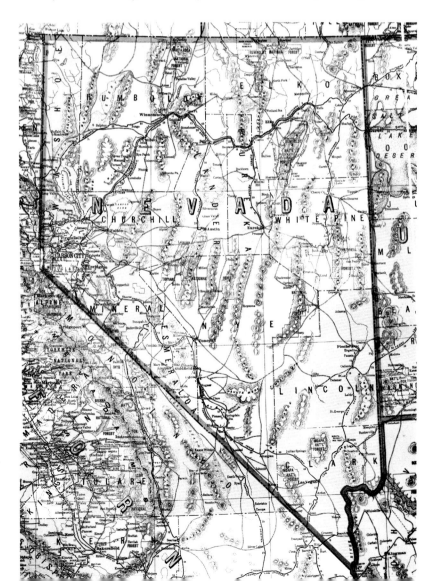

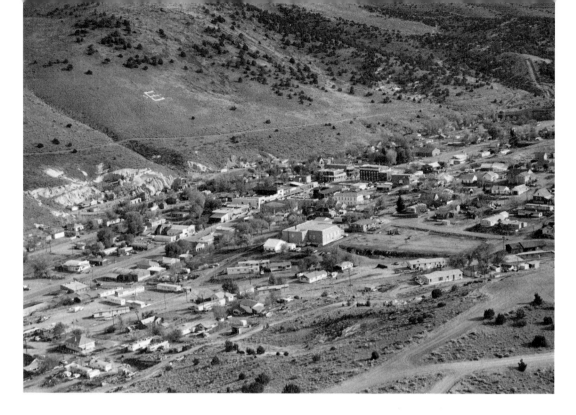

RIGHT: Aerial view of the town of Eureka, Nevada. The large "E" on the adjacent hillside, fashioned from whitewashed rocks, stands for the first letter of the town's name. Photograph by Blanton Owen, IAW-BO-B009-16

BELOW: The center of the town of Eureka and the hills to the west. The large brick building to the left is the Eureka County Courthouse, and the smaller building to the right is the old newspaper office, presently occupied by the local historical society. Photograph by Blanton Owen, IAW-BO-B021-17

They were covered with dirt and brush and burned in a fashion similar to that used in the circular pits. They were built on a slight slope, however, perhaps improving the burn along the length of the stack.[3]

There is one beehive-shaped stone charcoal oven still standing north of Eureka on the east side of Diamond Valley. Only a few of these permanent ovens were used in the Eureka district. Everyone has a theory about why stone ovens were used in some places and pits used in others, among them the availability of wood, the distance needed to transport wood to the oven, and the type of wood being used. It may be, too, that the ovens, which were built very early (the remaining one was built in 1869), were simply more trouble to build than they were worth. The existing oven is made without mortar, is twenty-five feet in diameter, thirty-five feet high, with walls eighteen to twenty inches thick. It was loaded through an opening near the top via a causeway built from the hillside to the oven.

The finished charcoal was packed and shipped in large sacks to the smelters via mule train, wagon, and rail. Eureka resident Al Biale recalls the distinctive ringing sound the bags of charcoal made when they were being handled or moved.

During the summer of 1879, Italian charcoal burners attempted to disrupt the making and delivery of charcoal to the silver and lead smelters in Eureka in an effort to rectify several grievances held against the smelters and their middle men. On August 18, a sheriff's posse confronted a large number of strikers at a charcoal ranch in the Fish Creek Mountains south of Eureka, and in the ensuing shoot-out killed five Italian *carbonari* and wounded several others. None of the posse was hurt. This event is variously called the Fish Creek War, the Charcoal Burner's War, the Italian War, and the Carbonari War.

Oral accounts of the Charcoal Burner's War maintain details and attitudes not seen in written accounts. Most of the burners were newly arrived Italians and could not speak English, a factor some present-day Eurekans think helped precipitate the fight. Benny Damele, a descendent of a charcoal burner, explained it this way:

There were so many people around that talked the language that they didn't have to learn [English], you know, their own people. They went to Italian boarding houses, Italian saloons and grocery stores the same. A few of them learned to talk a little [English]. They were mostly the dealers, and probably troublemakers, too, amongst them, because they knew the language and they'd make deals and they'd gyp the other guys. . . . They were probably the instigators of the strike. The smarter they got the more trouble they made, you know. People are that way.[4]

Al Biale, in talking about the English-speaking middle men, the people who contracted with the burners for the charcoal and then hauled it and sold it to the smelters, summed up his opinion by saying, "There's always somebody that's looking out for an easy dollar."[5]

Oral history accounts of the war rein-

Old charcoal oven in Diamond Valley, north of Eureka, Nevada. Built in 1869, the oven is thirty-five feet high and twenty-five feet in diameter. Photograph by Blanton Owen, IAW-BO-B008-16

force the folk belief, at least among the Italians in Eureka, that the strikers were justified in their actions and that the authorities attempted to cover up their roles. As Al Biale tells it:

I don't know, there's something funny there somewhere. They claim when these fellows were killed, the Italian consul, would it be, in San Francisco, [was headed for Eureka to investigate and help settle the dispute]. They got as far as Palisade and somebody talked him out of it and he went back, he never did come up [to Eureka after the shootings]. They had trials and everything, but they finally—I don't know just how that happened either—but they didn't jail anybody. And they still didn't give them their raise in wages, so they still blamed, according to what I could read, they still blamed the charcoal burners for starting it. Well, they did turn wagons over and interfere with things like that, but at the same time they were doing it for a purpose, and there's no question but what they should of had more, should have got more for their product.[6]

Al says the burners were striking for a three-cent-per-bushel of charcoal raise, from twenty-seven cents a bushel to thirty cents. This is no small amount when you consider that sixteen thousand bushels of charcoal were consumed per day during the height of the boom.[7] Written accounts, however, say the Italian consul did come to Eureka and helped calm the situation, and that the main demands of the strikers were for an increase in wages and the right of the charcoal producers to see the contract price between the middle men and the smelters. The "truth" of what happened, however, is irrelevant as far as the beliefs—and hence the behavior—of the people who retell the stories are concerned.

In Eureka the term *carbonari* seems to have had no political overtones, as it does in Italy. The Charcoal Burners Association, at best a loose organization composed of most, but not all, of the charcoal producers in Eureka, existed for only a few months and expressly to correct a specific economic problem faced by members of the group. There seems to have been no connection between it and the secret political organization (called *Il Carbonaria*) established in Italy to unify the disparate regions into a single national state.

Early Eureka had an Italian Benevolent Society and the Italian-dominated Charcoal Burners Protective Association was active for a few months, but the Catholic Church in Eureka, St. Brendan's, never had an Italian priest nor, apparently, a very strong Italian congregation. It seems, therefore, that except for a short period of time immediately after coming to central Nevada, Italians who elected to stay adopted those occupational and social practices that worked and helped them blend in with their neighbors. Miners of all nationalities had to learn to be hard rock drillers, heavy timber setters, and machine operators. Ranchers had to learn the cow handling practices that worked in the arid, thinly-grassed sage brush ocean of the great American desert. Even store keepers, especially after the mines closed, had to find merchandise and marketing techniques that appealed to a smaller, yet very homogeneous, clientele. The provisioning of Basque sheep herders and the supplying of large amounts of sugar for an illegal still operation are two examples.

Central Nevada's Italians are characterized more by their adaptability than by their retention of Italian cultural traditions.[8] There are no Italian social clubs, no bocce ball tournaments, no ethnic or religious celebrations and processions, no Italian restaurants and no Italian music or dance in Eureka or any other place in central Nevada today. Italians who stayed in the area when their main economic base of charcoal burning and mining disappeared adopted the occupational skills and attitudes that were necessary to become members of the larger community.

There are certainly some Italian cultural traits that survive within the Italian families in Eureka, but they prove to be the exception rather than the rule. Jeanelle Gibellini Dietrich, a third generation Italian born in Eureka (although she now lives and works most of the year in California) proudly remembers her mother and grandmother's ravioli recipe. She makes it, however, only for special occasions. She also has changed the main meat ingredient from beef brains to chicken to make the dish more palatable to modern tastes. The dish is now used as a symbol rather than as an everyday meal for nourishment.

The Gibellini ravioli recipe is more a symbol of family identity than of either Italian ethnicity or nationality. The two concepts are closely connected, but for most families and for Jeanelle Gibellini, the family comes first, Italianness second. Ravioli celebrates the Gibellinis as a family, one that happens to be Italian. Eureka's Italian families do not celebrate Italian traditions as such, they celebrate family traditions.

The Italians (and the Irish and the Germans) who elected to stay in Eureka when mining and smelting declined were the ones who still had a viable means of making a living. To do so, however, required that they be no different from their neighbors. To seem different (weird, standoffish, strange, cliquish) was a liability. Central Nevada, though large in geographic area, is thinly populated. People here clump together according to occupation, region, and religion more than according to ethnic origins.

To make such a concession was not hard. The people who stayed in central Nevada were of European origin. There was a significant Chinese population in Eureka during the boom years, but when the bust came, that community disappeared with very little trace. The Eureka Cafe, which still serves Chinese food, and the so-called opium den, a complex of tunnels and caves, are the last reminders of this community.

Perhaps another reason for staying in Eureka even when times got hard is that some folks were simply tired of moving and had too many roots; their migrating days were over. Contemporary descendants of the central Nevada Italians who stayed are invariably old-fashioned. They all pay serious attention to the past. Benny Damele's Dry Creek Ranch only recently rigged a solar- and battery-powered electrical system, and Benny still works his cows the old-time way. Louis Gibellini sharpens his drill steels "the old-fashioned way" without using "science." Al Biale is the town's foremost historian and is responsible for having a small monument erected where the five Italians killed during the Charcoal Burner's War are buried. Al's grandmother showed him the unmarked grave, and he never forgot.

Most immigrants to the American West, especially those who came to the rural West, almost immediately bought into the American dream of economic success; they came to make a stake. Central Nevada was not like Italy; it was dry, big, and sparsely settled. There were people from all over the world here rubbing elbows. During the period from 1870 to 1880, Nevada was proportionately the largest immigrant state in America: 44.2 percent of the state's residents were foreign born.[9] Most who came to the Great Basin intended either to go back to the old country (whether that be China or Italy), or to resettle in another, more hospitable environment as soon as they made their stake. And many did just that. Those who stayed, however, were successful adaptors, willing to give up those cultural traits

Local historian Al Biale at his home in Eureka. Biale's father and grandfather were both Eureka charcoal burners. Photograph by Valerie Parks, IAW-VP-B002-2

that set them apart from their neighbors in order to fit in.

The Italian ethnic experience in central Nevada, perhaps uncomfortably for contemporary advocates of "multiculturalism," is an example of a successful melting pot. None of Eureka's Italian families have denied or forgotten their Italian ancestry, but none consistently practice old-world cultural customs either; they exist in memory only, to be revived within each family according to each family's collective memory when desired.

Al Biale's uniform is gray-striped overalls. He is slight of stature and balding, and lives in the dressed-stone building that once was the manager's office for the Eureka Consolidated's smelter and mill, which was located across the road. His knowledge of the region's folk history, especially that which has occurred in his eighty-seven

years of residence in Eureka, is remarkable. He can produce names, dates, and other details, as well as general impressions, folk histories, anecdotes, and stories. He is gracious in manner, gentle of speech, and attentive to questions.

Al Biale's grandfather, John, emigrated from Genoa Province to Eureka in the mid-1870s to burn charcoal. He worked in the Fish Creek area for four years, but returned to Italy shortly before the Charcoal Burner's War of 1879. Soon after his return there, his daughter Clotilde and her husband Tom Pescio left for Eureka. Shortly thereafter, Al's father, also named John, immigrated to Eureka to be with his sister. He was fourteen years old. Their father never returned. Young John went to school in Eureka, starting as a fourteen-year-old in the first grade, but he learned English quickly. In 1881, his sister and her husband tried to enter the ranching business by buying Pinto Creek Ranch, southeast of Eureka, but they could not work out suitable terms. His sister and her family, therefore, returned to Italy, but John stayed. He burned charcoal, then worked in the mines and on ranches to make a living after the smelters shut down. While working for the Diamond Mine, he took time off to visit family friends in Utah. There he chanced onto a job as a clerk in a store run by an Austrian lady who could not speak Italian and was losing considerable business because of her inability to communicate with potential customers. John, however, had promised the manager of the Diamond Mine that he would return and operate the hoist, and he did. Nonetheless, at the first opportunity John quit the mining business and started the Eureka Cash Store. That was in 1903, the year his son Albert was born.

By 1903, Eureka had declined to a town of only seven hundred or so, down from a high in the late 1870s of nine thousand. The smelters were closed, and the mining that continued was small-scale. John Biale's store survived by carrying just about everything the townsfolk and surrounding ranchers needed except feed and dry goods. The store also catered to the growing sheep industry; it provisioned the burgeoning Eureka Land and Stock Company, which ran over eighteen thousand sheep, and the many itinerent Basque herders who passed through the area. During the 1920s, the Eureka Cash Store brought in up to thirty train car loads of merchandise a year.

By the 1910s, Eureka's Italian community was relatively small. Al's parents spoke both Italian and English, and his grandmother only Italian. But other children often made fun of Al when he spoke Italian, so he and the other Italian children his age very quickly dropped the language. Al also recalls as a youngster being called "dago" occasionally, plus various forms of anti-Italian discrimination.

The breakup of Eureka's Italian community, which began with the Charcoal Burner's War of 1879, spelled doom for the few communal Italian social activities and practices theretofore maintained. Al remembers that the main public celebrations during his youth were Thanksgiving, Fourth of July, St. Patrick's Day, and Labor Day. No special Italian holidays were celebrated. Public music usually consisted of saxophone, piano, drums, and trumpet, and town dances were held in the huge corrugated sheet metal dance hall, called The Pavilion, which still stands on the east side of town. These were community dances and not strictly Italian events. Al and others also remember that there was an Italian accordion player in town when they were kids, and that he used to play popular tunes of the day for family celebrations such as birthdays, weddings, and anniversaries. Again, he played for Italian and non-Italian families as well.

The single Catholic Church in Eureka, St. Brendan's, was never a center for the Italian community, and its priests were usually Irish. Al Biale does not remember special celebrations of Italian religious days or other holidays by Eureka's Italian families.

The disarray of the Italian community following the Charcoal Burner's War is illustrated by where those killed were buried. Although the victims were Catholics from northern Italy and southern Switzerland, they were not allowed to be buried in Eureka's Catholic cemetery. Instead, they were buried on the edge of the city cemetery. Al recalls that, as a very young boy, he used to accompany his grandmother on Memorial Day to pick wild flowers to decorate the family graves in the Catholic cemetery. "And then she'd always say," in her Swiss dialect, Al points out, "'now we have to go to the other cemetery, to put the flowers on the *carboneng*.'"[10] The depressions of the graves were still evident, Al remembers.

Until about the beginning of the second quarter of this century, many Italian families in and around Eureka raised a hog or two and made Italian sausage. A few people also distilled *grappa* and made wine. Interestingly, however, during Prohibition, the largest whiskey still operation in the region was run by a Tennessean named Gus Johnson. The Biale's store supplied up to sixty, one-hundred-pound sacks of sugar per week for the operation, plus a large number of charred oak barrels for whiskey storage. Al says the small-time, family operators, some of whom were Italian, were put out of business by the law, but the owners of the large still, who were not Italian, simply bought the law. The whiskey made at this still went mostly to Ely and Reno rather than to the local market, and hence it operated for about four years immune from prosecution. The Tennessean, incidentally, did not own the operation; he was simply hired to run it.

When the mines were operating, certain ethnic groups were associated with specific mines and their adjacent communities. The mine at Ruby Hill, about five miles west of Eureka, was worked by the Cornish and was owned by an English outfit. Al Biale's wife, Marie Harris, was the granddaughter of a Cornishman who worked as a hoist engineer at Ruby Hill. The Prospect and Diamond Hill mines, five miles south and twelve miles northeast of Eureka, respectively, were worked primarily by Italians, but owned by English. Both Al's father and his wife's father worked at these mines.

During the halcyon days of Eureka's mining, when the Italian community was fairly large and cohesive, there were a number of round, brick, beehive bread ovens in back yards. Al Biale remembers his grandmother using one when he was a child. She started a fire in the oven in the morning while the bread was rising. Shortly before it was ready to bake, she raked out the coals and ashes and wiped the bottom of the oven clean with a damp burlap sack wrapped around a flat wooden paddle. When the heat was right (determined by how a piece of brown paper bag curled when placed inside), she put the loaves onto the flat paddle and slid them into the oven. She always made special small loaves for Al and his sister. Al remembers that the Gibellinis and several other Italian families had ovens, too, and that one family baked bread as a commercial operation. There are no bread ovens in Eureka today.

Benny Damele sits down to an ample evening meal. The table is loaded with turkey, mashed potatoes and gravy, green beans, coleslaw, iced tea, coffee, and a large jug of red wine. Conversation ranges from politics to American Bashkir Curly horses to the old timers and beyond. After supper, everyone congregates around the fireplace as the daylight fades. A kerosene lamp is lit if something needs to be read or seen

more clearly, otherwise the light of the fire suffices. The day's events are discussed, and tomorrow's briefly touched on. The talk soon ranges toward the abstract, politics accounting for a goodly share, especially regarding the Bureau of Land Management (BLM).

Benny Damele is part of the third generation of Damele ranchers in central Nevada. His grandfather, John, came to Eureka in 1879 from northern Italy and worked as a *carbonari* for almost ten years. He arrived shortly after the Charcoal Burner's War and just as the mining industry was beginning to wane.

The inevitable mining bust, or borrasca, began in Eureka in the mid 1880s. Many of the mines shut down, and the two largest smelters, the Richmond and the Eureka Consolidated, closed in 1890 and 1891, respectively. The town of almost nine thousand people dwindled fast. Many of the Italians who worked in the mining industry, either directly or in related occupations, left, some returning to Italy, others moving on to other mining camps in the West. Still others left to seek their fortune in the fast growing areas on the west coast with established Italian communities.

John Damele stayed. During the hard winter of 1889–90, he found work on a cattle and sheep ranch near Eureka and never returned to work as a *carbonari*. He sent back to Italy for his wife and three children and, upon their arrival, leased his own ranch. Two years later they bought Three Bar Ranch. There they raised cattle, hay, and, for a time, sheep. When Benny's grandfather, John, bought Three Bar prior to 1900, the ranch buildings were already there. The same is true of all the ranches subsequently bought by the Dameles.

John Damele's son, Peter, bought Dry Creek Ranch in 1942 and most of the buildings on the ranch were already built by then. The main house was constructed around 1910–12 by Matt Hickison, who also built the stone stable and the smaller stone barn above the stable. It is this smaller barn that Benny thinks must have been built first, for it appears that half of it was lived in for a while, perhaps while the house was being built. It has windows, doors, and a stove flue. Today this barn serves as a chicken house and for storage. Benny's father, with the help of Benny and his brother Peter, built the large addition to the house in 1944. The cobblestone fireplace was built by a rock construction specialist, an Irishman named Bill Wholey (perhaps, Benny thinks, the proper way to spell the name is O'Holey). Wholey also helped Benny build the stone bunkhouse a few years later. In 1990 the old wallpaper was removed from

the "mud" (adobe) covered walls of the original part of the house. The newspapers behind were dated 1906.

The Dameles did very little building, with the exception of a few outbuildings, so there is no expression of old-world stone masonry or Italian building types on their ranches. By the time the Dameles entered the ranching business in the late 1800s, the buckaroo style of cow work was already entrenched in the region. Even though John Damele and his son Peter were Italian and spoke Italian between themselves, they immediately adopted the Spanish-derived regional style of ranching. Today, Benny Damele exemplifies the buckaroo heritage of cowboying.

The distinctive buckaroo style of cowboying harks back to the old *vaquero* days of

Aerial view of Benny Damele's Dry Creek Ranch, Lander County, Nevada. Clockwise from lower left: corral and stable, chicken house, Quonset hut used for machine storage, main house and bunkhouse (behind trees), and blacksmith's shop (right, foreground). The ranch was established as a supply and remount station for the Pony Express. Photograph by Andrea Graham, IAW-AG-B004-13

Standing at the stable on his Dry Creek Ranch, Italian-American buckaroo Benny Damele (right) and ranch hand Bob Eddy hold a horsehair mecarty. Photograph by Valerie Parks, IAW-VP-C014-12

Benny Damele's father, Peter, ca. 1940s. Born in 1890, Peter was the first Damele born in Nevada. Courtesy of Benny Damele

the late nineteenth century in California and northern Mexico. Charlie Russell character-izes the style this way:

Texas an' California, bein' the startin' places, made two species of cowpunchers; those west of the Rockies rangin' north, usin' cen-terfire or single-cinch saddles, with high fork an' cantle; packed a sixty or sixty-five foot rawhide rope, an' swung a big loop. These cow people were generally strong on pretty, usin' plenty of hoss jewelry, silver-mounted spurs, bits, an' conchas; instead of a quirt, used a romal, or a quirt braided to the end of the reins. Their saddles were full stamped, with from twenty-four to twenty-eight-inch eagle-bill tapaderos. Their chapa-rejos were made of fur or hair, either bear, angora goat, or hair sealskin. These fellows were sure fancy, an' called themselves buc-caroos, coming from the Spanish word, *vaquero.*[11]

Other characteristics of the buckaroo style that Benny adheres to are dallying rather than tying hard-and-fast, the making and use of horsehair mecarties, and the braiding of rawhide reins, bosals, romals and reatas. To dally is to take turns around the saddle horn after roping an animal. To tie hard-and-fast is to attach the end of your rope, usually only about thirty-five feet long, to the horn and let the animal run to the "end of his rope." A bosal is part of a headstall, like a hackamore. A romal is a quirt braided to the ends of the reins, which are never split. A reata is a rawhide rope.

Central Nevada is open range cow country. There are several large corporate ranches here, and on these ranches the cow-boy crew—the buckaroos—handle only the cow work. Haying, irrigating, and feeding hay are not considered buckaroo tasks; this is work for the ranchhands, often derisively called "rosin jaws" or "hay dinks" by the cowboys. The ideal buckaroo job is one where all of the work is done on horseback, but the realities of the job usually dictate some riding aboard tractors and in trucks as well. This is especially true on the smaller family ranches, such as Dry Creek, where all of the work must be done by the same one or two persons with perhaps the help of a hired hand or two.

Benny's father, Peter, was the first Damele born in Nevada, in 1890. Benny tells stories of how his father spoke Italian and Shoshone before he learned English, and how, in about 1907, when his father was a youngster, he rode through what is today Dry Creek Ranch. At that time there were only a few stockade corrals and a small cabin on the place. The original cabin, built of mud-and-willow and log, still stands, though in ruin. The place was then known as the Bates Ranch and, as Benny says, "was started by the ponies"—the Pony Express— which had supply and remount stations at Dry Creek and neighboring ranches in 1860. The water supplies and natural meadows at the Ackerman, Dry Creek, and Givens Ranches made them ideal stopover spots. The remains of the station at Dry Creek can still be seen below Benny's house.

When Benny's father, Peter, bought Dry Creek Ranch from John Hickison in 1942, there were Damele ranches in an almost unbroken line from Palisade in the north to Eureka and Austin in the south, a stretch of nearly a hundred miles. Today there are two Dameles still operating ranches, Benny and his cousin Leo's son Tony, who is at Sheep Creek Ranch fifty miles north of Dry Creek.

Benny Damele is a fine maker of horsehair mecarties. Nails and hooks used for holding the hair strings used in making them are located on the posts along the open front of the long, stone stable below the house. A mecarty is a combination lead rope and reins, and is often used with a bosal or a snaffle bit. Although some mecarty makers say mane hair is softer and easier on the hands and use only that,

Benny Damele (right) and Link Eddy (Bob's son) making a horsehair mecarty. Photograph by Blanton Owen, courtesy of Nevada State Council on the Arts

Benny uses tail hair, which he says is more plentiful and no harder on his hands than mane hair.

A finished mecarty is usually about twenty-two feet long and is made from four, three-eights-inch diameter, twisted "strings," which are themselves twisted together, but in the opposite direction. To make a string, Benny loops a few strands of hair over a hook in the end of a twist drill operated by an assistant, often young Link Eddy, the son of the couple who help Benny on the ranch. As he feeds the strands from a bundle of hair that was previously "picked," or separated and mixed up, Link twists and slowly backs up. Benny keeps feeding the hair. He determines the thickness of the string by how much hair he initially attaches to the hook and how many hairs he allows to slip between his fingers and thumb as the string grows. The tightness of the twist is adjusted by how fast he feeds the hair.

Benny Damele in his corral "parting out" cows to be sold. Photograph by Andrea Graham, IAW-AG-B003-20A

The annual cycle of work at Dry Creek is similar to that of the neighboring ranches, but remains uniquely old-fashioned in some ways. In the winter, Benny hauls hay to the cows and bulls, which are separated. Even though the cows are kept fairly close to either Dry Creek or Ackerman Ranch (which Benny also owns), the twice-a-day feeding chore in the worst of weather is cold, hard work. At one time, Benny became dependent, as have most ranchers, on tractors and trucks for hauling hay to his cattle. During one winter, however, an especially cold and snowy spell occurred. Temperatures of thirty to forty degrees below zero held for weeks. His tractors and trucks would not run, either because they would not start or the fuel truck from town could not get to his place. From that time on, Benny has never been without a good team of horses and a sled to feed with. He begins working them in the fall and keeps them busy throughout the winter.

Benny feeds sometimes as late as the end of April, depending on the weather. In March or April he brands calves and turns them out. They usually stay fairly close to home until the grass comes in on the mountains, at which time they move off. In June, he gathers his cows in the mountains and works the unbranded calves at corrals he has scattered around. He gathers in a circuit from south to north, finishing up at Ackerman. He is usually done by mid to late June. During the summer months haying is the order of the day.

Feed on the mountain begins to dry up in August and the cows start to move down to the flats. He puts them in the hayed fields below the house and gathers a number of yearlings to sell in September or October. He weans the calves in November and generally ships in December.

Unlike most ranchers today, Benny does not attempt to have all of his calves born within a short period of time, usually sixty days. This is partly because he has no adequate place to hold his bulls for any length of time, and because he knows the old-fashioned way has always worked well for him. "Yeah, I don't know. A lot of people [are] always wanting to increase their cattle and having trouble increasing. And me, I have more trouble keeping 'em down than I do increasing. I don't have no trouble getting [calves]."[12]

Benny shares the frustrations many ranchers in the West have with governmental control of the land, and BLM efforts to manage the range. He talks adamantly about his role as a steward of the land. "There's no way that anybody can stay in this business and abuse the country, you know, like they claim has been abused. I don't see how they can. I can't. I know if I do it, I'm out of business, I'm done."[13]

In 1989, Benny discovered he had colon cancer. He underwent modern chemotherapy to fight the disease, but also took two homemade medicines. One is an unidentified root he got from a Paiute friend of his and which he chews several times a day, and the other is a bitter-tasting, pasty concoction he calls "buckaroo medicine." Although usually taken internally, this buckaroo medicine is also reputed to be good for removing festering warts or moles; it "burns" them off over the course of a few days.[14]

Although Benny is a firm believer in his folk medicine, he is not so keen about another folk tradition. When he was a young man he decided he would take up the harmonica, an instrument played by his father. While riding in the mountains, he took the harmonica from his pocket and gave it a blow. His horse went crazy and bucked like there was no tomorrow. Benny clamped down on the harmonica with his teeth so he wouldn't lose it, and every time he came down into the saddle and the wind was knocked from him, the harmonica

squalled, and the horse kept bucking. Finally Benny realized what was happening and he spit the instrument out. The horse stopped bucking and took off up the hill at a gallop. Thus ended Benny's music-making efforts; he never went back to find the harmonica.

Louis Gibellini ascends the platform where the cube of granite sits, four feet on a side. It's the annual World Championship Single Jack Drilling Contest in Carson City. He arranges his eleven steel drills, hammer, and water bucket, assisted by his granddaughter, Jaqualeene, who paces his drilling and maintains the proper flow of water into the hole. The gun sounds and Louis begins a steady, driving rhythm, the sound of steel against steel ringing over the audience. He hardly seems to exert himself, but the four pound hammer keeps swinging and the hole keeps sinking, one steel replacing another. He maintains sixty-five strokes per minute, turning the steel after each blow. Many drillers lose their grip

Retired miner Louis Gibellini about to drive his "steel" deeper into a block of granite during the 1989 Single Jack Drilling Contest in Carson City, Nevada. Gibellini endeavors to maintain a steady pace with his four-pound hammer: at least sixty-five blows per minute over the course of the ten-minute contest. Photograph by Blanton Owen, IAW-BO-B002-9

after about six or seven minutes, and pause to flex their hammer hand. Louis never stops and the rhythm never falters. As the final minute starts, Jacque coaxes him to speed up his pace to seventy-six strokes per minute. He does. When the final gun sounds, Louis simply stops drilling, removes his steel, stands erect, gives the crowd a huge smile and waves. The audience goes crazy. They know they have seen the real thing; an honest-to-God hard rock miner who learned to drill in the mines, the hard way, not just for exhibition.

Louis never trains or practices for contests. As he says, he's "done it before," so he "doesn't exert himself" anymore. A fine understatement; Louis, at age eighty-four, regularly out-drills men sixty years his junior. After this contest he said, "When I got through, I didn't know I even drilled. I

never exerted myself, I felt just like when I started. And the rest, the way they exert themselves, they're crazy."[15]

Singlejack, hard-rock drilling contests are held today throughout the mining West. They probably began in the third quarter of the nineteenth century, at about the same time steam rock drills were converted to compressed air, making them suitable for underground use. This technological advance also stimulated the growth of hand-drilling contests as unique occupational celebrations in the West's many mining communities. It seems, however, that the mine operators were more interested in competitions between machine drills than human drillers:

The mine owners would be more interested in a competitive trial of rock-drilling machines [than of hand drillers]. In these days

Singlejack drilling contest at Tonopah, Nevada, 1904. Courtesy of Nevada Historical Society

[1892] machine labor in rock-drilling has so far displaced hand labor that such personal contests have no longer the value they formerly had. . . . All the mines of any size use the machine drill. . . . They do the work so much cheaper and quicker than men can do it.[16]

The earliest literary reference to a drilling contest is to one at the Boulder Industrial Association Fair in 1877. Accounts of earlier mining celebrations, such as the Miners' Union Day in Virginia City, Nevada, in 1874, do not mention drilling contests specifically, although they certainly could have been held.[17]

Drilling contests, like other occupational celebrations of skill, such as rodeos, loggers' jamborees, and firemens' musters, have very specific rules. Each driller is allowed eleven "steels," or drill bits of varying length. They cannot be smaller than three-quarters of an inch in diameter, and must have only one cutting edge; no star drills are allowed. The hammer can weigh no more than four pounds. A water bucket with a small hose out the side near the bottom with some sort of clamp to adjust the flow may be operated by one assistant. The object of the contest is to determine which driller can drill the deepest hole in ten minutes.

A driller begins at the gun by "collaring" the hole, getting it started even and straight, then continues to drill using successively longer steels until the final gun sounds. Colorado drillers tend to use a long, high hammer stroke, with fewer—but harder—strikes per minute. Nevadans generally use a quicker and shorter hammer stroke.

Doublejack drilling is more rarely seen today, although interest in reviving the technique is growing. Doublejack teams take turns swinging the hammer and holding the steel, and a good team can switch positions

Louis Gibellini's singlejack drilling tools: Bucket (used to hold water for flushing dust out of the hole and lubricating the "steel"), "steels" of various lengths (increasingly longer steels are used as the hole deepens), and a four-pound hammer. The tools are placed on top of Gibellini's "practice rock," a four-by-four-foot cube of granite he keeps in his backyard. Photograph by Blanton Owen, IAW-BO-B003-36

Louis Gibellini holds the engraved silver belt buckle he was awarded for winning the Nevada Silver Centennial Single Jack Drilling Championship in Virginia City on June 15, 1959. Photograph by Blanton Owen, IAW-BO-B012-16

**Louis Gibellini holds
the eight-foot-long
wooden skiis he made
and used in the 1920s,
when he traveled over
the mountains in the
winter from the Pros-
pect Mine to the Wind-
fall Mine. Photograph
by Blanton Owen, IAW-
BO-B013-2**

without missing a beat. In a doublejack contest, the steels are seven-eighths of an inch
in diameter, the team members must change
positions at least five times during the ten
minute allotted time, and a hammer must
weigh no more than eight pounds.

Louis has won the prestigious World
Championship Drilling Contest a number of
times in the past. Today, however, he participates only as a special invited guest, an
honored celebrity. Louis proudly wears a
silver belt buckle he received as first place
winner in a drilling contest held in Virginia
City in 1959 to celebrate the centennial of
the Comstock Lode's discovery. The buckle
was presented to him by then Vice-President
Richard Nixon.

Louis Gibellini's parents both came to
Nevada from southern Switzerland at age
fourteen, shortly before the turn of the century. His father ran a string of pack mules
hauling ore from the mines at Prospect to
the smelters in Eureka. After large scale
mining bottomed out and the smelters
closed down in the late 1880s and early
1890s, Louis's father continued to haul ore
from the remaining small mines to the narrow gauge railhead in Eureka, where the ore
was loaded and shipped to Utah for smelting. It was at this time that he became more
active as a miner and less as a packer.

Louis was born in Prospect in 1907.
While in Prospect, a heavily Italian settlement of about one hundred people, his
family and several others migrated in the
summers over the mountain to the Windfall
Mine. There they raised a small garden and
worked until fall, at which time they returned to Prospect, where the kids attended
school. Louis still has a pair of skis he built
and used to ski over the mountain from
Prospect to the Windfall Mine in the winter.
They are eight feet long, four inches wide,
and have old boot tops tacked to them
where the user's boots slipped in and were

laced tight. In those days Louis called his skis "snowshoes" and skied with a single pole, eight or ten feet long, rather than using the two poles common today.

Most of the mining activity in Prospect was shut down and the school was closed by 1921 when Louis moved with his family to Eureka. Even after this move, however, Louis continued to work in Prospect at the small, two- or three-man "gypo outfits" that persisted there, and at the Windfall Mine.

During a recent visit to the house where he was born in Prospect, Louis pointed out where his family's bread oven used to be, where the large boarding house once stood, where the school was, where the family's milk cow was kept, and just who lived where. There was never a grocery store in Prospect, so residents had to haul their provisions from Eureka and make their own food. He recalled how his grandmother made cheese and sausage, raised small gardens (in Prospect and at the Windfall Mine) and made wine, brandy, and *grappa* from imported California grapes. He also recalled how his parents spoke Italian in the home, but that he always replied in English. He says he never learned to speak much Italian, but understood it.

When Louis Gibellini started his career as a miner in the early 1920s, many of the mines around Eureka still drilled by hand. It wasn't until the late 1930s and 1940s that mechanized drilling equipment was commonly used in the smaller mines. Louis says that although he occasionally double jacked in the mines, most of the drilling was single jack. He also explained that with either method, the proper temper of the drilling steels was crucial. Each hardness and type of rock to be drilled required a correct temper. In order to be prepared—and safe—he took several sets of differently tempered steels into the mines each day. If steels of the wrong temper are used on the wrong

hardness of rock, he says, they can "break like glass."

Louis still sharpens his steels "the old fashioned way," just as his father taught him years ago. He does not use what he calls "science," like the younger competition drillers do today. He has a small, frame blacksmith shop next to his house where he sharpens and tempers his steels. He shapes them in the wash tub forge and does the final dressing on the grindstone. He tempers them by heating them to a cherry red, lets them air cool the proper amount, then takes a torch and heats them a little bit more to "draw the temper." When they are heated to the right color, he quickly cools the steel by immersing it in water. For hard granite, Louis draws it "a light straw," and for softer stone, he lets it remain a little more blueish.

The interior of Louis Gibellini's small blacksmith's shop, where he sharpens and tempers his drilling steels. Photograph by Valerie Parks, IAW-VP-B004-7

In the mines, wherever the working face is, is where the drilling has to be done—horizontally, below, or overhead. When drilling down, a trickle of water is run into the hole to flush the dust and grit from it, thus improving the drill's efficiency. Drilling horizontally or overhead, however, is done dry.

Louis continued to work in the mines off and on until 1967, primarily at the Windfall Mine and the Diamond Mine at Prospect. Because mining then was fairly small scale compared to the boom days fifty years earlier, Louis continued to drill by hand for years rather than use pneumatic machinery such as jack leg drills or drift drills. He has, of course, worked pneumatic equipment as well. In 1947, Louis and his wife, Josephine, now deceased, opened Louie's Lounge, a bar in Eureka, which Louis continues to run only on an occasional basis; he hates bartending.

Louis Gibellini beside his homeplace at the old mining settlement at Prospect, five miles south of Eureka, with researchers Andrea Graham and David Taylor. Photograph by Blanton Owen, IAW-BO-B011-14

The exterior of Louie's Lounge, a bar run by Louis Gibellini, on Main Street in Eureka. Photograph by Valerie Parks, IAW-VP-B004-3/4

Retentions of old-world culture are generally strongest where fairly large numbers of immigrants live in close proximity—as when northern Italians came to central Nevada in the 1870s to work in the mining industry there, specifically the making of charcoal for the smelters. The Charcoal Burners Protective Association was comprised mostly of Italians, and the Italian Benevolent Society thrived. Although current residents do not recall that there were specific Italian celebrations and pastimes, it is probable that there were. Furthermore, although no historian has yet to show that a *padrone* system existed in Eureka, oral accounts support the probability.[18] The large number of Italians who came to Eureka from a relatively small region of Italy and southern Switzerland is striking and is perhaps greater than would have resulted from word-of-mouth or family connections alone.

THE MELTING POT WORKS | 67

By the mid-1920s, old-world Italian cultural traits seem to have all but disappeared from Eureka. Because Italians who came to central Nevada did not retain old-world Italian customs and practices much beyond the time of initial settlement, however, does not mean their contributions to the area have been small or gone unappreciated. The Italians brought an ethic of hard work to the area, and provided a work force at a time when it was crucial for the region's survival. When that time passed, those Italians who stayed continued to contribute. The Dameles owned well-managed ranches throughout the region, the Gibellinis continued to work the mines and haul the ore, and the Biales continued to provide merchandise for the entire community and region.

Each of these families continues in the occupations of their forefathers. The Biale family still runs the Biale store, although Al's grandson-in-law now runs it as a hardware store and electrical supply shop. Louis Gibellini is still involved in the mining business; he holds options to several mine claims and participates in hard rock drilling contests. His granddaughter also has entered the family occupation as his assistant in the drilling contests. Benny Damele still ranches, and his nephews, Bernard and Tony, are in the wood cutting business just as their great-grandfather was in the 1870s. They have come full circle, a fact certainly not lost on Benny.

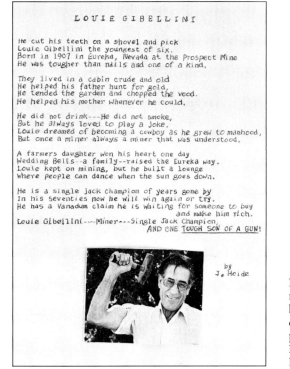

Poem about retired miner Louie Gibellini by J. Heide. Courtesy of Louie Gibellini; photograph by Blanton Owen, IAW-BO-B002-1

The communities that are central Nevada are not comprised of Italians or Irish or Germans, but rather of Americans or Nevadans or Eurekans who happen to have Italian or Irish or German ancestry. The communities are based on occupation and region, and are made up of individuals, some of whom are of Italian descent, who fit comfortably within the larger community. They are accepted members of that community and continue to contribute to its well-being.

PLACES OF ORIGIN

Calabresi in
Carbon County, Utah

PHILIP F. NOTARIANNI

Even though emigration from Calabria to Carbon County formed a tiny stream in the larger international flow of migration from Italy, it looms large within the contexts of the two places. I discovered this when I ventured into Decollatura, Italy, on an October day in 1987, unfamiliar with the town and its people. After stopping near a group of men and women absorbed in morning conversation, I introduced myself as someone studying Italian immigration history, and living in the United States. One woman quickly asked, "Have you every heard of Helper, Utah?" I choked, but immediately realized that for these Calabresi, the reference point to the United States was not Chicago or New York, but Helper. Her uncle, she informed me, is Raffaele Scalzo, an immigrant to Carbon County, Utah, in the early 1920s, who subsequently returned to Decollatura.[1]

Assessing the social and cultural effects of emigration and immigration requires knowledge of both places of origin and places of destination. The connections between Carbon County, Utah, and the southern Italian region of Calabria are cases in point. At first glance, the two places seem to be as far apart culturally as they are geographically, but a closer examination reveals that they are intimately involved in each other's history. Carbon County, where Calabresi settled in the early twentieth century as miners, railroad workers, and laborers, has in many respects become an extension of Calabrian history, while Calabria similarly shares in the history of the county and of Utah and the American West.[2]

Calabria, the toe of the Italian peninsula, has long been and continues to be a land of emigration. The dynamics of migration continue to shape the region, and Italian scholars differ on whether this process has been beneficial or harmful. Some see emigration as basically positive—a means of

sustaining a viable economic base and a vehicle for the maintenance of strong kinship ties (since emigration often transfers family relationships to the host country).[3] Others see it as disruptive; they claim that emigrants abandon more than their ancestral homes; they abandon a cultural landscape and a network of social relationships and economic ties that have developed over generations. This latter view holds that emigration robs both individuals and communities of their historical legacy.[4]

Scholars debate both views as they turn their attention increasingly to topics such as

Calabria, the region that forms the "toe" of the "boot" of Italy.

ABOVE: **Researcher Philip F. Notarianni (second from left) shares a glass of brandy with Raffaele Scalzo, Angelina Scalzo (Raffaele's niece), and Vincenzo DeFazio (Philomena and Vito Bonacci are Vincenzo's aunt and uncle by marriage), Decollatura, Catanzaro, Italy, March 1988. Raffaele Scalzo was an immigrant to Carbon County, Utah, in the 1920s. Courtesy of Philip F. Notarianni**

RIGHT: **Map of Utah. Detail, "Tunison's New Railroad Distance and County Map of the Golden West . . . ," 1913 Geography and Map Division, Library of Congress**

FAR RIGHT: **Map of Carbon County, in central Utah, showing railroad lines connecting the communities. Courtesy of Philip F. Notarianni**

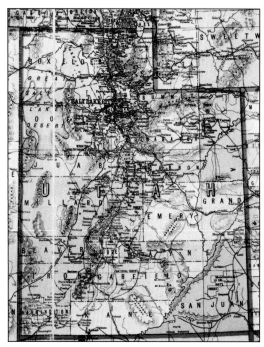

La Calabria dei Paesi (the Calabria of villages) and *il paese, la memoria* (collective village memory).[5] An examination of the cultural landscape, material culture, and folk traditions discloses that this collective memory has persisted in Utah as well as in Italy. The experience of Calabrians in Carbon County provides a case study of the maintenance of values and traditions in both the homeland and host country, and modifications of them over time.

In 1910, the United States admitted 718 Italian immigrants who gave Utah as their destination. Of that number 462 were listed as South Italian and 256 as North Italian.[6] In Carbon County, where this distinction between north and south would persist over the next generations, most of the southerners came from Calabria. Indeed most of them came from five villages: Aiello Calabro, Grimaldi, and San Giovanni in Fiore—which were in the province of Cosenza (CS)—and Cortale and Decolattura in the province of

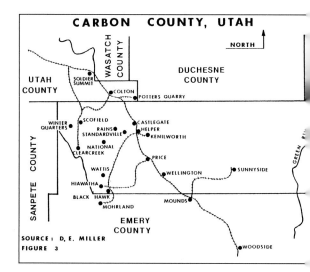

Catanzaro (CZ). Aiellesi, Decolatturesi, and Grimaldesi came to the coal camps of Carbon County to supply the labor required to run mines and railroads. The coal camp at Sunnyside was especially popular, for work was readily available in the mines and at the coke ovens. One of the Grimaldesi, Pietro Silvagni, became a contractor and built coke ovens there. Vito Bonacci of Spring Glen, Utah, remembers the coke ovens vividly. So does Raffaele Scalzo, who returned later to his home village of Decollatura CZ, carrying with him the stories of his experiences.[7] Such common memories were one of many links between the two regions.

With the immigrants came the language, foods, beliefs, customs, and values of the *paesi* or villages of origin. The landscape, for example, served both as context and as an expression of this cultural continuity. Scattered across the rugged Carbon County terrain are vegetable and spice gardens, chicken coups, pig pens, slaughter gallows (where animals are hung for skinning and cleaning), rabbit hutches, outdoor

kitchens, and domed baking ovens. Most of the gardens include basil, oregano, fennel, parsley, and garlic—all important in the maintenance of traditional foodways. The *barracche* (shacks or outbuildings), constructed of stone and wood, are similar to those found in the Calabrian countryside. The Calabrese immigrants erected familiar structures on the land, buildings that facilitated the production of familiar foods, such as *salsiccia* (pork sausage), *prosciutto* and *capocollo* (ham), *vino* (wine), and freshly baked bread. United States Geological Survey maps of Utah mining towns and Istituto Geografico Militare maps for various Calabrian towns show a surprising degree of similarity in terrain and layout. Thus rural Utah, unlike the urban immigrant destinations of the East, provided the Calabresi with suitable land and many opportunities to recreate their native landscape traditions.[8]

And when the Vito and Filomena Bonacci family traveled to Calabria in 1983, they discovered visual links between the Calabrian and Carbon County countrysides.

Carbon County coal miners, September 1942. Courtesy of Mary Nick Juliano, IAW-PFN-B007-2

ABOVE: **The Castle Gate Mine, Castle Gate, Utah. Photograph by David A. Taylor, IAW-DT-B036-28**

BELOW: **The town of Grimaldi, Consenza, Italy. September 1987. Photograph by Philip F. Notarianni**

For their son Joe Bonacci, the connection was triggered by:

the rock masonry that they did. I can see a lot of that here [in Carbon County]. . . . they all built their houses that way, over there, and that's the way a lot of Utah Italians in this area built their homes. . . . Everything was rock. . . . I guess that was something they learned from their youth, to build with that sandstone rock. . . . I thought of the old rock cellar that grandpa had over here in the front. . . . I guess that's what those people knew.[9]

Calabrese stone masons, such as Felice Gigliotti, also of Decollatura, have left a lasting legacy of stone work on the Carbon County countryside that continues to trigger the cultural memory.

The interaction of people with the land forms a theme common to the lives of Calabresi who remained in Italy and Calabresi who immigrated to Carbon County. An attitude toward the land, generally shared by Calabresi, is that it exists to be used. In Calabria, peasants work the land in patches and strips, often on steeply terraced hillsides, prudently using every available square centimeter. While Carbon County offered large tracts of land, the Calabrese practice of using land intensively persisted in Utah, nevertheless. This is still evident in the historic Saccomanno homestead in Spring Glen, even though it is now abandoned and being reclaimed by nature. Such practices are visible in the present-day Charles Saccomanno home, also in Spring Glen, and in

The distinctive rock formation that gives Castle Gate, Utah, its name. Photograph by Philip F. Notarianni, IAW-PFN-B008-16

the Catherine Verdi property in Helper. And Vito Bonacci of Spring Glen continues the "Italian way" of planting tomatoes, using wooden latticework to allow the fruit to grow upward.[10]

In the Verdi, Saccomanno, and Rudi Bruno homes, we see how spatial arrangements convey values. In each instance, the front yards are neat and orderly, somewhat artificial, and seldom actually used. The backyards seem completely disorganized, on the other hand, but the owners spend most of their outdoor time in the backyard and know the location and use of each thing there.

Calabresi place great emphasis upon the home. As in European peasant societies, the home becomes one's point of reference in space and time, central to a sense of identification.[11] Thus it was an "omen of great misfortune" to dream of the loss of one's own home. This attachment helps explain the recurring psychological and physical agony suffered by Filomena Bonacci, the wife of miner and labor organizer Frank Bonacci of Decollatura, as her family faced eviction from company-owned housing as punishment for her husband's labor union activity. As her daughter Marion once recalled, during the 1922 strike, coal company guards removed the family's furniture from their home, and the Bonaccis were forced to live in a shack. And because Frank Bonacci was out of work, Marion and her siblings went hungry. "My mother was never the same after this experience," Marion added. "She was silent and withdrawn." Anger over such evictions formed a primary issue in various Carbon County strikes.[12]

The concept of utility in the home (like the attitude toward the land) is also of primary significance. As with dwellings in Calabria, many Italian homes in Carbon County exhibit a sort of utilitarianism, driven by the attitude that there are particular times and places to accomplish particular tasks. For example, certain areas are designated for making wine in October; while others are for preparing hogs for slaughter in January. Devotion to the principle that one should derive maximum use from the space available is exemplified by the use of basements for second working kitchens and the use of out-buildings, called *baracche*, for putting up fruit and tomatoes or making soap. These homes also display the varied and creative uses of "cast off parts"—old railroad locomotive train springs used to run wine presses; railroad ties forming retaining and house and shed walls; and old bathtubs used as watering troughs for animals.

But items of personal and family attachment also abound in many Carbon County Calabrese homes. Photographs depicting family and friends, religious symbols, and various group identifications adorn walls and furniture, often in shrine-like exhibits. Mary Nick Juliano, born in San Giovanni in Fiore, and a resident of Price, possesses a myriad of such symbols.

Many Carbon County Calabresi equate the concept of home with relatives, whether in this country or in Italy, and the presence of family in Calabria solidifies the connection with the *paese* of origin.[13] If they lack family in Calabria, the attachment of Utah Calabresi to the place of origin is much weaker. John and Yolanda Bruno, for example, have no relatives in Italy, since most of the family emigrated. They have never visited Calabria. Vito Bonacci had a brother, Carmine, in Decollatura, but when Carmine died the link to the old country was diminished substantially and Vito knew that as a consequence he would never return to live in Calabria.

Central to the connection between personal identity and the uses of certain places is the object. Artifacts provide a "vehicle [for the] continuation and support of subjective identity,"[14] constituting a primary anchor for personal and cultural memory. Carbon County Calabrese households abound with objects that connect the generations to one another and Italy to America. The continued use of such objects by the immigrants' descendants indicate either a conscious or subconscious attachment to the *paese* and culture of origin. Such objects include implements for sausage making; ravioli and pasta makers; espresso machines and coffee grinders; wooden funnels and utensils; wine presses; outdoor domed baking ovens (*forni*); and cheese graters. Many of the smaller objects actually came from Italy, either during the immigration period or later. Other objects are contemporary artifacts representing the same value of utility, but conveying different forms. Vito Bonacci's "oven pullers" are a case in point: handmade wooden sticks with a hook on the end to pull out an oven grate and push it back in. Some of these gadgets find their way back to Italy to Calabrese friends and relatives there.

The Verdi and old Saccomanno homesteads retain the domed outdoor baking ovens called *forni*, once common fixtures of the Carbon County landscape. Historically, the *forno* exerted an important role in the personal economy of the peasant. Bread held a vital place in the diet of the people. Calabrian proverbs hold that "When in the home there is bread, there is everything. If there is flour, and oil, and wine, a home is full. . . . Those without fire live, that without bread dies." ("*Quannu alle case c'e' llu pane, c'e' tuttu; Si c'e' lla farina, l'uogliu e llu vinu, a casa e' kina . . . Chi eppi fuocu, campau; che eppe pane, muru.*)[15]

Vito Bonacci at his home in Spring Glen, Utah. Bonacci was born in Decollatura, Italy. Photograph by Philip F. Notarianni, IAW-PFN-B003-28

Mary Juliano recalls their oven, built by her "Papa Nick." (She remembers it well because she had to clean it!) The Nicks used a mixture of one hundred pounds of flour to bake one batch of bread. Homemade wooden *pale* (shovels, paddles) were used to distribute the hot coals and clean the oven. A fire was started in the middle of the oven using soft, sweet wood, "to enhance the taste." After heating, the oven was cleared of coals and the dough was put in to bake. A large iron door was closed over the central opening, but the flow of air was controlled through side vents. The use of *forni* continues in Calabria in basically the same manner, especially during holidays such as Christmas and Easter. But Mary and other immigrants replaced their outdoor ovens with coal stoves,[16] and later with gas or electric stoves.

Just as they keep objects from Italy a part of daily life in Carbon County, the Calabrese immigrants and their families demonstrate that there is a place for the dead in the lives of the living—another point of connection with their Italian relatives. The photographs that line the walls of many homes are but one manifestation. A more profound illustration is to be found in the numerous gravestones in the Helper and Price cemeteries that carry not only the names of the deceased and dates of birth and death but also inscriptions in the Italian language, birth places such as Reggio Calabria, and specific images, including photographs of the deceased.

The headstones of many of the Italian victims of the March 8, 1924, Castle Gate mine explosion in Helper are written in Italian and also refer to the Calabrian places of origin. Likewise, in the Calabrese town of Pedivigliano (CS), a headstone reads, "Frank Chiodo Family, U.S.A." In other locales, photographs of immigrant relatives are placed on grave markers even though the person is buried abroad. Both forms of honoring the dead reflect ways in which Italian relatives symbolically transport the souls of loved ones back to the *paese*.

There is another example of this connection between a common past and the two locales in Grimaldi, Italy, in the form of a monument honoring the city's World War I dead. The impetus for erecting the monument came from former resident Michele Jachetta (living in Pueblo, Colorado, at the time of the proposal) and his brother Antonio, who had settled in Columbia, Utah. Jachetta's newspaper, *Il Vindice,* sought subscriptions from Grimaldesi throughout the United States and Canada. By April 1922, the cause had collected some 18,515 lire from approximately fifty men, including some residing in Sunnyside and Helper. The monument still stands near the Grimaldi Municipio as a physical reminder to the Grimaldesi of the efforts headed by the *Americani.* [17]

For Carbon County Calabresi, foodways are the most enduring and visible of all the connections with an Italian/Calabrese identity. Food must be of high quality because it is given to the family, the wellspring of traditional values. And food also reflects directly upon the family, since conveying a *bella figura* (beautiful or positive appearance) is crucial to family honor. Preparing and eating certain foods allow a community to recreate its ethnic identity, maintain traditional boundaries with the dominant culture, and nurture familial closeness. Partaking of Italian foods enables the community to participate in Old World customs, evoking a nostalgic yearning for a simpler, pastoral life. Ultimately, these commemorative functions of food express different ways of experiencing the world (through its textures, tastes, shapes, colors, and smells) and different ways of organizing experience (as dynamic, holistic, and mysterious). [18]

Calabresi, both in Italy and Carbon County, prepare specific foods for specific occasions. Pasta and *sarde* (sardines), *bac-*

Gravestone, in the cemetery at Helper, of miners Domenick and Mike Bertolio, killed in the March 8, 1924, explosion at the Castle Gate Mine. Photograph by David A. Taylor, IAW-DT-B036-2

cala (dried salt cod), smelts, *crispelle* (a type of fritter), *finocchio* (fennel), and *lupini* (lupine seeds) evoke the traditional spirit of Christmas Eve dinner for many, including John and Yolanda Bruno of Helper. Others continue the process of making sausage, even exhibiting regional differences within Calabria.[19] For example, Utah immigrants and their descendants from Aiello Calabro use fennel in their sausage mixture, whereas those from nearby Colosimi do not, a variation still evident in the respective *paesi*.

Historically, in Calabria, the hog formed an integral part of the family economy,[20] and the slaughtering of hogs was a joyous event. Because fresh meat was seldom eaten, *l'uccisione del maiale* (the slaughter of hogs) became a feast featuring fresh meat and an abundance of wine that was celebrated by family members and friends. Although hog slaughterings rarely occur in Carbon County towns today, many slaughter gallows remain to testify to the importance of this yearly ritual. Mary Juliano and Filomena Bonacci vividly recall the tasks that fell to them, the

ABOVE: **Filomena Bonacci. Unlike her husband Vito, she was born in Carbon County. Photograph by Philip F. Notarianni, IAW-PFN-B003-14**

LEFT: **Mary Nick Juliano stands in front of a wall of family and religious photographs, images, and statues at her home in Price, Utah. Juliano was born in the Calabrian town of San Giovanni in Fiore, in 1904. Photograph by Philip F. Notarianni, IAW-PFN-B006-12**

jobs traditionally assigned to women: they cleaned pork entrails for use as sausage and *suppressata* (salami) casings, and prepared the large meal the day of the kill. Each part of the hog served a purpose—nothing was wasted.

Today in Calabria and Carbon County fresh meat is no longer a rarity; nevertheless, many families continue to make sausage and other preserved meats. For Joe Veltri, son of Italian and Greek parents, the making of homemade sausage connects him profoundly with his Calabrese heritage. For others, its popularity has declined, particularly as a result of the recent awareness that consumption of pork products is related to hypertension and high levels of cholesterol.

But even though the form of a traditional practice may change over time, it is often the case that its underlying values do not. For example, while the types of food or the ingredients of a dish may have changed, the value of quality in food preparation remains constant among Italians in Calabria and their relatives in Utah. Whenever possible, spices and basic ingredients are homegrown. And it remains important to know exactly what a food contains. In fact, various Calabrian families in Carbon County insist upon obtaining hand-picked aniseed (*aranzo*) from Calabria in making *fresine* (toasted biscuit), *taralli* (bread sticks), and other baked goods. Joe Bonacci, son of Vito and Filomena Bonacci, recalled the family's visit to Calabria in 1983 and how a neighbor, Jeanie Crocco, specifically requested that he bring her some *aranzo* from Calabria, which she wanted for her baking. John Bruno, originally of Domanico (CS), announced that anise seeds used to make *fresine* were from Italy. Whether purchased in Utah supermarkets or ethnic specialty stores, the domestic anise seed is just "not good enough."[21]

In the context of Carbon County, one may also observe other changes in foodways practices. For example, Rich Colombo, of Helper, uses knowledge passed down in his family to make sausage, but now makes it to sell at his market rather than solely for his family and friends. Implicit in his behavior, using a traditional form but "expressing" it in a new context, is the historical need for Calabresi to adapt in order to survive.

Language provides another link with past places. While most third- and fourth-generation Carbon County Italians do not speak Italian, those of the first generation (the immigrants) and some of their children possess a repertoire of words in Calabrese. Most often, to the amusement of their Calabrese relatives back in Italy, their lexicon reflects the dialect as it existed sixty years ago. Nevertheless, the usage of even a few words or phrases represents a connection that must be recognized as significant, both in conveying an identity and in demonstrating an ability to engage in linguistic code switching—the ability to move from one language to another.[22] For many descendants of Utah Calabresi, even when they are conversing in English, a colander remains a *sculapasta,* and one uses a *mappina* to dry dishes.

Linguistic code switching was apparent during an interview with Mary Nick Juliano, who was born in San Giovanni in Fiore in 1904 and came to Carbon County in 1909. Mary writes poems in English, but translates them into Italian because the language is "so emotional." As she answered questions, and became more comfortable with the interview, she switched from English to Italian. It was as though Italian conveyed more of her inner thoughts and beliefs. She recounted folk tales told by her father, again beginning in English but then reverting to Italian.

Owing to the lack of regular communication with the homeland that is a typical outcome of the immigrant experience, especially in the past, there are many instances of immigrant communities preserving customs that are no longer common in the old country. Accordingly, when Utah Calabresi return to Italy or when Calabresi from Italy visit Calabresi in Utah, a fresh awareness of Calabria's past is awakened. For example, during a visit to Salt Lake City, Giuseppe Maletta, of Colosimi, noted that Utah immigrants had told him about traditions and incidents in Colosimi's past that had previously been unknown to him. He was amazed that he had to travel to Utah to learn certain facets of Calabrian local history.[23]

Local Calabrian folklore, in turn, has been influenced by emigration. In writing of the Sila region in central Calabria, known to Carbon County Calabresi, one author maintains that emigration, as a social and human condition, has given many motives to song, popular poetry, proverbs, and "all that serves to express nostalgia, love, joy, and sorrow." With immigration there existed an exchange of popular culture.[24] Thus, when Raffaele Scalzo returned to Decollatura after living in Carbon County since the early 1920s, he recounted both fact and legend concerning the trials and tribulations of labor organizer Frank Bonacci. In this way portions of Utah lore became intertwined with that of Decollatura.[25]

Another immigrant who had arrived in Utah in 1954 recounted his 1977 return to Pedivigliano in Salt Lake City's *Deseret News*. Describing "The Pedivigliano Connection," Joe Costanzo wrote that perhaps everyone in the town "has heard about Salt Lake City, and some of the people walking along the steep narrow cobblestone streets know a great deal about the American city." He continued, "Back in Salt Lake, Pedivigliano is a household word in hundreds of

homes of Italians who immigrated to America and [to their] descendants."[26] That this connection proved of significance to the town is evident in a 1978 planning document which stated specifically that Pedivigliano's urban growth and development was a direct result of the "remittances from many immigrants."[27] As is the case with other towns, Utah money continues to find its way to Calabria for feast days or local restoration projects.

Telephone directories in Decollatura and Grimaldi contain many of the names listed in the Helper telephone book—Bonacci, Scalzo, DeFazio, Anselmo, Veltri, Bruno, Albo, and Gigliotti, for example. While looking around the Grimaldi cemetery, during my 1987 visit to Calabria, I was confronted by an older gentleman who suspiciously asked what I was doing near his wife's mausoleum. When I mentioned that I was from the western United States, his eyes lit up. "My father worked for the Denver & Rio Grande Railroad between Grand Junction, Colorado, and Helper, Utah."[28]

The *memoria* of the *paese* is still a shared resource, represented sometimes by land, sometimes by objects and activities, and more often by less concrete but equally compelling ties of tradition and of personal and family identity. It survives in records and documents as well as in memory and today is the object of renewed interest, not only among historians, but among the third and fourth generation of Carbon County Italian-Americans, who have learned that being an American does not require the renunciation of an Italian heritage. Raffaele Scalzo expresses the strong feelings he has for the two lands this way: "When someone talks bad about Italy, I get mad. But when someone talks badly about the United States, I get God-damned mad."

FOLKLIFE AND SURVIVAL

The Italian-Americans of Carbon County, Utah

STEVE SIPORIN

The dramatic landscape of eastern Utah may have seemed half-familiar to southern Italians like Giovanni Nicolavo when they first arrived in the early 1900s to dig coal out of the mountains and build railroads through them. Eastern Utah was arid and mountainous, like Calabria, but bigger, emptier, much colder in winter, and with fewer trees. What were the odds that the knowledge possessed by these immigrants—a (now) foreign language, farming skills based on Mediterranean weather and southern Italian crops, the medicinal uses of wild herbs that grew in Calabria, what each type of tree was good for—what were the odds any of this would be of use in Carbon County, Utah? Yet, this body of traditional knowledge was the only survival kit Nicolavo and his countrymen had.

Although they chose to leave a place where it had become increasingly difficult to earn a living for a place that symbolized unlimited economic opportunity, many threats to survival lay ahead. How would they, for instance, deal with the loss of family and homeland? What hardships—physical, economic, and emotional—were concealed beyond the proverbial "streets paved with gold?" How did they survive and what did they become?

The word *survival* has long been a key word in the study of tradition. Beginning in the 1870s, folklore itself was defined as "survivals," meaning "those processes, customs and opinions, and so forth, which have been carried on by force of habit into a new state of society different from that in which they had their original home."[1] This usually meant ancient, pre-Christian practices which were still to be found among European peasants at the time. Later, in America, the term was used to refer to "the survival of Old World customs that prove to be more conservative in the Americas than in Europe"—what might be called the sur-

vival of survivals (the wearing of amulets for protection against the evil eye by Italian immigrants, for instance).[2] Scholars like Melville Herskovitz, who emphasized the African element in African-American folk music, have been called "survivalists,"[3] and a dictionary definition calls survival "the act or fact of survival, esp. under adverse or unusual circumstances."[4]

To survive means, literally, to outlive, but the question in folklife studies is always *why?*—why has a particular custom lasted for fifty centuries, or why is a certain story still told when so many others have been

Empty coal cars rolling through Price Canyon, just north of Helper, Utah. Photograph by Steve Siporin, IAW-SS-B014-5

forgotten? The term *survival* is like a riddle in that it begs an answer; "force of habit" is not an adequate explanation.

Scholars and laypersons alike have tended to see traditional life-styles—even while they approve and appreciate the implicit aesthetic values—as a hindrance to success in modern industrial (and post-industrial) American settings. Nevertheless, the experience of Italian-Americans in Carbon County, Utah, seems to be saying something else: that traditional culture—folklife—has survived not as a drain on "real" life, not as something that has lasted in spite of its irrelevance, not merely as a testimony to sentiment; instead, their contemporary stories, houses, gardens, and recipes show us that traditional culture contributed in irreplaceable ways to the fundamental economic and social stability of Italian immigrants in the industrial, desert landscape of east central Utah. The folk culture of Calabria and Piemonte, of the Tyrol and Puglia, may have been the best of survival kits.

In folk culture, as in biology, endurance results from significance, not inattention, from persistence, not unconsciousness. "Survivals" depend upon *survivors,* real people—because it is *their* use, reinvention, realignment, and reconstruction of past culture

Two prints of Jesus and a crucifix on the wall of Rose Vea's living room, Spring Glen, Utah. Photograph by Steve Siporin, IAW-B016-16

that defines the present in relation to the past. Those who have not been overcome by history possess it and redefine it in their stories, their customs, and the objects they make and keep and even wear. If we listen and observe, their words and culture can tell us how they survived and what their history means to them.

But before seeing how their survival kits were "unpacked" and used, it is worth understanding something of the experience of immigration itself, including an appreciation for the trauma of leaving one's homeland, the first obstacle to survival.

I first saw Italy in October of 1967 as a student. I remember that the beauty of the landscape shocked me into realizing how difficult it must have been for anyone to leave. As the child of immigrants myself, I had been taught to be thankful for having been born in America—because America was, I was told, where *everyone* wanted to live; the "old country" was a bad place that the fortunate escaped. Italy was, obviously, not the same in 1967 as in 1907, but the idea that the old country was beautiful and worthy, that immigrants might have felt reluctant or at least ambivalent to leave, was an entirely new idea to me. I soon came to feel that there was probably no place on earth more beautiful, more deeply civilized, and more hospitable than Italy.

Was mine the naive response of impressionable youth? Perhaps, but it is also the typical response of hundreds of years of tourists, enraptured by olive orchards and vineyards seen and smelled in the golden autumn sun. And, more to the point, it is not just foreigners who love Italy. Listen for a moment to the words of Mary Nick Juliano of Price, Utah, as she recalls the moment of her parting from San Giovanni in Fiore, Calabria, Italy, seventy-four years before:

It's still a vivid dream. I remember the old cobblestone road—just an old road. We lived down there with my grandmother, my mother's mother, Serafina Sucurro. My dad's mother was way up the road, Angela Tangara, and my grandpa, Giambattista Nicolavo, my daddy's dad.

I remember the church, on the right side, and a few dear neighbors, on the left. I was just a little girl. . . .

Poppa didn't have any money, so he planned to come to America, and he left Momma and myself at Grandma Serafina's home. . . . My two uncles—no three!—Joe, Matteo, and Luigi—were home, and we lived with Grandma until Poppa sent money for Momma and myself to come to this country. . . .

There was a little scene in front of our home there in Italy that I'll never forget. I hung on to Grandma Sucurro, [voice shakes with emotion, on the verge of tears] and that's just as vivid as today. I wouldn't let go! It took two or three to unwrap my little arms. I was just five! And I screamed her name. My uncle grabbed me and hugged me tight. And the last thing I remember—is—that dear, dear little grandma, falling on the cobblestone road, screaming my name. We arrived in this country, but for a year, my mother thought I was going to die.[5]

Mary's narrative is more than a personal history. It is told and retold in the Nick family in Price, Utah, because it says something fundamental about immigration (the name *Nick* is an Anglicized version of Nicolavo). Being torn from one's grandmother is literal here, but it is also an apt metaphor for being torn from one's mother*land;* and leaving the place where one is secure, and sheltered by an extended family, sounds like the loss of paradise. Such an expulsion is the kind of trauma from which one may die—or grow strong.

In fact, many immigrants tell similar stories. Listen, for instance, to the story Til Davido tells of her mother, Elizabeth Marrelli, when she left the same town, San Giovanni in Fiore, for the same destination, Carbon County, Utah, to get married, at the age of twenty-one:

Til Davido: When she got in the carriage to leave, she said she could still see her mother running after the carriage and crying. She said, "That's something I'll never, ever forget—seeing my mother cry when I was leaving."

Steve Siporin: She probably figured she'd never see her again.

Til: Yes, and she didn't. The only member of their family that she ever did see again was her brother, because he came here.[6]

Parting from mother or grandmother was also a parting from family, home, and motherland—an event so painful for Mary Juliano and Elizabeth Marrelli that its memory has been inscribed not only in their own minds, but in the stories told by their descendants. These stories typify two different, but common, immigration experiences: those of a small child and those of a young woman about to be married. Both narratives begin in apparent helplessness, but both are life stories of survival and triumph.

Elizabeth Marrelli, Til Davido's mother, looked back at her journey over seventy years later, as she approached the age of one hundred:

When I was nineteen, I received letters from America. They were written by a gentleman named Francisco Felice. . . . Frank's letters and my responses were read and written by my aunt who was the village interpreter. After two years of corresponding, Frank sent me the money to go to America and become his wife.

I left my village, wearing a sign saying Salt Lake City, Utah and traveled by train to Naples. From Naples I traveled by ship to New York City. When I arrived in New York City, I was stranded for three days because I was thirty-five dollars short for my train fare. . . .

I had neither food nor money and I was only able to say "Helper, Utah America" in English, so I sat on the hard wooden bench alone in the big train depot. Finally, a shop keeper close by the depot came to help me. He was Italian and was able to speak with me. He wired Frank Felice in Helper, Utah and was able to get me the money. . . .

My long journey finally ended at Salt Lake City, Utah. There I met Francisco Felice. He was a very handsome man.[7]

Helen Papanikolas, a historian as well as a Greek native of multi-ethnic Helper, Utah, recalls that Elizabeth Marrelli's journey was not unique:

I often heard music coming from the Denver and Rio Grande Western depot [in Helper] where the uniformed Italian marching band met incoming passenger trains. They were hired to serenade immigrant picture brides, sent by their families to marry men they had never seen.[8]

Papanikolas's comment may explain the conclusion of Elizabeth Marrelli's immigration/marriage narrative: "He was a very handsome man." The brides were themselves "picture brides," but often they had not had a single opportunity to see images of the men they were to marry—until they met them.

The immigration experience of Mary Nick Juliano's father was also typical, but in other ways. He had left for America, to seek the family's future, even before his first child, Mary, was born. He had left his home village, San Giovanni in Fiore, because conditions had worsened, and it was harder for him to make a living than it had been for his parents. There was no hope things would improve in San Giovanni, at least not unless he could save enough money in America to return and buy his own land.

Once he arrived in America, he seized what opportunities he could. He worked in coal mines in Pennsylvania and West Virginia and silver mines in Nevada before coming to the coal camps of Carbon County, Utah. Here he found other Italians already working—some from his own province of Cosenza in Calabria, some even from San

Giovanni. The owners of several of the stores in the railroad and mining center of Helper were *mangiapolenti*—"cornmeal eaters"—North Italians, especially Piedmontese, who had arrived earlier. The old-world hostility between the northerners and southerners continued even here, exacerbated, perhaps, by the superior economic position of some of the earlier-arrived Piedmontese.

There were many other "foreigners" in the coal camps and towns: "Austrians" (meaning Croats, Serbs, and Slovenes), Chinese, Greeks, Irish, and Japanese, to name a few of the major groups. Fieldworkers for the Works Progress Administration counted twenty-eight different ethnic groups among a total Carbon County population of around twenty thousand in the 1930s.[9]

It is hard to know the emotions felt by that first generation of Italian immigrants to coal camps and railroad worksites in the American West. Was the vastness and remoteness of the western landscape more (or less?) daunting than the man-made metropolitan crush of the East? We do not really know for certain because these immigrants rarely articulated their feelings in written form, leaving behind, instead, stories about their hard work, modest needs, and camaraderie with each other. Doubtless, they faced tough questions and harsh choices. Although each of them possessed a great store of indigenous, local knowledge, it could not have been clear at first if such knowledge and skill would be of any value in America. They must have sometimes wondered if they had pulled the rug out from under themselves, putting everything, their lives included, in jeopardy. Ann Bonacci, of Helper, says that her father recalled a woman on ship screaming "*siamo perduti!*" ("we are lost!") as they steamed into New York Harbor.[10]

Garlic hung up to dry in an outbuilding adjacent to the Bruno house in Helper. Photograph by Thomas Carter, IAW-B006-27

Perhaps one reason many Italian immigrants to Carbon County survived and prospered was that they were not afraid to take risks. They were not foolish, either. Guido Rachiele, who today runs the Checkerboard Grocery in Price, says that his father left Reggio di Calabria for the United States when his friends wrote about the economic opportunities he would find. He was willing to work hard and did not give up readily. According to Guido, his father arrived in 1909 and first worked in Philadelphia as a cook for a construction crew. Then, based on the encouragement of others who had gone west, he headed for Southern California, because, as his friends had said, it resembled Southern Italy. But an encounter with cowboys in Elko, Nevada, threw his ultimate destination open to chance:

When they were in Elko, there was a holdover, and it was about the time one of these cattle drives came into Elko. And of course the cowboys were jubilant: they were hitting Elko. They began shooting, they began hollering, and so my dad and his two companions got scared. Not knowing what was happening, they jumped off the freight—the passenger train, and headed off into the sagebrush—worrying, that someone was af-

ter them, with all the shooting! So they stayed in the sagebrush all night. The next morning, when it became daylight, there was a passenger train, so they got on the passenger train. But not knowing that it wasn't going to California, it was heading back to Salt Lake. . . . So Elko was as close to California as he was able to get! . . .

There was a fellow in Salt Lake that said, "I'm going to Carbon County to get a job in the coal mines." So they got on a train and come back to Carbon County and was able to get a job . . . in Moreland. . . . And he and his two buddies got jobs in the coal mines there. And he became a settler of Carbon County.[11]

John Bruno, of Helper, recalled that beginning around 1900, his father and a friend named Colombo would come to the United States, work on the railroad for a year, and then return to Italy. He made several trips before "he got tired of going back and forth so they built a home here in Helper. And they sent for us in 1913."[12]

Was John Bruno's father originally trying to save up enough money in America to buy land in Calabria and remain there permanently? We do not know, but some estimates indicate that fully half of the Italian immigrants returned to Italy when they had enough cash to buy plots of land and thus gain control of resources (and their own destiny) in their home villages.[13] Was Bruno's father unsure of his ability to survive in the United States and thus kept returning to Italy? Or had immigration always been his plan, a plan set back periodically by economic depressions in the United States or by loneliness? That might be possible, for even today, Vito Bonacci—an immigrant who has lived in Spring Glen, Utah, for sixty years—considers the merits of returning to Calabria.[14]

Others in Carbon County, like Mr. Ariotti of Spring Glen (born in North Italy, near Novalese in the region of Piemonte), tell of parents or relatives who "couldn't make up their minds" and traveled back and forth, from villages in Italy to western towns in the United States, for their entire lives. Ariotti says that his father liked Italy when he was in the United States and the United States when he was in Italy. Finally, his mother said that she was staying put; she was in the United States at the time. Her husband went back to Italy—but when he decided to return World War II intervened. His children brought him back to America, long after the war.[15]

The province of Piemonte, in the far northwest of Italy, seems to have been the other major source of Carbon County's permanent Italian immigrants. Edna (Borla) Romano's great-grandfather and grandfather left the French-Italian border area around Noli and arrived in Helper early enough (1895) to witness Butch Cassidy's hold-up at Castle Gate, according to family tradition. The great-grandfather and son worked in Carbon County's mines, but the son returned to Italy to marry, then returned to Carbon County, and finally sent back to Italy for his wife. He himself eventually returned to Italy to live the rest of his life, but his wife, Edna's grandmother, stayed and raised six children in Castle Gate.[16]

Those who remained in the mining and railroad towns of the intermountain West succeeded against difficult odds; they solved the riddle of survival. As I suggested earlier, scholars and laypersons alike have tended to see traditional culture as a hindrance to success in twentieth-century American settings. As much as we may applaud efforts to conserve tradition, we have—at least until recently—viewed traditional cultures as neutral at best, as impediments at worst, to full participation in American life. This attitude has not yet ceased; witness, for instance, the recent law making English the official language of the state of California, a law based on the unproved assumption that solid grounding in ancestral languages other than English impedes economic and social integration.

Many members of the first generation of Italian immigrants to Carbon County did not feel this way. As Helen Papanikolas writes,

Although America was ostensibly a melting pot, the immigrants did not know they were supposed to melt in it. In their neighborhoods they continued their age-old customs: they married and baptized their children in joyous communal affairs; they played their folk songs on ancient instruments; they sang of their nations' tragic history under waves of foreign invaders; they called midwives and folk healers to attend them; and they keened for their dead at the side of open coffins or buried them according to their ancestral customs.[17]

But how did traditional culture solve the immediate, economic problem of survival?

First, coal mining was not the regular, dependable, year-around occupation that we may assume it was. There was more work in the winter (although the number of days per week varied), when people heated with coal, but virtually none in the summer. Lou Colosimo recalls that when he lived in Moreland, Utah, where he was born, his father had only about one day's work per month.[18] For miners, income was not steady or even predictable. Most families lessened their dependence on cash income through the enormous gardens they planted, the animals they raised, butchered, and preserved, and the bread they baked with wood they gathered, in the outdoor ovens they built. These traditional skills gave them an economic self-sufficiency without which they could not have survived in Carbon County.

Other uncertainties existed, too. Although the men came to Utah because of economic opportunities, many were killed or crippled in the mines, and their families were left without means of support. Survival then became an even more difficult riddle. Elizabeth Marrelli, whose immigration narrative was recounted earlier, provides an example of someone resourceful enough to find a solution and become a survivor. First, she gives us the old-world background:

In my village, I was known for my bread making and crocheting abilities. I remember one time when I was about thirteen years old a woman from the village went to my mother asking for me so that I might make her some bread.[19]

Elizabeth (then "Sabella") corresponded with Francisco Felice for two years before coming to Helper to meet him and marry him. But after twelve years of marriage, tragedy struck when Frank died:

I was alone. This time I had four mouths to feed. What did I do? I baked my bread. Every morning at five o'clock I kneaded one hundred pounds of flour into many loaves of my good bread. These loaves were baked in an outside oven. It was not easy, but we had each other and we made the best of life at that time. You do what you have to do and think about it later.[20]

Most families appear to have baked their own bread in outdoor ovens, usually once a week; Elizabeth Marrelli baked every day

and earned a cash income by supplying single miners. In other words, the humblest of traditional skills enabled the Marrelli family to survive with dignity and ultimately triumph.

Survival periodically became an acute problem for many during railroad and mining strikes, especially when strikes failed. As Philip Notarianni writes, after a 1905 strike and organizing effort was broken, some Italians began "truck farms" along the Price River.[21] The traditional agricultural skills of the Saccomano family, for instance, allowed them to develop a diversified farm that supplied fresh fruit and vegetables to the working miners in the remote company towns in the mountains:

These are the boxes that we used to peddle with in the wagon. We special-made these. There'd be sixteen, in the wagon. We'd fill these with potatoes and tomatoes and vegetables. . . . We made them ourselves— there'd be four across and four down . . . [to] fit the wagon.[22]

The Saccomanos raised sheep for wool and spring lamb, slaughtered their own pigs to produce a wide variety of sausages and salami, and started their vegetables growing as early as February by using framed "hotbeds." They were self-sufficient. The wagon and specially made boxes were eventually replaced with a truck, and they continued

Drawing of the domed bake oven (*forno*) in the yard of the Antonio and Marie Verde house, Helper, Utah. According to family history, it was Antonio "Tony" Verde (born in 1914) who built the oven, much in the style of those found in Calabria. Prior to use, a large quantity of wood—cedar or juniper—would be burned in the oven until it was very hot. The coals and ashes would then be swept out and radiant heat would be used to bake bread. The oven is six feet across at the base and nearly five feet high. Drawing by Susan Anderson

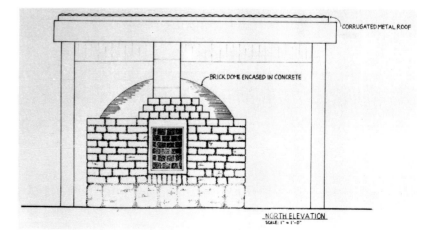

NORTH ELEVATION
SCALE: 1" = 1'-0"

CORRUGATED METAL ROOF

BRICK DOME ENCASED IN CONCRETE

Shoe repairman Dominick Besso at work in his shop in Price. Besso's father was a shoemaker in Italy, and he continued in the trade when he moved to Carbon County. Photograph by Steve Siporin, IAW-SS-B022-16

peddling fruit at the mining camps until the late 1960s. Today, Charlie Saccomano still raises pigs (for sale), rabbits, chickens, and a huge garden. There are also orchards and fields of alfalfa.

Not everyone mined or worked on the railroads, though these were the major employers. Dominick Besso's father was a shoemaker in Italy and returned to his craft in Price—the craft Dominick still practices today.[23] One immigrant became a goat herder in the mountains above Helper. The western landscape offered possible continuities with Italian folklife unimaginable in the eastern metropolises, for all their greater numbers of Italians. Ann Bonacci recalls the goat herder and his cheeses, a familiar part of the Helper milieu of the 1920s:

We used to have a goat herder. He lived way up in the mountains. . . . He'd make cheese out of goat's milk. And I grew up on that kind of stuff. On *rigotta*—Americans say "ricawta" [laughs]—and all kinds of cheese. Something like mozzarella, that would melt— it's even tastier than the mozzarella we get in the stores. . . . They used to make cheese that you'd grate for your spaghetti. . . .
He used to come down with the wagon and his horse—little one horse wagon— and he'd bring all his stuff. . . . He had his family up there; they all worked together.[24]

According to Ann Bonacci, it was the lack of modern pasteurization—not lack of demand—that put the goat herder out of business. Until quite recently, the Calabrian cheese-making tradition has been carried forward by Mrs. John Vea, of Spring Glen (originally from Cosenza province). She made provolone, ricotta, and *tuma* cheese. Although cheese-making has ended, her family continues to butcher several pigs each November, storing the resulting prosciutto, capacolla, soprasatta, salame, and sausage in their traditional outdoor cellar.

The immigrant generation was not completely dependent on wage labor to feed and house itself; it was not dependent on cash to entertain itself, either:

"Cuoco, cuoco della cucina, Che fa il re Con la scava regina?"	"Cook, cook of the kitchen, What is the king doing with the slave queen?"
"Suona e canta e balla."	"He plays, sings, and dances."[25]

This rhymed refrain is part of a fairy tale (perhaps a *cante-fable*) recalled by Ann Bonacci of Helper. A witch has turned a prince into a butterfly; he flutters at the window of the palace, asking what has become of the queen.

Ann Bonacci and Til Davido recall the magnificent fairy tales told by Frank Scavo, Carmana and Margaret Felice, Nick Vecchio, and Fred Nicastro in their Italian neighborhood of "Townsite" in Helper. One told the tales from "A Thousand and One Nights"; another told "*Cicirinella*" (Cinderella). Such stories were told in the evenings when people visited each other, especially in the winter when everyone gathered around the coal-burning kitchen stove:

There was a lot of storytelling when we were kids. Lots of storytelling. We'd get together at nights with neighbors. . . . He [Fred Nicastro] used to come up every— maybe three times a week, and oh!— he'd tell the most fantastic stories. . . . we would just *wait* for the night that he'd come over. . . . He started to tell us the story of "A Thousand and One Nights," and . . . we just were fascinated. We just could not wait for him to tell us those stories.[26]

There were other forms of entertainment as well. The traditional game of *bocce*, a kind of bowling, was played in the sand by the river in Helper, though this was mainly a north Italian (male) game.[27] Italian card games like *briscola* and *scopa* were also played by the men, and, to a lesser extent, still are in homes and pool halls.[28]

But the most significant and widespread form of entertainment was probably socializing itself. As Edna Romano put it, "People liked people then,"[29] and it sometimes seems as if people did like each other more than they do today. There appears to have been less privacy, but more camaraderie. There were the many bars on Main Street in Helper, patronized mainly by men, but there were also numerous social occasions marked by plentiful home-made foods, including wine. (As Kerry Nick Fister said, "We were gourmets, but we didn't know it."[30]) These occasions included performances of traditional dances like the tarantella, and traditional music and singing; the button accordion, for instance, was a common instrument. Al Veltri recalls:

I remember many neighborhood house parties, especially in Joe Bruno's basement. Dominic Albo would sing, dance, and entertain us. We kids would eat, play games, sing, and dance. They would throw quarters at our feet when we danced the tarantella.[31]

Parties also took place in celebration of traditional events like weddings and baptisms:

I think they looked forward to the baptisms just for a party [laughs]. . . . We were all baptized together. . . . They'd celebrate for two or three days. . . . to be with their own people. . . . It was very noisy around here.[32]

Perhaps Italians are stereotyped (even by themselves) as being noisy and knowing how to party. What may not be so well recognized is that shared merrymaking and emotion create social bonds that can have real economic force in the struggle for survival. These bonds may be called upon in times of crisis, like strikes:

Steve Siporin: How did they survive the strikes?

Edna Romano: By helping each other! Those that had the farms and the cows and the milk helped the others. . . . They had huge gardens . . . and, all kinds of animals. . . . I think about all people ever bought, my mother said, was the coffee and sugar. But they all helped each other. . . . They could stay out on strike and hold up because they really stuck together.[33]

Northern Italians in Helper created their own mutual aid society, the *Stella di America*. Informally, members sometimes bartered their goods and services—Edna Romano recalls how her mother, then a young girl, was paid in milk bottles for helping a mother with her newborn baby.[34]

Italians in Helper created not only their own economy and entertainment, they created their own landscape as well. Parts of this landscape, like the outdoor bake ovens that were once a regular feature in so many yards, are mostly gone today, but driving or walking around Helper, one begins to realize that there is a particular balance to the yards that is quite unlike other American towns and neighborhoods. Outbuildings like small shacks and converted garages (usually with smoke stacks) are bunched at the back or side of the yard, often adjacent to a fence. Some yards have two or three such sheds—and few have none. These were once used for making and storing sausage, prosciutto, capacolla, soprasatta, and wine, for baking bread, and for drying oregano and garlic. (In contrast, only twenty-five miles away is the mining town of Scofield, Utah, which was home to many Finnish immigrants. Scofield lacks stonework, and the outbuildings are saunas rather than sausage-making sheds.) These outbuildings make Helper unique; they create a dense, intricate network, an industrial, urban village texture in the midst of a landscape dominated by rock-rimmed canyons, mountains, and the sky.

The contributions of Italian folklife reached beyond the Italian immigrant community. Common skills the immigrants brought with them, stonemasonry in particular, were used to lay the foundations of towns and industry, to transform "that awesome space" of the West into a human place.[35] But one locally told anecdote about a Calabrian stonemason who built a jail suggests that Italians were punished just for being Italians rather than acknowledged for their useful stoneworking skills:

According to family tradition, after Felice Gigliotti completed the jail [in 1904] and was paid by the United States Fuel Company, he entered the saloon in Hiawatha and offered to buy drinks for everyone. Two "Americans" announced that they would not drink

Yolanda Bruno removes a batch of *frazzini* from her oven. The biscuit-like bread, flavored with aniseed, is usually eaten for breakfast. Photograph by Steve Siporin, IAW-SS-B007-3

with a "God-damn Italian." The highly in-
sulted Gigliotti started a fight with the two,
and as a result, he is credited not only with
building the Hiawatha jail but also as being
its first occupant.[36]

But even today, towns like Helper are,
from the ground up, the visible creations of
Italian stonemasons. Gigliotti's son, Ross,
who was eighty-seven in 1990, can point to
the buildings and railroad bridges his father
made. Other names of Italian stonemasons
recur in conversation—Barzaga, Bianco, Bis-
cardi, Borla, Elegante, Falsetti, Manelli, Manina, Putri, Seppi; their stonework forms the
physical base upon which Helper still stands
and Carbon County still runs. Their work is
solid, resisting time, surviving. Stonework
was one area where Northern and Southern
Italians had skills in common, for the roll of
stonemasons is as filled with Piemontese as
it is with Calabrese.

Italian stonemasons from both the
North and the South were called upon not
only to build houses, stores, and boarding
houses for private entrepreneurs; they also
built the company-owned mining camps,
including railroad beds, bridges, foundations, and buildings. And for city, county,
and state government, they built embankments, highway bridges, and retaining walls.
All were built of native sandstone—timber
was not plentiful. The sheer volume of the
stone masonry in Helper and in mining
camps like Columbia, Kenilworth, Hiawatha, and Standardville is astounding in itself.
Al Veltri, a retired pharmacist in Helper,
asked to comment on the abundance of
stonework, said, "I think everybody in Italy
was some kind of a mason, weren't they?"[37]
In other words, wasn't it just another of
those many remarkable skills that all these
immigrants came equipped with? Wasn't it
ordinary, barely worthy of mention?

ABOVE: **Stone masonry
wall at Standardville,
Utah. Italian masons
built a wide variety of
stone structures in
Carbon County, includ-
ing houses, stores,
mining camp buildings,
bridges, and retaining
walls. Photograph by
Steve Siporin, IAW-SS-
B001-36A**

LEFT: **Detail of sand-
stone wall at Standard-
ville. Photograph by
Steve Siporin, IAW-SS-
B001-33A**

Perhaps the historic stonework of Carbon County can serve as a metaphor of Italian ethnicity today, as well. Stonework is everywhere, underlying everything—a whole economy was built on it, and it still provides the structure, literally the foundation for life today. Newer frame houses in Kenilworth, for instance, lie on older stonework foundations. But you may not notice the stonework unless you train your eye to look for it. The more time one spends looking, the more one realizes that stonemasonry is everywhere.

Maybe Italian ethnicity in Carbon County is also that way. It is not readily apparent with signs saying "look at this, it's Italian" or in obvious genres, like language and song. But at a deep, structural level, that of behavior, Italian—and especially Southern Italian—values undergird the lives of many members of this society. The enduring Italianness of Carbon County is apparent not only in buildings, houses, fences, embankments, retaining walls, and highway and railroad bridges—the works of native sandstone that form an unmistakable regional landscape shaped by skilled, immigrant hands—but also in foodways, matriarchal families, large gardens featuring favorite Italian vegetables and herbs, historical gravemarkers (in Italian or with Italian reference), and the Stella d'America Lodge—the oldest fraternal organization in the state of Utah.[38]

In other words, members of that remarkable, and even heroic, first generation realized that the solace of a familiar culture did not have to be sacrificed for economic security. Just the opposite: they survived *through* the practice of their traditional arts. Hardly a hindrance, it was a necessity. Their

A few of the many examples of stonework found in Carbon County. This house in Helper has a stone lower story that is built into a retaining wall (left). Another retaining wall can be seen on the hillside above and behind the house. Photograph by Steve Siporin, IAW-SS-B005-15

traditional knowledge was general enough to allow them to cope with, and to adapt to, a radically different environment, yet specific enough to give them concrete skills and to be useful in developing social bonds with fellow immigrants. Their farming and food-preserving skills supplemented an unpredictable, boom-and-bust, industrial wage-economy that could not sustain families by itself. At the same time, what were essentially economic acts (gardening, preserving pork products, making wine, and baking bread, for instance) involved social occasions that strengthened bonds of affection and created a sense of community among Italian immigrants. That sense of community—of social solidarity among equals—was itself another critical economic tool in the face of mining companies' resistance to unionization and strikes.

Traditions from an utterly different world proved to be the best of survival kits. Ironically, they provided what a liberal arts education is supposed to provide for college students today—the skills and knowledge that are general enough to enable them to adapt to unforeseen and unforeseeable circumstances in a rapidly changing world. Most Italian immigrants to Carbon County may have been illiterate, but their traditional culture served them well in enormously trying circumstances. Folklife equipped Italian immigrants to Carbon County not only to

Richard Colombo making sausages at the R & A Market in Price. Photograph by Steve Siporin, IAW-SS-B013-26A

survive the traumas of immigration and to take care of themselves and each other; it also enabled them to make lasting contributions to the communities in which they settled. The northern and southern Italian folklife they brought with them was economically meaningful, adaptive, and essential.

THE ARCHITECTURE OF IMMIGRATION

Documenting Italian-American Vernacular Buildings in Utah and Nevada

THOMAS CARTER

In 1990 when the American Folklife Center invited a team of teachers and students from the University of Utah's Graduate School of Architecture to document with photos and measured drawings buildings constructed by Italian immigrants in central Utah and eastern Nevada, some colleagues were skeptical. Italian architecture in the West? Was there such a thing? For these people, as for many westerners, hyphentated America, the world of Italian-Americans and other immigrant groups, lay to the east in the big urban centers of Boston, New York, and Chicago. They told us to forget about Italian buildings and look on the ranches and in the mining towns for real western architecture.

And that is what we did. We went to the ranches and mining towns and found what we knew we would find, both Italians and, not surprisingly, buildings constructed by, lived in, and used by Italians. We knew they were there simply because the West is and always has been a land of cultural diversity. Particular stereotypes die hard, but the old image of the West as the exclusive domain of cowboys and Indians is one that badly needs discarding, simply because it is wrong. Western historians such as Patricia Limerick have worked diligently in recent years to remind us that western America shared, as she says in *The Legacy of Conquest,* "in the transplanted diversity of Europe. Expansion [westward] involved peoples of every background: English, Irish, Cornish, Scottish, French, German, Portuguese, Scandinavian, Greek, and Russian." And Italians. Or better yet, Italian-Americans, since once in their new surroundings these immigrants became Americans, and their experience became an American experience. For many, Italy was now only a memory. The reality was making a living and, more specifically, making a living in the American West of the late nineteenth and early twentieth centuries. Jobs for Italian-Americans came initially in the region's mines. Later, some of the newcomers switched to farming and ranching. And it is in mining towns of Utah and Nevada and to a lesser extent on the ranches of Nevada's high desert that we may find the architecture of Italian-American immigration.

The idea of an architecture of immigration is nothing new: people have been studying America's imported building traditions for years. Nonetheless, simple definitions are hard to find. For many, immigrant buildings are roughly synonymous with ethnic buildings, with "ethnic" implying the presence of a set of special, culturally derived architectural traits that serve to distinguish one immigrant group both from other immigrant groups and from the dominant host culture. Thus, immigrant architecture is the architecture of ethnicity: the self-conscious expression of old-world identity through buildings. Ethnicity in architecture may be expressed through the simple retention of traditional building practices, in new architectural forms evolving from older ones, or it may even be invented by singling out a certain architectural image of the homeland for highlighting, thereby creating a new form. All these kinds of ethnic architecture are found in Utah and Nevada Italian-American communities.

Yet in planning the work for this project, our team knew there was another, less well-known side to immigrant architecture that also deserved attention. Most Italian-Americans in the West did not build in the style of their homeland. In the western United States, as in the nation as a whole, great numbers of immigrants adopted the architectural styles of the mainstream American culture. What should we do with buildings that express Americanization rather than ethnicity?

Are they not part of the architecture of immigration? If some of the Italians coming to the West chose to reveal their old-world affinities through architecture, there were others who affirmed allegiance to their new homeland by building American houses, a house being, after all, the most conspicuous and lasting of personal symbols. Still other immigrants (and this may be the majority) simply had no choice in the matter.

The American West encountered by most of the arriving Italians was already heavily industrialized. After all, it was the news of jobs in the mines and smelters and on the railroads that brought them there in the first place. The immigrants' West was an urban one of blackened skies, smokestacks, piles of detritus from the smelters, and small houses perched precariously on hillsides. In this world, newcomers became renters, bought existing houses, or, if they could afford to, built in the expedient style of the western mining town. Not surprisingly perhaps, western mining town housing looks much the same from Arizona to Montana, being part of a larger industrial system that covered much of the region during the period of immigration. Such housing, although overtly nonethnic, is nevertheless part and parcel of the immigrant experience. It is an architecture that calls attention to the simple truth that for many immigrants the expression of ethnicity through architecture was simply unaffordable.

This is not to say that Italians left no special mark on the urban environment. They did, certainly. But the signs are not always obvious. In western towns one has to look carefully for the architecture of Italian-American ethnicity. You can see it in the quantity and quality of stone buildings, for one thing. Masonry was one area where Italians excelled, and where there were Italians there was likely to be finely crafted stonework of all kinds. It is visible too in outbuildings—buildings out behind the main house—where sausage and wine were made, tomatoes canned, herbs dried, and bread baked. Structures like these were often makeshift affairs, created of necessity from whatever materials were available, but they were nevertheless indispensible features in a domestic landscape subtly but stubbornly oriented toward the production and processing of food.

The architecture of Italian-Americans in the West, then, displays great variety. Some of it—mostly buildings found in the more rural areas where social and economic constraints were less rigid—looks as if it could have been built in Italy. Other examples are purely American. We felt that our work should show both sides, the Italian and the American, and we therefore wanted to include the widest possible range of buildings in our survey. Accordingly, we chose to focus our attention on two urban centers, Helper, in Carbon County, Utah, and Eureka in Eureka County, Nevada, as well as several outlying farms in Carbon County and two ranches in Nevada known to be owned by Italian-Americans. The following illustrations were chosen to represent the Graduate School of Architecture's contribution to the Italian-Americans in the West Project. The drawings are by graduate students Susan Anderson, Bee Bergold, Steve Simmons, and Doug Banks. Professor Darla Linberg-Berreth provided the artistic supervision. Background information on the individual sites was supplied by Steve Siporin, Phil Notarriani, Blanton Owen, and Andrea Graham. Special thanks to Pete Tony and Jody Delmue, Lavange McNeil, Yolanda Bruno, Lester and Edith Verde Pitts, Arvetta Satterfield, and Ivan McCourt for access to and information on the buildings.

Camillo Manina House, Spring Glen, Carbon County, Utah. The Manina House was constructed during the late 1920s and early 1930s by immigrants Camillo Manina, Domenic Conca, John Manina, and Virginio Marzo. Its partially subterranean design and stone construction are typical of housing in the Manina's native village of Novalesa, in the Province of Torino, Italy. Camillo Manina worked in the Carbon County coal mines, but raised most of what he needed to live on at the house in Spring Glen. Photograph by Thomas Carter, IAW-TC-B004-9

Graduate students Susan Anderson and Bee Bergold pulling measurements off the goat shed on the Manina farm. Besides goats, Manina also kept chickens, rabbits, and a donkey. Photograph by Steve Siporin, IAW-SS-B006-18

Front elevation and first floor plan of the Camillo Manina House. The Manina House was built in two stages. The original dwelling was single-story in height and consisted of two rooms—a bedroom and a kitchen—built halfway into the hillside. Later, a second story was added of brick rescued from the demolition of the Denver and Rio Grande Western Railroad Company roundhouse in nearby Helper. In Italy two-level houses like this often had animals stabled on the ground floor, and Manina perpetuated this tradition in Carbon County by locating a small donkey stall next to the kitchen. Drawing by Susan Anderson

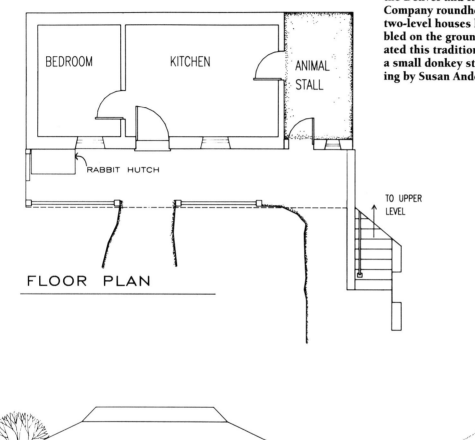

FLOOR PLAN

FRONT ELEVATION

Aerial view of the Joseph Delmue Ranch, Lincoln County, Nevada. Joseph Delmue was born in Biasca, Switzerland, an Italian-speaking town on the Italian-Swiss border. He emigrated to Lincoln County in the 1870s to cut timber for the mines at Pioche. Turning to ranching in the 1880s, Delmue took up land in nearby Dry Valley, where he built a small wooden house and a timber-frame barn. These structures were replaced by a substantial stone house in 1900 and a large hay barn in 1916. Both of these new buildings were patterned after those in Delmue's native country. Photograph by Blanton Owen, IAW-BO-BO20-11

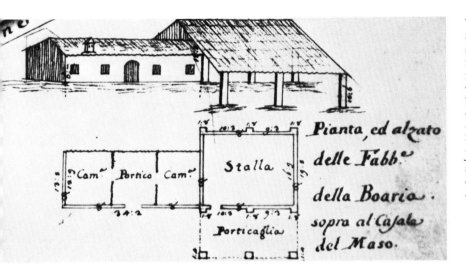

This plate is from Francesco Bocchi's *L'architettura Populare in Italia: Emilia-Romagna* and shows a combined house and barn complex from northern Italy. The buildings are typical of the region and consist of a symmetrical three-part villa-type house and a large aisle-and nave-type barn. The house is of masonry construction, while the barn roof sits on large free-standing pillars. The spaces between the pillars are either left open or enclosed with stone or wood. Joseph Delmue built a similar house and barn, albeit detached from one another, in Nevada during the first two decades of the twentieth century.

Section drawing of the Delmue House looking south. As this drawing shows, Delmue used the mountainside for the rear wall of the house, chiseling away the soft stone to make the fireplace (the flue is not depicted) and a cave-like entrance to a rear storage corridor. Drawing by Doug Banks

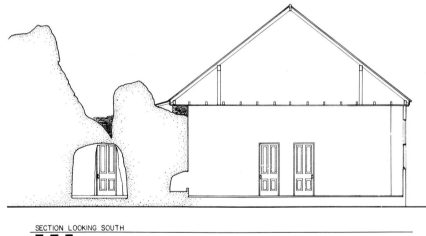

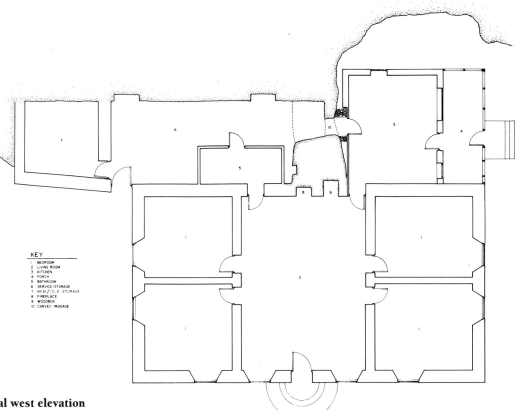

KEY
1 BEDROOM
2 LIVING ROOM
3 KITCHEN
4 PORCH
5 BATHROOM
6 SERVICE/STORAGE
7 MEAT/COLD STORAGE
8 FIREPLACE
9 WOODBOX
10 CARVED PASSAGE

PLAN

Joseph Delmue House, principal west elevation and groundplan. The design of the house Joseph Delmue built in 1900 is that of the small three-part villa. Such houses were popular with Europe's burgeoning middle-class during the nineteenth century. In choosing the villa form, Delmue made reference to a symbol of economic attainment familiar in his home country, although the imposing stone building probably had the desired effect in Nevada as well. By the turn of the century, Joe Delmue was doing well in America and it showed in the kind of house he could afford to build. Sixteen years later, it showed in his barn too. Drawing by Doug Banks

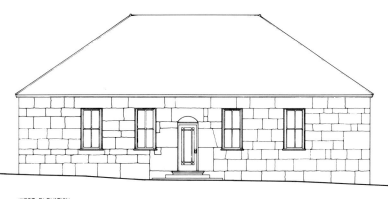

WEST ELEVATION

Fieldworker Steve Simmons braves the December cold to sketch the elevation of the Delmue Barn. Photograph by Thomas Carter, IAW-TC-B008-27

Axonometric drawing of the Delmue Barn. The 1916 barn is truly monumental, measuring approximately fifty feet wide and eighty feet long. The distinctive plan, composed of a long aisle with flanking naves, is based on European prototypes. The Delmues stacked hay in the main aisle, stabled their horses in the north side, and used the south section for feeding cattle. The roof is Swiss-Italian style, where the plate timbers are supported by free-standing pillars. In the Delmue barn, there are four stone pillars along each side of the center aisle and four supporting the shed roof in the south side. The northernmost wall is carved out of the hillside. The outer walls are made of horizontally stacked railroad ties. Drawing by Steve Simmons

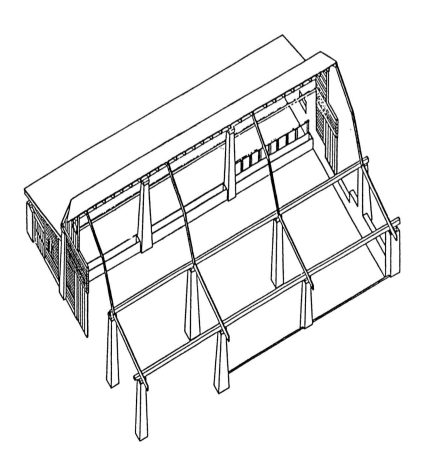

Stone pillars of barn under construction at the Delmue Ranch. An unidentified man is sitting on top of one of the pillars. Courtesy of Pete and Marlene Delmue, and Pete Tony and Jody Delmue. Copy of original photograph by Blanton Owen, IAW-BO-B018-17

Andrea Graham and Thomas Carter document a miner's cottage in Eureka, Eureka County, Nevada. As in other parts of the West, Italians in Eureka and Helper, Utah, found expediency and necessity winning out over ethnicity, at least in housing. Small one- and two-room cabins such as this stone example on Morris Street in Eureka typified the immigrants' architectural experience. Photograph by Blanton Owen, IAW-BO-B026-11

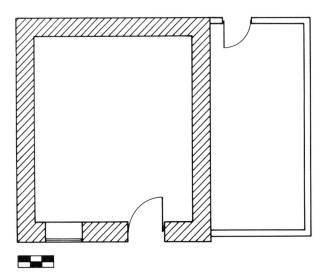

Single-cell floorplan of the Morris Street miner's cottage, Eureka, Eureka County, Nevada. Drawing by Thomas Carter and Alan Barnett

Stone miners' houses along Milano Court, off
Welby Street, Helper, Carbon County, Utah. Joe
Milano had these stone houses built in 1911.
They are single-story examples of the ubiquitous
foursquare house type, a house type identified
by its square, box-like shape and pyramidal
roof. The Milanos occupied several of the houses
while renting the rest for extra income. Mi-
lano was a blacksmith who came from Forno
Canavese in the Province of Torino, Italy. The
stonework is believed to have been done by
Felice Gigliotti, a mason from Decollatura in
Calabria, Italy. Photograph by Thomas Carter,
IAW-TC-B005-7

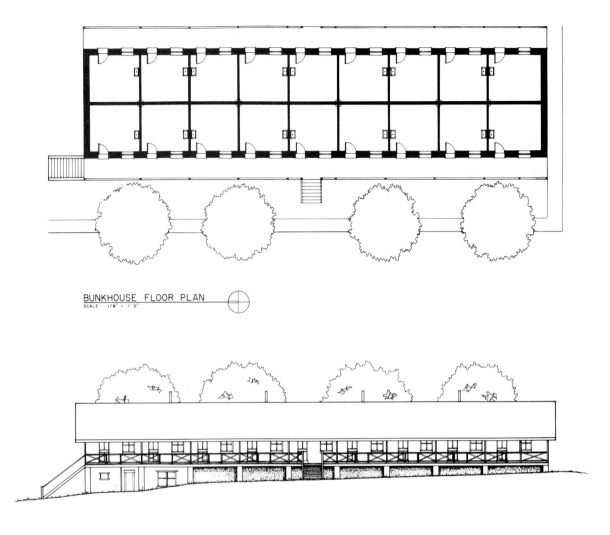

BUNKHOUSE FLOOR PLAN
SCALE: 1/8" = 1'-0"

WEST ELEVATION
SCALE 1/8" = 1'-0"

West elevation and groundplan of the Columbia Steel Company Bunkhouse, Columbia, Carbon County, Utah. This large stone bunkhouse was built by the Columbia Steel Company as a residence for unmarried miners. Constructed between 1922 and 1923 by Italian stonemason Michael Seppi, the bunkhouse formed part of a large residential complex that also included a dining hall and bathhouse. Drawing by Bee Bergold

South elevation of the Columbia Steel Company bunkhouse. Italian mason Michael Seppi acquired a fine reputation in eastern Carbon County for his work with the local sandstone. Photograph by Thomas Carter, IAW-TC-B007-10

West elevation of the Antonio and Marie Verde House, Helper, Carbon County, Utah. The Verde house is a side-passage type dwelling that was built around 1903 for the Verdes by a local contractor by the name of Leute. Side-passage houses—another common mining town house form—have an off-center entrance passage and a rectangular plan that has its narrow end facing the street. Photograph by Thomas Carter, IAW-TC-B004-20

Verde bake oven, Helper, Carbon County, Utah. Outdoor bake ovens (*forni*) are found in Italian-American communities throughout the West and signal a widespread persistence of traditional immigrant foodways in America. According to the Verde family history, it was Tony Verde, born in 1914, who built the domed bake oven, much in the style of those found in the Calabrian countryside of southern Italy. Cedar or juniper would be burned in the oven and then the ashes raked out, leaving the bricks hot and ideal for cooking. Photograph by Thomas Carter, IAW-TC-B004-22

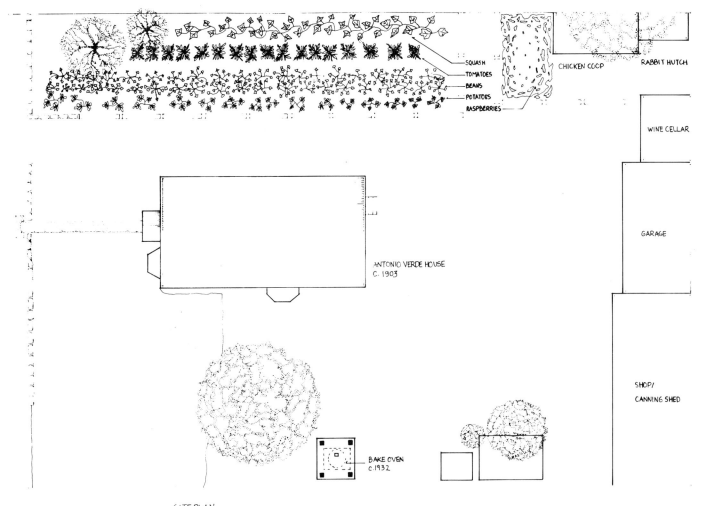

SQUASH
TOMATOES
BEANS
POTATOES
RASPBERRIES

CHICKEN COOP

RABBIT HUTCH

WINE CELLAR

GARAGE

SHOP/
CANNING SHED

ANTONIO VERDE HOUSE
C. 1903

BAKE OVEN
c. 1932

SITE PLAN
SCALE : 1:10

Site plan of the Verde House Lot, Helper, Carbon County, Utah. Elsewhere in this volume folklorist Steve Siporin argues forcefully and correctly for a rethinking of the immigrant labor experience. Siporin notes that during the early twentieth century miners in towns like Helper did not work year-round. The mines operated on a supply-and-demand basis, and the miners often found themselves working short weeks or not at all during months when the need for coal dropped. An unpredictable income coupled with already low wages made it important for miners and their families to produce much of their own food, and to develop other sources of revenue. In mining towns like Helper it is customary to find Italian-American houselots cluttered with outbuildings of various kinds, places where raw materials—mostly produce from the garden and animals such as pigs, chickens, and rabbits— were processed into food. The Verde place is a good example of the Italian-American houselot: there is a large garden, a canning shed, an outdoor bake oven, a wine cellar (where sausage was also stored), and a rabbit hutch. Drawing by Susan Anderson

Joe Bruno House, Helper, Carbon County, Utah. Italian immigrant Joe Bruno came to Helper in 1903 to work in the Carbon County coal mines. His family followed ten years later in 1913 and lived in a small house Bruno had acquired on the south side of town. In 1927 the family's fortunes had increased to the point where they could build a new brick bungalow-style house on the more fashionable north side. Photograph by Thomas Carter, IAW-TC-B002-14

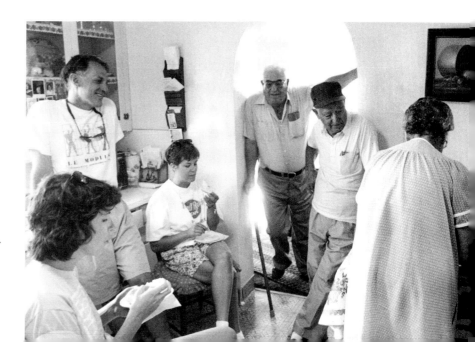

One of the fringe benefits of architectural fieldwork: Bee Bergold, Thomas Carter, and Susan Anderson eating baked *frazzini* and drinking coffee with John and Yolanda Bruno, Guy Bruno, and other members of the Bruno family. Photograph by Steve Siporin, IAW-SS-B007-17a

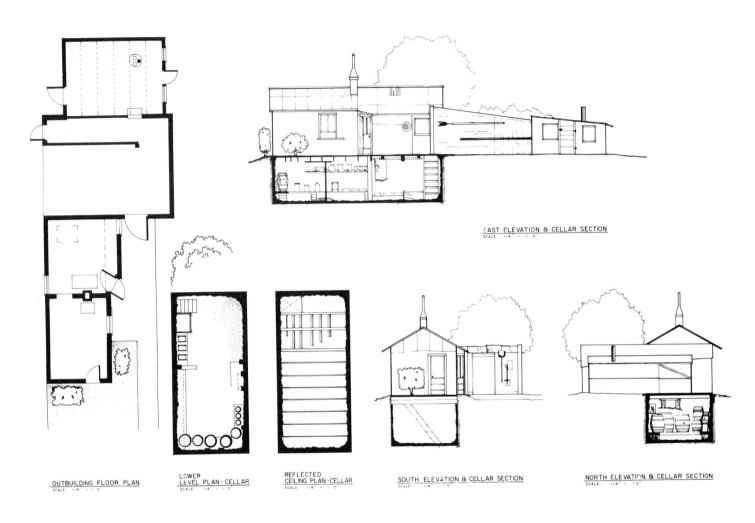

OUTBUILDING FLOOR PLAN
SCALE : 1/4" = 1'-0"

LOWER
LEVEL PLAN-CELLAR
SCALE : 1/4" = 1'-0"

REFLECTED
CEILING PLAN-CELLAR
SCALE : 1/4" = 1'-0"

EAST ELEVATION & CELLAR SECTION
SCALE : 1/4" = 1'-0"

SOUTH ELEVATION & CELLAR SECTION
SCALE : 1/4" = 1'-0"

NORTH ELEVATION & CELLAR SECTION
SCALE : 1/4" = 1'-0"

Bruno outbuildings, elevation and ground plan, Helper, Carbon County, Utah. Like many other immigrant families, the Brunos raised and processed most of their own food. They also supplemented their income by taking in renters and doing small jobs for the mines. The center for this activity on the Bruno houselot was a small wooden building, unassuming in appearance, that played a significant role in the family's life in America. As he was finishing his new house, Joe Bruno also dragged a two-room building from an adjacent lot and placed it over a newly dug cellar. The south room was then rented out to single miners, while the north room was used for canning tomatoes, drying herbs like garlic and oregano, and for making sausage, wine, and lard. The wine barrels, ceramic lard vessels, and dried sausage were stored in the cellar. In the late 1930s a garage for the family car was attached to the north end of the building and then in 1960 another room was added where the family earned extra money by taking on maintenance jobs for the Denver and Rio Grande Western railroad. Drawing by Bee Bergold

Bruno houselot plan and garden, Helper, Carbon County, Utah. The Bruno property was and continues to be oriented toward the production of food. Water—the key element in the production system—is brought into the lot from both the north and east from one of the town's main irrigation canals. Smaller ditches then move water to the orchard on the north and the main vegetable garden on the east. After it passes through orchard and garden, the water is piped onto the lawn around the house, and whatever is left over is funneled in an underground pipe to a daughter's house in the next block. The Brunos have always had apple, apricot, peach, pear, and plum trees; and their garden yields the necessary herbs for Italian cuisine like basil, oregano, and parsley. Peppers came in all sizes and temperatures, and the vegetables usually consisted of fava beans, zucchini, and other kinds of squash. Finally, out along or across the ditch there were rabbit hutches, a chicken coop, and a hog pen—the humble dwellings are the stuff of life for an Italian-American household. Drawing by Bee Bergold

RABBIT PENS

KEY

1	APPLE TREE	16	OREGANO
2	APRICOT TREE	17	PARSLEY
3	BASIL	18	PEAS
4	BELL PEPPER	19	PEACH TREE
5	BRIDAL WREATH	20	PEAR TREE
6	CHERRY TREE	21	PEONIES
7	CUCUMBER	22	PLUM TREE
8	FLAGS	23	QUEEN ANNE'S LACE
9	GARLIC	24	RASPBERRIES
10	GRAPES	25	SNOWBALL BUSH
11	HONEYSUCKLE	26	STRING BEANS
12	HORSEBEANS	27	TOMATO
13	HOT PEPPERS	28	TULIPS
14	LILAC	29	WALNUT TREE
15	NECTARINE TREE	30	ZUCCHINI
— — —	— — —	— —	WATERING SYSTEM

CHICKEN COOP

OUTBUILDING

COW AND PIG BARN

SITE & GARDEN PLAN
SCALE 1" = 10'-1"
0   5   10   20

John and Yolanda Bruno's home and their vegetable garden and fruit and nut trees. Photograph by Thomas Carter, IAW-TC-B006-30

WALLA WALLA SWEETS

Onions and Ethnic Identity in an Italian Community in the Northwest

JENS LUND

Un gruppo di pionieri si insediò in una colonia agricola, ancor più a nord della California, in una cittadina del mitico West con un nome attraente, Walla Walla, nello stato americano di Washington.[1]

A group of pioneers settled in an agricultural colony even further north than California, in a village in the mythical West with an attracting name, Walla Walla, in Washington State.

So reads the town history of Lonate Pozzolo, a suburb of Milan. Other Italians also came to the village with the attracting name. They founded a community far from other Italian settlements, endured prejudice, pursued agriculture and horticulture, and kept their Italian identity. There they erected the first Christopher Columbus statue on the West Coast and established the Northwest's first Columbus Day parades, both in 1911.

More than a century later, there are still many Italians in the valley. A revival of ethnicity, inspired by the Bicentennial, *Roots,* and the 1989 Washington State Centennial, and led by a new Italian Heritage Association (IHA), puts red-white-and-green-clad marchers and dancers in the streets during Columbus Day week. But it is in family life that people have sustained their ethnic identity. They have expressed it through the Church, the food, and ties to specialized horticulture—especially to a local variety of onion with the attracting name "Walla Walla sweet."

The onion is best characterized by its pungent flavor and odor, and there may be something paradoxical about a sweet onion. Yet, several varieties have been developed specifically for their mildness and sweetness, such as the Bermuda and the Vidalia. But the sweetest of all is the "Walla Walla sweet," developed during the 1920s and given official recognition and its own "Walla Walla Sweet Onion Commission" in 1981.

The "Walla Walla sweet" onion has been a significant part of Walla Walla Italian-American life for seven decades. Historian Ernesto Milani called it "the emblematic vegetable among the American-Lonatese."[2] But the "Walla Walla sweet" is of a more complex ethnic origin. It descended from a so-called French onion brought to the valley about 1900 from Corsica. Through the 1910s and twenties, several immigrant growers (including southern Italians, as well as Lonatese) experimented with its development. To further confuse matters, the U.S. Department of Agriculture (USDA) classifies it as a "sweet Spanish-style" onion. The stories of the Walla Walla Valley Italian-American community and of this strain of onion are closely entwined.

A unique characteristic of today's "Walla Walla sweet" is the labor-intensiveness of its cultivation. Having the highest moisture content of any commercial onion, most of the harvesting and other handling must be done by hand. It is also an open-pollinated

A crate of Walla Walla, Washington's, famous sweet onions at Virgil Criscola's farm. Since their development in the 1920s, these onions have played an important role in the lives of Walla Walla's Italian-Americans. They are now considered a symbol of the Italian-American community. Photograph by Jens Lund, IAW-JL-B-WW028-17

onion, unlike the other commercial onion varieties of today, which are hybrids. Most "Walla Walla sweet" growers select and grow their own seed and harvest and prepare the seed by hand. By hand-selection they try to produce the ideal onion narrowly defined by the commission.

Detail from advertisement for "Genuine Walla Walla Sweet Onions." Peaks in the Blue Mountain range, east of Walla Walla, are shown in the background.

Walla Walla onion-grower Virgil Criscola in his onion field, December 1989. Photograph by Jens Lund, IAW-JL-B-WW028-4

The Walla Walla Valley straddles Walla Walla County, Washington, and northeastern Umatilla County, Oregon. To the north lie the Snake River and the Palouse farmlands, to the west, the Columbia River, and to the east and south, the Blue Mountains and the Umatilla National Forest. There are three small towns in the valley, Walla Walla and College Place, Washington, and Milton-Freewater, Oregon. Total population of the valley is about forty thousand.

The landscape is covered with wheat, vineyards, orchards, and truck farms. Much of the employment in the area is agricultural, but large employers include the Corps of Engineers, a beef packing plant, a can factory, and a penitentiary. The nearest large city (158 miles away) is Spokane, Washington, also home of the nearest Italian-American community.

Walla Walla is a European-American mispronunciation of a Nez Perce Indian word meaning "abundant water." The climate is benign, much milder than most of the inland Northwest, and the farmland is excellent, with over sixty-six thousand acres of prime farmland in Walla Walla County alone. The annual growing season is over two hundred days. Walla Walla and College Place are largely residential, Milton-Freewater is an agricultural service center. The area has a substantial Mexican-American population, mostly recent settlers. Other ethnic groups include people of Volga German, Irish, French-Canadian, and Scandinavian descent. There was once a sizeable Chinese community in the valley. Many of them were also produce growers.[3] Many local Italian-Americans claim that 25 percent of the people in the valley are of at least partial Italian ancestry.

Italian settlers came to the Walla Walla Valley in the nineteenth century. The first was orchardist, baker, and grocer Frank Orselli, who settled in Walla Walla in 1857.[4] Today's Italian-American community began with the arrival, in 1876, of Pasquale Saturno, from Ischia, near Naples.[5] Several other early Italian settlers probably came by chance, but sending home for friends and neighbors for labor or marriage increased the population, with immigration continuing into the 1920s. The presence of the community inspired other Italians to trickle in, especially from railroad-building crews. A number settled first in the little Northern Pacific railroad town of Starbuck, about forty miles to the northeast.

Among the earliest Italians to come to the area were Joe Tachi (1880), Tony Locati (1886), John Arbini (1890), all three from Lonate Pozzolo, and Louis Rizzuti (1886 or 1887), a Calabrese.[6] All became truck gardeners. (The Italian produce growers in the Walla Walla Valley have preferred to call themselves "gardeners.") Most of them had lived elsewhere in the United States first and had heard of the availability near Walla Walla of good, inexpensive farmland.

Saturno and Tachi became partners soon after Tachi's arrival, but after a few years they went separate ways. Tachi later sent for his nephews, Locati and Arbini. Rizzuti was the first southern Italian after Saturno, but he may have come on his own.

Italians pose for a photograph at Tony Locati's place in Walla Walla, 1910. Tony Locati (front row, hand on chin) is one of Walla Walla's earliest Italian settlers. Front row, from left: Emilio Airoldi, Carlo Locati, Mary Locati, Jacob Locati, Sam Castoldi, Tony Locati, Frank Arbini, "Nel" (last name unknown), Carlo Ponti, Henry Locati, August L. Locati. Back row: Joe Arbini, Henry Grassi, Tony Zaro, Ambrose "Jim" Locati, Joe "Pign" Locati, John Arbini, Andrea Castoldi, Angelo Castoldi, "Sandrin" Ferrari, and Joe Fausti. Courtesy of Carrie Criscola and Joe J. Locati, WWI-BJL002-32

Tachi and Rizzuti seem to have begun the cycle of sending for relatives who, in turn, sent for more relatives. By 1900, there were two distinct Italian communities in the valley, the Milanese or Northern Colony (most of whom were from Lonate Pozzolo and the Ticino Valley) and the "Calabrese" or Southern Colony, southern Italians not all of whom were from Calabria.

Locati and others remember that the immigrants usually spoke the Milanese or Calabrese dialects. Some, who had attended school in Italy, also spoke standard Italian, and most members of both groups could at least understand it. Bert Pesciallo, whose Genovese father, Giuseppe, was a viticulturist on the Oregon side of the line, remembers when groups of Milanese and "Calabrese" came down to buy wine grapes. Giuseppe Pesciallo spoke standard Italian to both groups. Pesciallo also remembers that the Southerners paid deference to the Northerners, who were considered a superior class by virtue of language and origins.

Saturno, Tachi, and Rizzuti were the first Italian gardeners to prosper and they often employed newer arrivals, later renting them land until they were able to purchase their own property. The poorer Italians paid them the deference due *padroni*.

Interviews with their descendants indicate that these settlers had not been farmers in Europe but laborers of various sorts, some of them having traveled to France or Switzerland first to work in construction. But they avidly sought the opportunity to acquire productive land, and they followed the example of their predecessors, becoming small-scale produce farmers, raising such vegetables as spinach, onions, beets, and carrots.

From the beginning, the Italian gardeners tended to settle in two locations. Most of the Milanese settled in an area called Blalock, which bounded western Walla Walla

and northern College Place. Many Southerners eventually bought cheaper land in the area known as "South Ninth," south of Ninth Avenue, from southern Walla Walla to the state line. At one time, so many Italian children attended the Braden School south of Walla Walla that it was known locally as "the Italian school."

The mainstream community, of northern European origin, did not consider the immigrants or even the American-born Italian-Americans to be "American" or even white. In his book, *The Horticultural Heritage of Walla Walla County, 1818–1977*, Joe J. Locati, son of Tony, cited local newspapers routinely referring to Italians as "foreign elements" and "Dagos." The local monthly, *Up-To-The-Times*, reported:

In the vegetable industry, John Chinaman and the sons of Italy cut considerable figure. As gardeners, these two classes have few superiors. . . . Of late years, however, attracted by the profits of the business, many white men and those representing the best citizenship have become holders of valuable vegetable lands.[7]

As Locati points out in his history, practically all of the "white men" and "best citizenship" soon left the business.

It was probably prejudice that inspired a number of the early Italians to anglicize their names. Spagnuoli became "Spanish." Magnoni became "Manuel." Saturno became "Breen," and his descendants remained Breens until the 1980s, when his great-grandson, Doug Breen, legally changed his name to "Breen Saturno." An amusing community legend explains how Saturno became Breen. In the words of Joe J. Locati:

One day, when we had the 1976 thing, we borrowed some Italian dresses and things of that nature from an aunt of mine, Mrs. Jim Locati. . . . My wife and I went there and I was talking to her and she was well in her eighties and I said *"Zia,"* or "Aunt, tell me how is it that Pasquale Saturno became 'Breen?'" Now her sister is the Locati who married Pasquale Saturno's son. "Oh," she says. "That's because he couldn't talk very good and when he went to market he'd say, 'I breeng-a spinach, I breeng-a the onions, I breeng-a thees,' and they started calling him 'Breen.'" . . . But Pasquale Saturno then becomes "Frank Breen," and because of his accent. That's what my aunt told me and she ought to know.

The "Breen" story is a favorite in the community. I heard versions of it at least five times. The community sense of humor includes a considerable dose of ethnic self-mocking.

Response to prejudice may have been a factor in the decision of Frank Yuse, a Walla Walla Italian barber (who later became a lawyer and judge in Spokane) to mount a campaign, in 1910, to erect a statue of Christopher Columbus on the Walla Walla County Court House lawn. The Columbus statue was paid for entirely by subscriptions of local members of the Italian community. Tony Ambrose, a retired barber who was Yuse's apprentice, remembers the subscription drive well:

Well, he got the people together, to donate some money to build it. They all bought part of it, they donated five, six dollars, whatever they could. That's how they got the thing going. Yeah, they all donated some. And then they all came to the parade on Columbus Day. They all marched in it.

On October 12, 1911, the Columbus statue was dedicated, before a crowd of three thousand people, including the local Italian Drum Band, a company of militia, a platoon of police, and the local schools, which were dismissed for the day. Tony Locati served as grand marshal of the ceremony. Chiselled on the back of the pedestal were the names of the ninety-eight subscribers, a "who's who" of the local Italian community. A flag of the Kingdom of Italy was

ABOVE: Statue of Christopher Columbus in front of the Walla Walla County Court-house. Photograph by Jens Lund, WWI89-BJL002-7

LEFT: Names of the sponsors of Walla Walla's Christopher Columbus statue, engraved on the back of the statue's base. The statue was paid for entirely by subscriptions from members of the local Italian community. Photograph by Jens Lund, WWI89-BJL001-1

ABOVE: A Columbus Day parade by the local Italian community in the early 1910s. In the front row, Giuseppe Maiuri (left) carries the Kingdom of Italy flag, and Arthur Maiuri carries the flag of the United States. Courtesy of Doug Breen Saturno, IAW-JL-B-WW011-25

RIGHT: Pasquale Saturno's badge from the 1911 dedication of the Columbus statue. Photograph by Jens Lund, IAW-JL-B-WW012-5

purchased and flown for the occasion. For years it belonged to the Walla Walla Gardeners Association, who recently donated it to the Fort Walla Walla Museum. The statue still stands on the court house lawn.[8]

Yuse also established an Italian newspaper and founded an "Italian Workingmen's Association." However, at the time, the social distance between Northerners and Southerners was so great that the association soon fell apart.

The difficulty of getting fair prices for their produce led the Italian growers to establish the Walla Walla Gardeners Association (WWGA) in 1916, with John Arbini as president. Locati remembers the meeting in College Place in the spring of 1916, when the organization was begun. By 1917, it had its own packing house. Until it became a corporation in 1983, the WWGA claimed to be the oldest packing cooperative in the West still operating under its original charter. To this day, it is still an Italian-American institution.

The WWGA has served not only as a packing house and marketing cooperative. It has also served its members as a credit union and a buyers' club for groceries. The association purchased bulk food, which it sold its members at cost, even for credit against future deliveries. They also operated a retail grocery store. For a long time, the WWGA was the only source of Italian food ingredients available in the valley. During the years when many made their own wine, the WWGA purchased traincar loads of grapes from California. In recent years, the WWGA has supported the ethnic revival through the Italian Heritage Association and Italian Heritage Days.

The other leading institution providing ethnic continuity for valley Italian-Americans has been St. Francis of Assisi Roman Catholic Church in Walla Walla. Although St. Patrick's Catholic parish was already there when the Italian pioneers arrived, most did not take part in Catholic religious activities because of cultural differences. An Italian priest, Father Oscar R. Balducci, was assigned to St. Mary's Hospital as chaplain in 1914. Although a Florentine, whose dialect was scarcely understood by Milanese and Calabrese, Fr. Balducci started saying Mass in private homes for members of the Italian community. He convinced the Spokane Diocese to establish a missionary church for the Italians, separate from the already existing parish. It remains so today.[9]

In 1915, St. Francis of Assisi Roman Catholic Church was erected and dedicated. Its establishment revived religious participation among Catholic Italians. (Some Italian families had become Protestants, some of them Seventh-day Adventists.) The old wooden church was replaced in 1939 by the stuccoed structure that still stands on West Alder Street today. Father Balducci died in 1937. He was St. Francis's first and last Italian pastor. The stained glass windows in the present-day church were paid for by subscription. On opposite sides near the front pew, are two windows inscribed "Donated by the Northern Colony" and "Donated by the Southern Colony." It is said that these windows told the Northerners and Southerners which side to sit on in the days when they still kept separate.

Much of the history of the Italian colony in the Walla Walla Valley is the history of horticulture and of the daily lives of horticulturists. Locati's *Horticultural Heritage* explores this in great detail. The early Italian gardeners planted and shipped a variety of produce, but after the 1920s, as the "Walla Walla sweet" emerged, onions increased in importance. Increasing demand for asparagus also spurred cultivation of that crop. Most of the gardeners worked small plots, which they cultivated intensively.

Farm work was shared by the large Italian-American families, as men, women, and children planted, thinned, weeded, and harvested together. Although the work was hard, many remember the positive aspects of family work-parties. Immigrant Maria Daltoso remembers her children and herself singing together as they worked, and they often asked her to sing from her repertoire of old Italian songs. A much younger woman, Marilyn McCann, remembers looking forward to the work parties she went on with her grandparents' family. She described them as picnics, during which they located and harvested *giunci* (rushes) in local wetlands, used for tying "bunch crops" (spinach, carrots, beets, and other fresh vegetables) at harvest. They were most plentiful in a marsh in the Blalock area where the

Members of the Walla Walla Gardeners' Association pose for a portrait at the WWGA packing house, ca. 1910. Courtesy of Francis and Nadine Christiano, IAW-JL-B-WW010-1

Blue Mountain Mall is now located. Charlie Paietta also remembers *giunci*-cutting parties.

In recent years, the larger holdings south of Walla Walla, and some farther out in the county have come to be the only ones to turn a profit for the full-time farmer. Many of the second- and third-generation growers have continued to plant and intensively cultivate small crops of onions and asparagus after retirement. Some retirees prefer asparagus, as they are perennials, and not subject to "white rot," a fungus pest.

The onion has become a symbol of the local Italian-American community. Onions were one of the first crops to be shipped out of the Walla Walla Valley, as early as 1863, and many of the Chinese gardeners grew them. Locati believes that Italians were growing them before 1900. His mother remembered that when she came to be Tony Locati's bride in 1900, he already grew several varieties. They were a profitable crop that did well in the local soil and climate.[10]

Much local lore centers around the origins of the "Walla Walla sweet." According to Joe Locati, the "sweets'" ancestral seed came to the valley from Corsica around 1900 with Pete Pieri, who had served there in the French army. Hearing about agricultural opportunities in the American West, he acquired some seed and set out for the New World, ending up in Walla Walla County. (Locati emphasizes that Corsica, though a part of France, was Genovese territory until 1768, is still largely Italian in heritage, and that the onion is therefore Italian.)

Pieri's onions did well and some of his Italian neighbors acquired seed from him. The strain was especially valuable for its ability to winter over in Walla Walla's climate, thus giving it an early start and bringing it to maturity weeks before the spring-planted onions already grown locally. They came to be known locally, in the local version of the Milanese dialect, as *la cipulla francaisa*. By 1915, local newspapers reported the increasing cultivation of "French" onions by Italian gardeners.

The early "French" onions were remarkable in their productivity. In Locati's words:

It would seem that the Italian grower, with his third-grade-or-less education and his fine Walla Walla soil produced about 220 percent more onions per acre than the U.S. average. And that ain't bad, no matter how you say it, for those early days.

The early "French" onions were seeded directly in the fields in early September and wintered over like winter wheat.

In the spring, on hands and knees, using a putty knife, plants were thinned out to some three or four inches apart and some of the thinnings transplanted to new patches.

The self-reliant growers selected their own seed. Early in the 1920s, John Arbini noticed that some "French" onions matured as early as late June, and he began to select these. He was thus able to market his crop earlier than other gardeners. This led his competition to begin saving their earliest seed as well. The "early Arbini" strain was stabilized by 1925. A hard freeze in 1924 had destroyed most of the onions in the valley, but some supplies of "French" and "early Arbini" seed survived. Onion prices were high in the 1920s. This encouraged Walla Walla's Italian gardeners to revive and improve the strains and to raise larger crops.

During the 1930s, the valley gardeners double-cropped spinach and onions. According to Locati, they would alternate rows of "early Arbini" and ordinary "French." Since the onions were open-pollinated, the two strains cross-fertilized, and out of this came three strains, "early Arbini," "early French," and "late French," all harvestable in succession. Individual sub-strains of these three also proliferated. All together they came to be certified by the inspectors as "yellow globe onions, sweet 'Spanish' type." And it is this type that became today's "Walla Walla sweet," although that term did not start being used until much later, probably in the late 1940s or early 1950s.

In the early decades of this century, the onions were hand-harvested and graded right in the field by the gardeners' own family members. Even when harvesting machines became available, the high moisture content of the "Walla Walla sweet" strains (over 90 percent, supposedly the highest for any onion variety) prevented their use.

Planting and harvesting methods remained basically the same until the early 1950s. Truck gardening in the Walla Walla Valley was largely a family affair. Italian gardener families were large and children and young people planted, transplanted, thinned, graded, harvested, and bagged or crated onions during respective seasons. Onion-growing families shared a work culture derived from ethnic, occupational, and family traditions, and intimately connected with the seasonal work cycle, the relationship of the *padroni* to the poorer gardeners, and the social and economic relationships around the WWGA.

Third-generation onion-grower Jim Vinti farms a large area south of Walla Walla, raising "sweets" and hard hybrid winter onions. When Vinti was a boy, onions were first planted in seedbeds in late August and transplanted in rows in October. They wintered over and matured in June or July. The big change, which came around 1970, was the introduction of direct seeding, in September, thus eliminating the transplanting step.

Before the 1950s, onions were graded, sized, and sacked right in the fields, usually by family members, who learned grading at their parents' knees. During the grading,

they selected the next year's seed. During the late 1950s, sacks gave way to boxes, and in the early 1960s to large bins, which were hauled to the WWGA packing house for grading and sacking. A few families, such as the Bossinis, also do their own packing. Many of the larger growers also raise considerable acreage of hybrid winter onions, which they harvest mechanically.

Selection, preparation, and planting of seed onions by hand has changed little over the generations. Individual onions are chosen for shape and size, earliness or lateness, as desired. Seed onions are planted in late August or early September. They sprout almost immediately and winter over. In May, their umbels (seed-cluster stalks) appear. In Virgil Criscola's words:

We cut off the seed pods, and usually that's in like the first of August, and set them out to dry and then we trash it. . . . In the old days we used to take and put a burlap gunny sack, fill it about half full, tie a knot in the end of the sack and then beat it with a baseball bat. That was the way we used to do it. Well, nowadays we'll still put them in a gunny sack, but we'll run over them with the duals of a truck on some concrete, on a

Lewis "Louie" Colombo thins Walla Walla sweet onions in his field in College Place, Washington, April 1989. The selection, preparation, and harvest of seed onions by hand has changed little over the years. Photograph by Jens Lund, WWI89-BJL006-13

Italian-American women with variations of deep-fried Italian pastry called *crustelli* they have made in Carmela "Carmy" Destito-Buttice's kitchen. Left to right: Carmy Destito-Buttice, Ellen Anthony, Mary Gunberg, and Elveda Elia. Photograph by Jens Lund, IAW-JL-B-WW015-30

concrete driveway. Run over them three or four times and that just smashes them all. And then we'll take and wash them in a tub, just a regular old washtub, and then set the seed out to dry. . . . The seeds settle in the bottom of the tub and the chaff and junk floats to the top.

Although onion-growing is perhaps the most visible manifestation of ethnic continuity in the community, other Italian customs survive in the community foodways. Of particular interest is the survival of both Northern and Southern foods not usually associated with the red sauce and pasta-based cuisine that most Americans know as Italian food. Families of Milanese origin know the northern origin of such dishes as *polenta* and *risotto,* both still prominent in the local diet.[11] One Southern dish in the local cuisine is *cucia,* a wheat-and-meat-stock porridge, which has never become a popular Italian-American food. In the early days, both *polenta* and *cucia* were made of game after a successful hunt.

Isolation from other Italian communities affected local recipes. *Risotto* is traditionally spiced and colored with rare and expensive saffron. A similar color (but a different flavor) can be achieved using safflower blossoms, which are easy to grow. Today, *risotto* in Walla Walla is often flavored and colored with safflower, which they now call "saffron." As Francis Christiano, who grows it in his home garden, puts it, "Of course, it's not the same as Middle Eastern saffron, which is much stronger and much more expensive."

The gardeners' association made it possible for people in this isolated community to purchase ingredients used in Italian cooking. Despite this, many people who grew up in immigrant families remember that their everyday diet was not that different from the diet of their non-Italian farmer neighbors. Italian dishes were more likely to appear at specific seasons such as Christmas and Lent, as they do today during Italian Heritage Days.

Onions do appear in many Italian recipes. However, the "Walla Walla sweet" is not a cooking onion. There are a few recipes, such as baked onions, casserole, and fried onion rings, in which they can be used, but "sweets" are primarily a slicing onion. They are not part of traditional Italian or Italian-American cuisine.

Winemaking is very much a part of Italian tradition, of course, but in this country it is sometimes associated with uncomfortable memories. The early immigrants were avid winemakers. Soon after his arrival, Pasquale Saturno built a two-story brick shed to use as a winery and wine-cellar. It is still standing in somewhat collapsed condition, and in it are casks, demijohns, a cooperage fermenting vat, and a press.

Washington is one of the leading winemaking states in the union, despite the fact that almost all of its vineyards were planted since the 1950s, but local Italians have not had a prominent role in this industry. There were, however, a few who did raise wine-grapes and make wine commercially. Frank Sabucco raised over twenty varieties of grapes on the banks of the Columbia River near Attalia, Washington, from the 1920s through 1953. Some of the local home wine-makers picked their own grapes at Sabucco's orchard, and he sold the rest to a Seattle winery.

Other winemakers included father and son, Giuseppe and Bert Pesciallo, who lived across the Oregon line near Milton-Freewater. Some Italians bought their grapes from the Pesciallos, who also made licensed wine on a small scale. There is one small but very successful Italian-American winery inside of Walla Walla's city limits, the Leonetti Cellars, operated by Gary Figgins, whose mother was a Leonetti. Several Leonetti wines have won national and international prizes.

The negative side of the winemaking tradition is its association with anti-Italian prejudice in the valley, especially during Prohibition. In traditional Italian society, wine-drinking is part of mealtime. The mentality of the Prohibitionist Anglo community associated it with drunkenness.

During Prohibition, Walla Walla had a reputation as a "wide-open" bootlegging town. Certain corrupt officials, who looked the other way at protected transactions, made a great show of raiding Italian home winemakers. Many Italian families, who made, at most, a few gallons for their own consumption were ostentatiously raided. Officers would destroy any container found in the house of a violator, which could be used to store the illegal product. Many Italian families lost every pot, pan, and fruit jar (including jars of canned fruit and vegetables) during these punitive raids. There were, of course, also a few Italian wine-makers who were willing to risk arrest to

Old label for Blue Mountain "Black Prince" wine, produced in the Walla Walla Valley by Blue Mountain Vineyards, near Milton-Freewater, Oregon.

Joe Basta (left) and Angelo Locati enjoy a glass of wine out in the garden, in the late 1920s. The child is Basta's daughter Rose. Courtesy of Francis and Nadine Christiano, IAW-JL-B-WW009-27

make some money selling wine, and their activities affected the entire community's reputation.

Italians who did not make wine, or who made it only for their own consumption, were sometimes harassed by non-Italians who came to their homes demanding to buy wine, as it was assumed by many that all Italians had some for sale. Joe J. Locati remembers, from his childhood, a drunk man appearing at his parents' door in the middle of the night demanding that they sell him wine. When they protested that they had none, he became belligerent, claiming that he was a judge down in Oregon and that they had better be forthcoming.

The negative stereotype, in the Walla Walla Valley, of Italian as winemaker and Prohibition-violator ensured that winemaking did not persist on any substantial scale in the second and third generations, unlike in California or the Northeast. Discussions of the winemaking tradition are ambivalent. Most local people are aware of how the old immigrants were avid winemakers and

wine-drinkers. Most are quick to affirm that this tradition is moribund, and many are uncomfortable talking about it at all. A very few men of the second generation still make wine at home.

People of Italian ancestry were not the only truck gardeners in the Walla Walla Valley. But those who were, shared not only their involvement in the WWGA. They were also part of an informal group of people who could claim to have developed and sustained the unique "Walla Walla sweet" onion strain. Pride in this accomplishment helped make the 1980s ethnic revival possible.

American society has seesawed between extolling pluralism and demanding assimilation since the beginning of our nation's history. The most recent tilt towards ethnic pluralism began in the late 1960s, first prompted by the movement for black civil rights. By the mid-1970s, as preparations for the American Revolutionary Bicentennial proceeded, American popular culture accepted ethnic pride as a positive virtue. Many local Bicentennial celebrations were, in effect, ethnic festivals, thus popularly verifying ethnic identification as a form of American patriotism. The aftermath of the Bicentennial included a profusion of local celebrations and festivals that persists to the present day. And in 1978, the popularity of Alex Haley's *Roots* and its dramatization on television evoked extensive interest in genealogy and national origins.

This movement also affected Walla Walla. The Walla Walla *Union-Bulletin* issued a special Bicentennial supplement, with articles on the Italians and other ethnic communities in the area.[12] Also in 1976, a group of local Italian-Americans and other citizens organized a ceremony to rededicate the Christopher Columbus statue on the court house grounds.

Two-story brick winery and wine cellar built by Pasquale Saturno (Frank Breen), in College Place, Washington. Saturno, who arrived in 1876, was Walla Walla's second Italian settler. Photograph by Jens Lund, IAW-JL-B-WW025-12

Members of Walla Walla's Italian Heritage Association celebrate Columbus Day on the steps of the Walla Walla County Courthouse, 1989, with visiting members of the Vancouver, B.C., Italian Folk Choir. Holding the association's new banner are Carmela "Carmy" Destito-Buttice, Elveda Elia, Carmy's grandson Justin Destito (holding staff), and Emilio "Millie" Buttice (right). The banner is being dedicated as a memorial to Carmy's father, the late Salvatore "Sam" Perfetto. Photograph by Jens Lund, IAW-JL-B-WW002-23

At about the same time, Joe J. Locati, recently retired as a federal-state fruit and produce inspector, was asked to give a lecture on the local Italian community to a history class at Whitman College in Walla Walla. While preparing for this, he discovered that there was little source material on the subject so he began research. The result of his work was the 1978 publication of his book, *The Horticultural Heritage of Walla Walla County, 1818–1977 . . . With a Section on the Italian Heritage*. Locati delved into government and private business records, and interviewed other knowledgeable citizens. He uncovered the history of the "Walla Walla sweet" onion, including its Corsican origins via Pete Pieri, and its gradual evolution through selection by such gardeners as Joe Arbini and Joe Locati's father, Tony. Before, local legend had it that the onion was developed by one grower, usually Tony Locati or Joe Arbini, and this turned out not to be the case at all.

The Horticultural Heritage was not warmly received by all members of the community. A few took issue with some of Locati's conclusions. But the strident discussions that these controversies sparked had the positive effect of eliciting even more interest in local Italian-American history and culture.

In 1982, the Walla Walla Gardeners Association commissioned Tom Moro, a sculptor from the local Italian-American community, to carve a small statue of an Italian boy sitting on a sack of onions. Eighty bronze castings of this sculpture, titled "Walla Walla Sweet," were made, and many of the gardener families have purchased copies. The piece received considerable publicity at the 1983 Southeastern Washington Fair, thus giving more recognition to the Italian contribution to local agriculture.[13]

Francis Christiano collects historical memorabilia, organized the local muzzle loaders' association, and is a summer National Park Service employee at nearby Whitman Mission-Wailatpu National Historic Site. He credits Bill Burk, manager of the Fort Walla Walla Museum, with organizing the first ethnic celebrations in recent years. They include a series of public festivities held at the fort in the fall of 1982, celebrating the Italian, Mexican, Native American, and Volga German communities. It was during the 1985 commemoration of the seventieth anniversary of St. Francis of Assisi Church, that the possibility of establishing a local Italian Heritage Association (IHA) was first discussed. After the church anniversary, a group of interested individuals, led by Christiano, Richard Campanelli, Carmela "Carmy" Destito-Buttice, and others, started meeting to discuss establishing an Italian association.

Christiano credits Locati's book and Burk's "Ethnic Days" with providing the impetus for the organizing of the IHA. His wife, Nadine, who is of Volga German origin, belongs to the local chapter of the American Historical Society of Germans from Russia. AHSGR members advised Christiano and his friends how to proceed.

Walla Walla never had a local Sons of Italy lodge, although a few local people belonged to the lodge in Spokane. In establishing an Italian association, affiliation with the Sons was discussed, but a majority decided against it. Unlike the days of Yuse and the Workingmen's Club, the old friction between Northerners and Southerners was long forgotten. Many second-generation Italians, including Christiano, were children of one parent from the north and one from the south.

The proposed establishment of a heritage association was not without controversy. According to Christiano, some of the older Italian-Americans were opposed to the very idea, feeling that they had finally lived down negative stereotypes and become Americans, and that emphasizing the Italian heritage risked reviving old prejudices. Christiano and others advocated opening the association to people of all faiths and a few older Catholics objected to this. One prominent older second-generation man, who later became an active supporter of the organization, complained at first that the Italian ethnicity had long died out and that their efforts were "nothing but a bit of nostalgia."

Some of the most avid supporters were people who had come to Walla Walla from elsewhere in North America, and who thus had no bitter first-hand memories of prejudice in the Walla Walla Valley. A few examples are Carmy Destito-Buttice, a native of Spokane; Richard Campanelli, who also taught evening school classes in the Italian language, born in the vicinity, but raised in California; Louis Rizzuti, retired Walla Walla city employee, originally from Steubenville, Ohio; and Jan Eaton, a young high school counselor from the Italian mining community in Trail, British Columbia.

The IHA was established and chartered in 1986, and the first Italian Heritage Days were held in October 1986. Christiano believes that fear of a revival of prejudice scared away some of the more prominent older members of the community until the organization had been in existence for over a year, so they missed becoming charter members. From the start, however, the organization and the festival were supported by the Walla Walla Gardeners Association, and by several Italian-American-owned businesses.

Despite "white rot" fungus, the third generation's abandonment of agriculture for the professions, and an agricultural economy that made onion-growing profitable only for the larger operators, the onion-growers were finally getting the respect that they felt they deserved. It was also during this period that the "Walla Walla sweet" began to be noticed by gourmet food writers and that the WWGA began to ship "sweets" by air freight to Alaska, California, the East Coast, and even Japan. Yet, it was the educated third- and fourth-generation who flocked to the association in the greatest numbers. Third- and fourth-generation women, Geraldine Hartley, Mary Kleyn, and Cheryl Knotts, revived Italian dancing, especially among the children.

Italian Heritage Days begins with a parade down Main Street on Saturday morning, ending at Walla Walla County Court House. At a ceremony there, the Knights of Columbus place a wreath on the 1911 Columbus statue. In the afternoon, there is singing, musical performance, and dancing. Participants include the Famee Friulani Dancers and the Italian Folk Chorus, both from Vancouver, Canada. The local adults' and children's Italian Heritage Dancers also perform. The IHA's sausage booth sells great quantities of "hot" and "mild" sausage. In the evening there is a banquet.

Sunday afternoon begins with the "Grape Stomp." For all its festivity, it is about a negative stereotype of the Old World Italian crushing grapes with bare feet, now dealt with in a humorous way. Local businesses sponsor teams, who compete to see who can squeeze the most juice out of a measured amount of grapes in a five-minute period by stamping on them in casks on a flat-bed truck before a crowd of cheering onlookers. The event was first seen at winery festivals further west in the upper Columbia Valley by IHA members who then brought the idea to Walla Walla. The "Grape Stomp" is followed by more dancing, singing, and sausage selling.

Walla Walla Valley Italian-Americans

H. Atlas "Doc" Bailey offers sausages for sale at the Italian Heritage Association's booth during Walla Walla's Italian Heritage Days, October 1989. Initiated in 1986, Italian Heritage Days is a prominent expression of the recent ethnic revival. Photograph by Jens Lund, IAW-JL-B-WW003-30

have risen in status and economic circumstances in the century they have lived in the valley. They have overcome internal cultural divisions, and, as many of the Anglo surnames attest, they have assimilated into the mainstream North American West. And history and ethnicity, as these people now practice them, have become mainstream American pastimes and hobbies. At the time of the valley's ethnic revival, the informal folk ethnicity of narratives told around family albums and of pictures displayed on mantelpieces still survived.

This community has maintained its ethnic identity in part because of the unifying role of the onion crop, and most recently because of the ethnic revival. Both the continuity and the revival are, in part, products

Maria Daltoso performs a song for researcher Jens Lund. Photograph by Jens Lund, IAW-JL-BWW029-27A

of specific individuals' efforts at maintaining or raising Italian identity. The leaders of the revival are well-known to all. The heroes of continuity are less visible. They include the second- and third-generation people who maintained at least a smattering of the language and dialects, and the women who kept and passed on the recipes for traditional food.

This was especially important as such southern Italian-influenced foods as spaghetti, pizza, lasagne, and ravioli became part of mainstream popular culture. The fact that Milanese foods are so different from these entrees has sustained family recipes for *polenta* and *risotto*.

Continuity has also been fostered by individuals who have served informally as community photo-archivists. Frank Fazzari's publicly displayed collection in The Pastime Cafe is one example. Joe J. Locati, Tony Ambrose, Francis Christiano, Doug Breen Saturno, Charlie Paietta, Carrie Criscola, Carmy Destito-Buttice, and others all have collections, about which they can expound.

Other heroes of continuity are the community's rememberers, like Charlie Paietta and Carrie Criscola, who can talk of the old days with friend or stranger alike. Old-timers like Locati and Paietta, and younger people, like Doug Breen Saturno and the Christianos have curated family albums, framed pictures, and such artifacts as Pasquale Saturno's 1911 parade badge and Tony Locati's old parade sash.

Immigrant farm-wife Maria Daltoso often performs ballads, other songs, and traditional verse (all in Italian) for family and neighbors. She is often asked to sing the grisly murder ballad, "Una bella e graziosa fanciulla." With its graphic violence and profound sense of tragedy, it may serve as a necessary counterpoint to the festive nostalgia of celebration. As Dave Deccio plays the lively tarantellas during Columbus Day weekend, there still lurks in some memories the story of the local girl who was whipped for refusing a valley *padrone's* dance, the smashed belongings of suspected winemakers, and the taunts of prejudiced neighbors.

The institutionalization of the "Walla Walla sweet" gourmet onion coincided with the local ethnic revival, and the two phenomena supported each other. The community turned first to festive ethnicity, beginning as re-creative events, such as the revived Columbus Day parade and ceremony at the statue. The Italian Heritage Dancers, both adults' and children's, are an obvious immediate link with Italian heritage, visible, colorful, easily presented in the context of a parade and festival. But they learned the dances from books and from the Vancouver dancers.

Walla Walla Italian-Americans have often been apprehensive about ethnicity, and to some extent, this unease still persists. Since the revival, there has been a certain amount of tension between those who quietly sustained tradition over the years and those who quickly embraced the association and the festival. But in the long run, these two approaches to ethnicity probably reinforce each other. The festival's celebration of Italian heritage has made ethnic continuity a source of community and individual self-esteem.

The status of the sweet onion and the status of the gardeners and their progeny increased proportionately. Once ethnic festivity became a common feature in small-town America, the stage was set, not only for an ethnic revival, but also for a deeper appreciation of those who had quietly kept Italian traditions alive—traditions of savory foods and lively dance-tunes, and the memories of a culture finding its way in a new world, a legacy of both joy and pain.

The "Walla Walla" is indeed sweet, but it is also an onion, with all that implies. Once merely a local variety of a not-very-glamorous vegetable, it is now a "gourmet" export onion. A little colony of Italian-Americans, isolated from the vigorous communities in California and the Northeast, have nurtured this strain from its humble beginnings to its present standing. As they integrated into the mainstream culture of Western American farmers, many families continued to nurture Italian traditions at home. And when the third and fourth generation left the farm and became teachers,

engineers, and real estate agents, they learned to cherish their Italian heritage, turning it into an expression of public pride and celebration.

Walla Walla sweet onions growing in Louis and Greg Bossini's field, south of Walla Walla, Washington. Photograph by Jens Lund, WWI89-BJL003-11

TRADITION IN A BOTTLE

The A. Conrotto Winery of Gilroy, California

DAVID A. TAYLOR

Salute!" he seems to be saying as he raises a small glass of red wine. Anselmo Conrotto, in a photograph taken in 1929, is seated fourth from the left on a long wooden bench, outdoors near the Hecker Pass Highway in Gilroy, California. Dressed in a three-piece suit and holding his trademark high-crown felt hat on his knee, the sturdy, thirty-nine-year-old Conrotto looks every inch the prosperous farmer. His fellow members of Gilroy's Piemonte Club—all with ties to the Piedmont region of northern Italy—exude a similar prosperity. Scagliotti, Viarengo, Giachino, Pappani, Colombano, Giretti, Balanesi, Marchetti, Ortalda, Bellini, and Serafini are their surnames, and their fine clothes, cars parked under an oak tree, and expressions of contentment bespeak the success they have achieved in California. Like Anselmo Conrotto, most of them were immigrants who purchased land along Hecker Pass and

planted orchards and vineyards. Some built small wineries.

Over sixty years later, a number of these vineyards and wineries remain. Many have changed hands over the years, but a few have remained in the founders' families. One such operation is the winery founded by Anselmo Conrotto three years before the photograph was taken. The continuity of this family business provides both a case study of California winemaking and, more important, insight into the reasons why the "Italianness" of winemaking in California is rooted as much in the structure and values of family businesses as in the process of wine production.

Anselmo Conrotto was born in the village of Coconato d'Asti, Piedmont, on March 6, 1890. His father, Battista, was a farmer, and young Anselmo began to learn about agriculture as he carried out routine chores on the family farm. According to

Anselmo Conrotto (fourth from left in the front row) and other members of Gilroy's Piedmont Club at a meeting near Hecker Pass Highway in California in 1929. Front row, left to right: Emilio Scagliotti, Joseph Viarengo, Giachinto Conrotto, Anselmo Conrotto, Enrico Giachino, Felix Pappani, Camillo Colombano, Virginio Pappani, Serafino Giretti. Back row: Albert Balanesi, Enrico Marchetti, John Giachino, Dominic Ortalda, Joe Bellini, Dominic Serafini, Ed Scagliotti, John Marchetti. Courtesy of Aldo and Aurora Viarengo, IAW-DT-B016-31

information in a published biographical sketch, Anselmo decided to leave Italy because "he had heard and read of the great opportunities in California, and his ambition was stirred to cast in his lot with this favored section."[1] According to family tradition, Anselmo came to California because two of five brothers—Giachinto and Peter—were there already.

Sixteen-year-old Anselmo arrived in Gilroy, Santa Clara County, in 1906. Like his brothers, he found employment on farms and orchards as a laborer. In the main, the Conrotto brothers and other immigrants worked for Anglo-American farmers who, by the end of the nineteenth century, had transformed the Santa Clara Valley from wheat-centered general farming into specialized agriculture featuring fruits, vegetables, and seed production. Soon Santa Clara County became not only the top fruit producing county in California, but one of the largest fruit producing areas on earth. Indeed, it came to be known as "the garden spot of the world." Anselmo's son Chinto ascribes the transformation of the county's agricultural base to Italians:

When [my father] came to Gilroy, most of this was oats and wheat. There was a lot of cattle in those days. Then, when the Italians came in, they all started digging holes and planting trees and vineyards and all that. It changed the whole thing. In about eight or ten years it was a different country.[2]

In 1919, 98,152 acres were planted in fruit trees and 2,850 acres planted in grape vines. Primary fruit crops included prunes, apricots, peaches, cherries, and grapes. The county's prune production in 1919 totalled more than all the prunes grown elsewhere in the United States.[3] According to one survey of the area's resources, "Santa Clara County means prunes."[4] The acreage used for vineyards had previously been consider-

ably larger,[5] but the profitability of the fruit industry led many vineyardists to pull up their vines and plant fruit trees. In 1919, Prohibition cast a pall over the entire California wine industry.

Winemaking in Santa Clara County began around 1800 at the Santa Clara Mission, northwest of the San Jose presidio, under the auspices of Spanish and, later, Italian Jesuit priests.[6] French immigrants founded the commercial wine industry in the 1850s, originating all three of the county's largest and best-known firms: Paul Masson, Mirassou, and Almaden. The initial center of winemaking was in the northwestern foothill district now known as Silicon Valley, but by the end of the nineteenth century a secondary grape and wine producing area was established in the upper valley around Gilroy.[7] In 1896, nearly all of the vineyardists in the upper valley were of Anglo- or German-American origin. However, Italian winemakers had moved south from the San Francisco peninsula to the northwestern section of the county, and by 1915 several winemakers with Italian surnames were recorded in the Gilroy area.[8] Vincent Picchetti, who began by working in the Jesuit vineyards and then started a winery of his own in the 1880s, was apparently the first.[9] By the early twentieth century, many Gilroy farms had small wineries where wine was made primarily for home consumption, with the surplus sold for extra money.[10]

In 1911, Anselmo Conrotto returned to Italy in order to fulfill his military obligation. He served in the Alpine Regiment of the Italian Army for two years, a little more than half of which he spent at the front during the Tripoli War. After his discharge from the army in 1913, he stayed on in Italy, taking a wife, Rose Conti, in the spring of 1914. Anselmo's son Chinto recalls this period in his father's life:

When he became twenty-one he went to Italy to serve the army and when he was there the Turks and Italy, they got in a beef. So, he fought [in] that . . . Tripoli War. He had a few bucks then from the United States and he became [a] very good friend to a colonel. So, they were on a boat in the Mediterranean going home after the war and he took my dad aside and he says, "Well, you better pack your grip and get the hell out [because] there's going to be a *big* war." That was World War I. So, my dad got married. He did everything, I guess, in three, four months. [Then] he was on a boat coming home with my mother.[11]

The Conrottos arrived in Gilroy later in 1914, and Anselmo again secured work on local farms and orchards. In order to earn extra money for the purchase of land, he took on additional work baling hay. Later, along with a man named Bonfante, he bought a vineyard and grew grapes, which were sold to a Gilroy winery operated by the California Wine Association. After a year in this venture, Anselmo and his partner sold out to another local Italian, and he used his share of the profits to purchase a house in Gilroy.[12] He then hired himself out to vineyards in the Gilroy area until 1919, when, along with his brother Peter, he took out a four-year lease on the Doyle Ranch on Stevens Creek in Cupertino (about forty-two miles northwest of Gilroy), where he tended five hundred acres planted in fruit trees (prunes, apricots, and peaches), grape vines, hay, and grain.[13] Under the Conrottos' care, harvests increased from year to year, and in 1923, grapes and prunes—the two main crops—totaled 650 tons and 200 tons respectively.

Although Prohibition went into effect in 1919, an amendment to the Volstead Act permitted households to produce up to two hundred gallons of wine per year for home consumption. Consequently, the grape market was supported by a strong demand from home winemakers and pre-Prohibition

Anselmo Conrotto as pictured in Sawyer's *History of Santa Clara, California*, published in 1922.

prices in the $10-to-$20-per-ton range rocketed to over $100 per ton within a year. As a result, vineyardists who secured these high prices reaped windfalls. Apparently, Anselmo Conrotto was one of them since he reported that he sold grapes grown on the Doyle Ranch for as much as $135 a ton.[14]

In 1923, Anselmo purchased a home on Harrison Street in San Francisco and then took his family back to Italy to visit his relatives. They stayed for about a year. According to his son Chinto, who would have been eight years old at the time, his father intended that the family would remain in Italy but, for whatever reason, conditions were not favorable.[15] Subsequently, the family re-

Anselmo Conrotto at work in his prune orchard in Gilroy, ca. 1950. Courtesy of Chinto and Rose Conrotto, IAW-DT-B018-12

At first, Anselmo grew prunes and apricots and also purchased grapes from local vineyards that he sold to his old customers in Cupertino. In 1926, though Prohibition was still in effect, he erected a large wooden winery building on his property.[16] Initially, the building was used to store crops of dried prunes and apricots, which were air-dried outside and brought inside to be sheltered from rain. The building was also used for some surreptitious distilling. In a space beneath the floor that was further hidden by racks of drying prunes, a small still was set up and used to make grappa, a type of brandy.[17]

In 1933, with the repeal of Prohibition imminent, Conrotto purchased winemaking equipment in San Francisco, installed large storage tanks, planted new vines, and performed other chores necessary for the operation of a winery. After the repeal of the Eighteenth Amendment later in the year, he bought grapes from local growers and, probably in 1934, made his first wine for commercial purposes.

The design of the Conrotto winery is noteworthy. While other local wineries were constructed on flat land, the Conrotto winery was built into the side of a small hill with one level (the fermentation room) higher than a second (the storage room). This arrangement allowed newly fermented grape juice to flow from the upper level into storage tanks in the lower level by gravity, thus eliminating the need for high-speed pumps. And the fact that the building is constructed into the side of a hill helps maintain a relatively cool and constant temperature inside the winery. According to family tradition, there are analogues of this gravity-flow winery in Anselmo's home region of Italy, where he first encountered the design.[18]

The winery's upper level or fermentation

turned to San Francisco and opened a small restaurant. But Anselmo longed to return to farming, and so, in 1924, he purchased fourteen acres on the Hecker Pass Highway in Gilroy and moved the family there. At that time, the Italians who were attracted to the valley were mainly Piedmontese from the north of Italy or Calabrese from the south. Regional distinctions were played out in Gilroy, since the Piedmontese tended to settle around Hecker Pass, on the west side of the town, and the Calabrese settled on land they cleared on the south side of town.

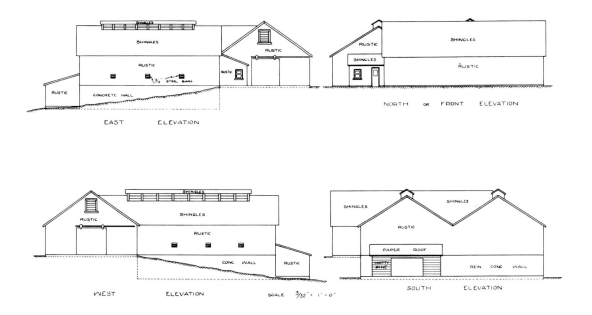

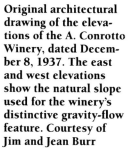

Original architectural drawing of the elevations of the A. Conrotto Winery, dated December 8, 1937. The east and west elevations show the natural slope used for the winery's distinctive gravity-flow feature. Courtesy of Jim and Jean Burr

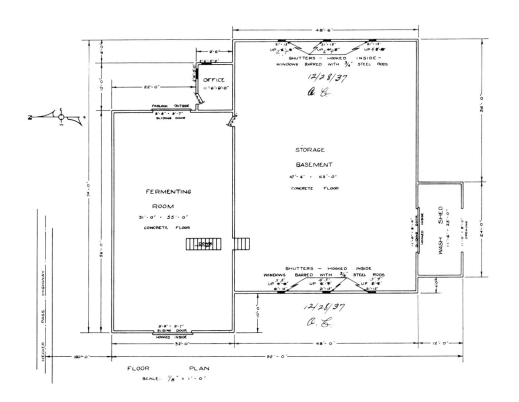

The original floor plan of the winery showing the office, the fermenting room, the storage room, and the wash shed. Courtesy of Jim and Jean Burr

Anselmo Conrotto in the storage room of his winery, ca. 1960s. Courtesy of Chinto and Rose Conrotto, IAW-DT-B018-6

room is primarily occupied by four large cement vats called fermenting tanks. After grapes have been crushed, the juice and pulp (collectively, the "must") are pumped into these tanks, where they ferment for approximately seven days. During this period, winery workers periodically walk across the top of the tanks on boards and use poles to punch down the "cap"—the floating layer of skins—so that juice and skins come into contact. Known as "punching down," this is the traditional European method used to keep fermenting wine and floating skins in contact, thus enhancing the color and composition of red wines.[19] After the juice has finished fermenting, it is transferred into a settling tank, where solid particles settle to the bottom. The solids that remain in the fermentation tank are pressed to extract juice, and this juice is also placed in the settling tank. After settling overnight, the juice is drawn off again and transported into large storage tanks in the lower level of the winery. The wine will remain in the storage tanks until it is clarified by being pumped or syphoned into another container, thus

leaving sediment behind. This procedure, called "racking," may be repeated several times. According to Jim Burr, the husband of Anselmo's granddaughter, who now operates the winery, Anselmo used to "rack by the moon."

He would always state, and I think it's true a lot of times, that your solids at a certain time of your moon are really hard. They wouldn't move. You could draw that liquid off with no problem. [But] another period during the moon cycle that solid would be more liquified and so . . . it would start to move and mix back in the wine a little bit . . . . And that was always his theory: rack by the moon, the quarter moon changing.[20]

Originally, the storage area of the winery was jam-packed with redwood storage tanks and oak puncheons. The storage tanks were fabricated by coopers from San Francisco who built them, took them apart, and reassembled them inside the winery. The largest tanks are about twenty-two feet high and hold 15,000 gallons each. The puncheons were purchased at the beginning of Prohibition from a winery cooperative in Gilroy.

Those that Anselmo purchased range in size from 160 to 4,940 gallons. After the winery was expanded in 1938, it had a total capacity of 134,000 gallons.

When the wine has aged sufficiently in the storage tanks, it is bottled, labeled, and sold.[21] In the early years, the winery produced only red wine. Referred to as burgundy, it was a blend of wines made from zinfandel and carignane grapes, varieties commonly planted by Italians in the Hecker Pass area. Later, smaller quantities of white wine, called sauterne or chablis, principally made from French Colombard grapes, were also produced.[22]

Most of the wine was sold in gallon jugs or in barrels. The jugs were filled with a small hose that syphoned wine directly from a wine barrel. In the first year of operation, the winery sold its wine for as little as twenty-five cents per gallon. Customers were residents of Gilroy who bought wine for home use, and also proprietors of restaurants in the Santa Clara and Salinas valleys who purchased wine in bulk. According to Anselmo's son Chinto, who worked with his father in the winery and later took over the operation, eventually about 90 percent of their wine was delivered to various customers, mostly restaurants. "I had all the restaurants in Salinas Valley," he recalled.[23]

The Conrottos purchased grapes from other vineyardists in the Gilroy area to supplement the grapes grown on their own land in Hecker Pass. In 1943, Anselmo purchased a seventy-five-acre "ranch" in Morgan Hill, ten miles northwest of Gilroy, and grew grapes on fifty acres and walnuts on the rest.

During the early years of the Conrotto Winery, other Italians operated small wineries in Gilroy and Morgan Hill. For example, in Gilroy, wineries were established by A. Bertero (1906), Caesar Roffinella (1910), Eduardo Scagliotti[24] (1912), and the Cassa brothers (1935). And in Morgan Hill, others were founded by the Marchetti family (early 1900s), Camillo Colombano (1923), and Emilio Guglielmo (1925).[25]

Anselmo continued to produce rather coarse, inexpensive wine with help from his son Chinto and local Italians (mainly Piedmontese) who were hired to perform various chores in the winery. After the expansion of the winery in 1938, little about the operation was changed until 1962, when the property in Morgan Hill was sold because of the bother of running back and forth between Gilroy and Morgan Hill and also because of the difficulty in finding laborers to prune the Morgan Hill vineyard.[26]

As Anselmo got older, more and more of the winery's management fell to Chinto. Nevertheless, Anselmo, a confirmed workaholic, maintained an active involvement. According to Jim Burr, up until the end of his life Anselmo was a hard worker and constantly in motion. As Jim put it:

He never stopped to have coffee. No, no, no, you didn't do that when he was around. He had to work. Keep those brooms [moving], do something. You never sit down. . . . There was always something to be doing. He didn't believe in resting or coffee breaks.[27]

Anselmo's second wife, Lena, picking grapes at the Conrotto's ranch in Morgan Hill, ca. 1950. Courtesy of Chinto and Rose Conrotto, IAW-DT-B018-16

ABOVE: During the annual grape harvest, Jim Burr tosses grapes into the crushing machine as American Folklife Center researcher Paola Tavarelli lends a hand. September 1989. Photograph by David A. Taylor, IAW-DT-B021-23

RIGHT: Anselmo Conrotto's son Chinto with his wife, Rose, and daughter Jean. In 1983, Chinto handed over the operation of the winery to Jean and her sister Jermaine, and their husbands. Photograph by David A. Taylor, IAW-DT-B019-2

Jim Burr married Chinto's daughter Jean in 1969, and, following employment with Standard Oil, he began to work at the Conrotto Winery on a full-time basis in 1973. He learned about winemaking in the traditional manner—by watching Anselmo and Chinto and the hired men, and by taking part in the various operations, gaining experience and confidence over time. He remembers being captivated by activities at the winery from the start.

Oh, it was exciting. You know, coming down, seeing them in there . . . crushing those grapes. [Really], going to town. Of course, it was a lot of hard work and they needed help. And there used to be a lot of guys working and everything was done more physically. . . . Oh, its always been exciting, you know, to see the different aspects of what's going on.[28]

Anselmo died in 1980 at age ninety and the winery was passed on to Chinto. Three years later, sixty-eight-year-old Chinto decided to retire, and the winery was taken over by his two daughters, Jean and Jermaine, and their husbands, Jim and Jerry. Jim and Jean handle day-to-day operations at the winery with help from their son Scott and daughter Renée and from Jean's parents, Chinto and Rose. Jermaine and Jerry Case and their children, who live in Stockton, California, contribute labor when they can take time to come to the winery.

Unlike her husband, Jean grew up at the winery. "It was a great place," she remembers.

When you're a child you don't realize how important all these things can be, but it was fun. It was fun watching . . . . And they were busy, both my dad and my grandfather. And they had helpers. And then . . . as I got older, in high school, I worked harder because I wanted the money.[29]

Most of the work she did in the winery was simple manual labor:

As a child I didn't really do too much, but as I got older I labeled and helped. And it was just gallons and half-gallons. And my dad would fill the bottles up, cork them, and we'd cap them and put a little band over them and label them. And a few bottles were broken. And when my dad got the empty cases we'd have to help store.[30]

Since they took over the winery, Jim and Jean haven't made many changes in the winemaking equipment or in the winemaking process. In fact, says Jean, "we have everything that my grandfather started with. And some of these things, we hope every time we press the button for it to start . . . it works again this year."[31] Indeed, the tiny, family-run A. Conrotto Winery offers a sharp contrast to California's large, modern wineries with the latest in double-jacketed, temperature-controlled stainless steel tanks, and other high-tech apparatus.

The biggest change they have made is in the kind and variety of wines they produce. With the growing sophistication of wine drinkers following the post-1960s California wine boom, they quickly realized that the winery's unadorned wines—the generic burgundy and sauterne produced since the winery was founded—held little appeal for wine connoisseurs. Therefore, they decided to switch to the production of varietals. These wines are made from and named after varieties of *Vitis vinifera,* the old-world grapevine from which most of the world's fine wines are made. And so, in addition to a chablis and a burgundy, the winery now produces a chardonnay, a white zinfandel, a Johannesburg reisling, a carignane, a cabernet sauvignon, a petite sirah, and a zinfandel.[32]

For Jean and Jim, there are multiple satisfactions that flow from their involvement with the winery. For example, they enjoy the freedom that comes from running their own business and, of course, the profits they earn. And they savor the opportunity to create a high-status product that gives pleasure both to themselves and to their customers. For Jim, there is much obvious pleasure in the physicality of the work and in the challenge of mastering the many operations involved in winemaking. For Jean, the more outgoing of the two, there is excitement in socializing with customers in the winery's small tasting room and introducing them to the wine. And both enjoy the camaraderie they share with other wine makers in the area, many of whom, like the Burrs, belong to the Santa Clara Vintners' Association.

Jean Conrotto Burr removes leaves and foreign matter from boxes of grapes before the grapes are crushed—one of the chores that is part of the annual "crush." Photograph by David A. Taylor, IAW-DT-B021-15

It is clear, too, that Jim and Jean enjoy the relatively relaxed lifestyle that comes from running a small winery in a region that does not attract hoards of visitors. Unlike the famous Napa Valley wineries, for example, Santa Clara Valley's wineries do not lure large numbers of tourists who create heavy traffic on the roads. Jean reports with satisfaction that more than one customer who has visited Napa Valley wineries has told her, "I didn't realize this area was so quiet and we don't have to be herded like cattle."[33] And the scale of their operation is integral to Jean and Jim's enjoyment of their winemaking business. As Jean explained, "If you get it too big it isn't fun anymore."[34]

Jean and Jim also find pleasure in the knowledge that the operation of the winery will probably continue in the family for at least another generation. Their twenty-three year-old son, Scott, has decided to become a winemaker and is now in his third year in the enology program at Fresno State University. If his plan is successful, he will represent the fourth generation of the family's involvement with the winery and will become the first family member to receive formal training in winemaking. Scott's training will consist of a convergence of two modes of learning: informal/traditional training, through a kind of apprenticeship at his family's winery, and formal/scientific training at the university. As he expressed it during his first year at Fresno State:

I know everything from the old-world methods. I mean, this has been handed down to my grandfather, my great-grandfather, and keeps on going down the ladder. And there are a lot of new techniques I'm learning, you know. But the basic principles are all still the same. There's just [different] techniques. Most people don't use the wood tanks now. They all go into stainless steel [tanks] with jacketing. . . . It's very expensive, though, and we'd have to remodel our whole winery to do that. But . . . [if we] do have the opportunity [to do that, I'll] have

that knowledge behind me. But then I'll also have the knowledge to run *this* winery. So I think a blend of the two will make a better person.[35]

As the prospective inheritor of the family business, Scott will likely take on "curatorial" responsibilities.[36] That is, like some participants in other family businesses, he will inherit primary responsibility for the conservation of the material assets of the business—the winery and its accoutrements—as well as its cultural assets, the meanings attached to artifacts and activities. Like his parents before him, and his grandparents before them, with regard to the family's cultural assets he will endeavor to maintain the values and traditions from previous generations that help order life in the present and reify links between family members. The items within his curatorial responsibility will likely include stories about his great-grandfather that convey Anselmo's attitude toward work; objects, like the old gallon-size glass bottles that once contained Conrotto burgundy and sauterne (now on display in the winery's tasting room), that represent an important part of the winery's history; and artifacts, like photographs of Anselmo and his bronzed felt hat (mounted on the wall in Chinto and Rose's living room), that serve as memorials to the winery's founder and reminders of his goals.

What is Italian about the Conrotto Winery and other wineries run by Italians? Obviously, there is the ethnic descent of the proprietors. There are also elements of Italianness in the physical product of the wineries—the wine itself—in that wine has long been an important component of traditional Italian foodways, and that winemaking, home winemaking in particular, is a traditional skill Italian immigrants brought with them to America. Yet, commercial winemaking carried on in California today by Italians (not to mention scores of non-Italian vintners) is largely derived from French practices introduced in California in the nineteenth century and later reinforced by formal training provided by enology programs developed by the University of California and Fresno State University.

However, while the techniques used for the commercial production of fine wines are not of Italian origin, examples of Italian traditionality can be found in other forms. For example, some vintners make wine from grapes of Italian origin, such as barbera and grignolino, varieties from Piedmont. And Italian craftsmanship, in the form of stone-masonry and coopering, continues to be in demand in the winemaking districts of California. Another prominent instance of the continuity of Italian tradition is the family-based management of wineries. One salient characteristic of the Italian style of management is an emphasis on the participation of family members in decision making. According to Jean, the success of the A. Conrotto Winery is dependent upon the engagement of family members. Success results "if we all work together," she remarked.

Oh, sometimes we lock horns, too, but we do all work together, which is very important. And both my sisters have helped, too. My older sister and her husband and then my middle sister, who is a nun, has helped in other ways. I think she's prayed for us a lot, too. But, you know, she gives us advice, or suggests things. So, we've all worked together. And we're very fortunate that we were able to do that.[37]

Because there are negative as well as positive aspects to running family businesses, not all families can do what Jean and her family have been able to do. For example, members of younger generations can sometimes feel pressure to enter into the business. In addition, intra-family tensions

Contemporary label from the A. Conrotto Winery with an illustration of the main winery building. The phrase "four generation vintners—since 1926" calls attention to the longevity of the family's winemaking tradition. Courtesy of Jim and Jean Burr

Label from the Emilio Guglielmo Winery in Morgan Hill, California, that includes a statement (right) combining family history, sense of place, and pride in the family's occupational tradition. Courtesy of Emilio Guglielmo Winery

about how the business should be run can lead to open breaches. Cases in point within the California wine industry are the celebrated public feuds between members of the Mondavi family and between members of the Sebastiani family. Both resulted in the division of land owned by these two families. In the Santa Clara Valley, disagreements between two members of another family resulted in one leaving to start his own winery while the other retained the winery they had run jointly.

At the core of family-based management is the desire for closeness between family members, and the winery provides a nexus for the attainment of this goal. In other words, in addition to the winery's obvious worth as an income-generating enterprise, it also has worth as a means of connecting family members with past generations, with members of their own generation, and, potentially, with members of future generations. Family closeness is reinforced through the medium of the winery in a number of other ways. First, the continuity of the winery as a family enterprise depends on transmission of knowledge from one generation to the next, knowledge concerned with grape-growing, winemaking, business practices, and family traditions. Second, the operation of the winery, particularly at times of peak activity, such as the annual harvest, requires the mobilization of the family for the purpose of supplying labor. Third, the ability of family members to consume the product of their labors, often at family reunions, anniversaries, weddings, and other occasions of great symbolic importance, enable them metaphorically to imbibe a tradition (winemaking) within the context of the enactment of other traditions. And, finally, the winery connects family members with a particular place that is of great significance in the family's history.

Because it is a family business, the winery is a means for family members to share aspects of their corporate identity, not only with each other but also with their customers and the public at large. Thus the family creates products—bottles of wine in this instance—that are infused with family traditions. At the A. Conrotto Winery and other wineries, the qualities that family traditions bring to winemaking are promoted in various ways. For example, many of the labels the Conrotto winery puts on its bottles call attention to the continuity of the family's business by stating simply: "Four Generation Vintners—Since 1926." The Emilio Guglielmo Winery in Morgan Hill, another four-generation operation, uses labels to make a stronger statement about the Guglielmo family's winemaking tradition. The text on the label of wine marketed under its "Mount Madonna" vintages interweaves family history, sense of place, quality of product, and pride in occupational heritage, and invites the customer to participate in the Guglielmo family tradition:

The Mount Madonna name, first used by our family in 1946, comes from a section of the Santa Cruz mountain range which overlooks the beautiful Santa Clara Valley. In 1925 our founder, Emilio Guglielmo, first settled in this valley and began a tradition of producing a quality wine in a clean *natural* style. With an uncompromising concern for quality and a sense of pride, we invite you to share our wines with us and take part in a tradition.

Obviously, the presentation of information of this kind and the display of family photographs and other artifacts in public tasting rooms are attempts to market the concept of kinship to the public.[38] This sort of marketing implies that products and services purveyed by family businesses are imbued with special qualities, qualities directly related to longevity, continuity of tradition, personal service, and sustained commitment to high standards.[39]

While connections to Italian winemaking traditions are relatively superficial (though the social connection to Italy is strong), what is particularly Italian about the Conrotto winery is the structure of the family business, a structure evident in family-run farms, grocery stores, restaurants and many other businesses. Thus it is arguable that a large number of Italians are involved with winemaking in California because the industry happens to mesh neatly with the traditional concepts of family business structure and permits the expression of values of great significance to many Italian families.[40]

Two of the many barrels of wine in the storage room of the A. Conrotto Winery. These contain wine from Santa Clara Valley carignane grapes crushed in 1984. Photograph by Ken Light, IAW-KL-B138-12

"GET ON ONE END OF THE ROPE AND PULL TOGETHER"

Italian-American Life and Work in Pueblo, Colorado

RUSSELL FRANK

Along route I-25 south of Denver, the Front Range of the Rocky Mountains bends west, and the landscape below Colorado Springs gets drier, scrubbier, hotter, browner, as it shifts subtly from high plains to high desert. The region is an unlikely setting for Steel Town, U.S.A., but like the brick-and-beer-joint working-class towns of the Ohio Valley which it so surprisingly resembles, Pueblo, Colorado, came into being because of its location near the coal mines, coke ovens, and limestone quarries.

The interconnected empire of mines, ovens, quarries, and railroad that became the Colorado Fuel and Iron Corporation (CF&I) was launched in 1870 with the organization of the Denver and Rio Grande Western Railroad. During the next ten years, founder William J. Palmer bought lands and mines along the D & RG line, and in 1880 built a blast furnace south of Pueblo. The company town that grew up around the steel mill was called Bessemer.

Southern Italians from Sicily, Calabria, and Campania who came to New Orleans to harvest Bayou sugar cane[1] and to New York and Philadelphia to work on the railroad got wind of this sudden burst of opportunity on the Rocky Mountain frontier and headed west. Coal towns like Brookside and Rockvale near Cañon City and Berwin near Trinidad became almost entirely Italian. The Italians of Pueblo lived first on Goat Hill and in the old downtown area along the Arkansas River to be near their zinc smelter jobs, then began making their way south to Bessemer when the smelters closed, the river flooded, and opportunities opened at the steel mill.

By the 1920s, a Bessemer neighborhood bounded by Northern Avenue to the south, Abriendo Avenue to the north and west, and the railroad tracks to the east was almost entirely Italian: Currie, Elm, El Dorado, Box Elder, Evans, Routt, and Spruce streets. The principal street, the one with the grocery stores, the school, and Gus' Place, was Elm. Even now, said Lil Sciortino, "there's a bond between people from Elm Street."[2]

"Everyone worked at the CF&I who lived on that street," said self-described "Elm Street baby" Sandy Holman, who tends bar at Gus's, as does her mother, Vera Gurovich, née Califano. "They all walked to work and they all walked back."[3]

And they all stopped in at Gus's for beers. Freddy Masciotra has a simple explanation for the popularity of his late father's

Steelworker Lou Riccillo with rails in the "rail mill" of the Colorado Fuel and Iron (CF & I) Steel Corporation, Pueblo, Colorado. Photograph by Ken Light, IAW-KL-B295-15

bar: "We had the coldest beer in town"[4]—a claim that really meant something in the days before refrigeration, especially to the guys who worked at CF&I.

The mill was a place of infernal heat and insidious discrimination against non-Anglo workers. Joe Genova, born in 1926, went to work part-time in CF&I's open-hearth furnace while still in high school. There was no protective clothing and the heat was so intense, he recalled, that it blistered your feet. According to brothers Ralph and Pete Montera, the workers wore two pairs of pants, two pairs of socks, and two pairs of gloves. The planks they walked on were soaked in water. Even so, if not replaced frequently, they would burst into flame. Jim DiIorio remembers strapping on tire sections as protective leggings to work

in the fourteen-inch mill summers and after school when he was a teenager. The one good thing about the heat was that it enabled the men to bring pork chops to work, put them in hand-held wire grills, and cook them for lunch.

Then there were the injuries. Louis Paglione's dad was blinded in one eye by a recoiling wire in the wire mill. "It gave him a hard look," Louis recalled. "He looked like he was mad all the time."[5] Russell DiSalvo's father was killed. In the rod mills, Tony Martellaro said, you had to grab long, hot strands of steel with tongs "and if you missed it, man, you had that stuff flying around like spaghetti all over."[6] One guy had a rod go right through his stomach. They cut the rod at both ends with a bolt cutter, brought him to the hospital and

Steel-making in progress at CF & I, ca. 1950. Courtesy of Jim DiIorio, IAW-RF-B031-11

pulled it out. The guy not only lived, he went back to work. Asked if the company was remiss when it came to safety, Paul Palmero put it this way: "It was a lot easier to replace a person than it was to replace a piece of machinery."[7]

Little wonder that Joe Genova tried to get off the floor and into a safer and better-paying job as a crane operator, only to be told by his supervisor, "As long as your name ends in a vowel you're gonna stay down in the cellar."[8] Some Italians changed their names to move up the ladder. Others had their names changed for them by employers who did not want to take the trouble to spell or pronounce their names correctly. Louis Paglione talks bitterly about this "loss of identity."[9] "I didn't know what discrimination was 'til I went to work in the mill," said Paul Palermo.[10]

Palermo and others use the term "League of Nations" to describe the ethnic harmony that supposedly prevailed among the Italians, Mexicans, blacks, and "Bojons" (Yugoslavs) who lived in the vicinity of the mill. But the reference to the ill-fated league takes on ironic overtones when you listen to those whose memories of Pueblo between the wars are less rosy. During the twenties, according to Russell DiSalvo, there were Ku Klux Klansmen in Pueblo's city government and on the police force. In 1924, the city would not issue a permit for the Columbus Day parade. The parade took place anyway, with shotguns poking out the windows of all the cars. Around the same time, a cross was burned at Northern and Abriendo. DiSalvo said he got shot at—by police officers, he thinks—while trying to put out the fire. "The Italians were looked down upon," Nettie Montera said flatly. "It was hard for them to get a job in the mill and elsewhere."[11]

As recently as 1940, out of 125 cranemen, three were Italian, two were "Bojons,"

and two were Mexicans. It was only when the union came in in 1942 that promotions became strict matters of seniority. "Before the war," said Ralph Montera, "you didn't have a chance to go nowhere."[12] Sam Catalano finally made foreman in 1964, after twenty-five years in the blast furnace. "The name just wasn't right," he said. "Before it was just the pale-faces."[13] That same year, ironically enough, the Civil Rights Act was passed. Instead of being passed over in favor of northern Europeans, southern and eastern Europeans suddenly found themselves being passed over in favor of Mexicans, blacks, and Indians. "Before," Paul Palermo said, "we were just lousy wops." Now they had magically become coequal with the Anglos. "There were a lot of hard feelings," according to Joe Genova.[14]

Despite the risks, the shift work, and the ceiling on Italian ambition, mill jobs were plums and the men who worked there remember the place fondly. The mill, said Joe Genova, "was like family. The old man worked there for a while, the kid worked there, the brothers all worked in there, it was all pretty well generation, generation down the line. Let's face it. It was the only place in town where you could make money. . . If you weren't afraid of molten metal, that was the place to work. Good-paying jobs."[15] When Louis Paglione was made a foreman in the wire mill during the 1950s—an active union man, he thinks management was trying to co-opt him—he had to supervise his own father, a particularly awkward state of affairs for an Italian family. The first time he told his father what to do, Louis said, "he looked at me like he was going to give me a backhand." After much agony, he got himself transferred to a different shift: "Our relationship got back to father and son instead of boss and employee."[16]

Sam Catalano started at sixty cents an

Tearing down an old blast furnace at CF & I. Courtesy of Jim Di-Iorio, IAW-RF-B031-10

hour—twice what they were paying in the railroad yard. The families of the steelworkers were grateful for the living those jobs provided. Nettie Montera remembers clothes hung outside to dry taking on a rust color from the smoke exhaled by the pig iron machine. "Nobody squawked," she said. The old-timers' saying, according to her brother-in-law, Pete Montera, was, "You don't have to worry when the smoke is coming out of the stack. You better worry when it don't come out of the stack because then we're in trouble."[17]

When smoke stopped coming out of the stack, when CF&I quit cooking steel in blast furnaces and went to melting scrap in arc furnaces, the men mourned the toppling of these landmark brick towers that for years dominated the Pueblo skyline. Sam Catalano equated tearing them down with "knocking down the Statue of Liberty. That's what built Pueblo."[18] Catalano and others think one of them should have been turned into a museum. Every year since the last of the blast furnaces went cold in 1982, the men who worked there have held a reunion at a Northern Avenue tavern where mill memorabilia—old hard hats, leggings and face shields, carbon bricks and blobs of pig iron, hammers and jacks, old signs and photographs—are auctioned off to help pay for the food and drink. "Blast Furnace Survivor" T-shirts are hawked for the same purpose.

Further layoffs since the blast furnace shut down—the work force has shrunk from a high of 8,500 to less than 2,000— have many in Pueblo predicting the demise of the entire CF&I operation. The impact on the Italian community would not be great because so few Italians work there nowadays. During the Depression, when the plant shut down for about five months, the impact was not as great as one might think because the Italians had never abandoned the foodways they had brought with them from the old country. Foods like pasta fagiole and polenta "stuck to your bones," Paul Palermo said.[19] Most of the women made their own pasta, macaroni, and lasagna, but usually bought spaghetti in twenty-pound wooden boxes. Jim DiIorio slept in such a box as a baby. Spaghetti was eaten several times a week and always on Sunday. Then the men would play bocce in the unpaved street and repair to Gus' Place for beers and songs— there was often an accordionist.

The men would hunt rabbit, deer, elk, quail, pheasant, duck. The women would can tomatoes, roasted peppers, pickles, relish, ketchup, cauliflower, peaches, and pears. Caponato, a mixture of celery, olives, peppers, onions, and eggplant, or eggplant layered with oil, hot peppers, and garlic were put up in crocks. The tomatoes were cooked outside over a wood fire. Parsley, oregano, basil, mint, and chilis were dried and put in jars. "Everything from scratch," said Paul Palermo.[20]

Many of the houses in Bessemer had chicken coops, rabbit hutches, and goat pens. "Italian families didn't need help from anybody," Sam Catalano said.[21] Except each other. If you were building a barn or a chicken coop, said Charles Conatore, "the whole damn neighborhood was there to help you."[22] The advice Rose Conatore's father gave her when she married Charles seemed to be the ethic that governed life in

ABOVE: **During the 1990 Blast Furnace Reunion, retired steel worker Pete Carleo (right) gazes at a scale model of the old CF & I blast furnace sitting atop a pool table in Hogan's Tavern, Pueblo. Photograph by Russell Frank, IAW-RF-B022-15**

LEFT: **Rose Conatore crocheting in the living room of her home on Evans Street in Pueblo. Photograph by Ken Light, IAW-KL-B248-11**

the neighborhood as well. Instead of engaging in a tug-o'-war, he said, "get on one end of the rope and pull together."[23]

The great communal activity was the annual winter hog-butchering and sausage-making. Tony Martellaro remembers the men hitting the hog on the head with a sledge hammer and his dad sticking it through the neck between the ribs with a twelve-inch blade. Charles Conatore claimed his dad "could stick a hog and never miss."[24] Martellaro remembers them dipping the pig in a fifty-five-gallon vat of boiling water to loosen the hair and then five or six guys scraping it until it was as white as paper. Conatore recalls the hogs being hung by their hind legs and sawed down the middle

and the women scraping the hair off until it was "clean as that mirror."[25] The skin would be pulled off in two-inch strips, rolled up and frozen, to be used in spaghetti sauce. After skinning, the fat would be taken off and pork chops and steaks cut. The hind quarters and shoulders went for sausage. The intestines were scraped out with a spoon and used for casings. The sausages would be put up in five-gallon crocks covered over with rendered lard and stored in the basement. The ears and the feet were pickled. "We used to lose the hair and the squeal and that was about it," Martellaro said.[26] But then he noted that the seat of his old pickup was stuffed with hog's hair.

Most Italian households in Bessemer

The single remaining domed bake oven (*forno*) in the backyard of a house on Currie Street in Pueblo's Bessemer neighborhood. Photograph by Russell Frank, IAW-RF-B028-8

had a brick oven or *forno* in the backyard, used primarily for bread baking. Typically, fifteen loaves were baked at a time. "You've never had a good piece of bread 'til you've had one that's been baked outside in the oven, right on the hot brick," Sam Catalano insisted.[27] Gathering the wood, lighting the fire, waiting for the oven temperature to be right—Tony Martellaro said his mother could tell by putting a piece of newsprint in: if it turned brown without bursting into flame, it was time to bake—mixing, kneading and shaping the dough, and hauling the loaves from kitchen to *forno* and from *forno* to kitchen was hard work. Joe Genova's job after school on Fridays was to load the *forno* with wood so his mom could light the fire early Saturday morning. With the leftover dough the women made sausage bread or *foccaccia* (little loaves dipped in olive oil, salt, and pepper) for the kids. Charles Conatore remembers his father trading six dollars and a quart of wine for a truckload of railroad ties for the *forno*. The loaves, stored covered in a barrel, usually lasted two to three weeks. When the last of it started to get hard it would go into cooked cabbage or a bowl of beans.

Another staple that everyone made themselves was wine. Gus Masciotra bought boxcar-loads of California grapes for sale to the neighborhood winemakers. "All this district here, Box Elder, El Dorado, Abriendo, Evans would order, 250, 300 boxes of grapes," said Domenick Bucciarelli.[28] Paul Palermo's family used to buy seventy-five crates and Paul had to carry them all down the basement steps: "That's one of the things I used to hate yearly."[29] Fred Masciotra claims Italians drink wine because it "cuts the starch."[30] Joe Genova remembers his dad keeping his gallon of wine under his chair at table. "That's the difference between Calabresi and Sicilians," he said.[31]

During the years when Prohibition and the Depression overlapped, and making a living was a "catch-as-catch-can" proposition, many Italian men tried their hand at distilling and selling whiskey. "This was bootlegging country," said Ralph Montera. "They called Pueblo 'Little Chicago,'" agreed his brother Pete. "Every other family sold whiskey," said Ralph's wife, Nettie. "It was Depression," Ralph explained. "There was no money."[32]

On Thanksgiving Day 1928, according to Domenick Bucciarelli, federal agents raided ninety-six households, including his own. Bucciarelli remembers the feds pulling up and getting out of all four doors of their car "like a bunch of chickens." Frightened, he ran to the back of his father's store and tripped over some empty pop bottles. The agents came looking for him thinking he was breaking whiskey bottles. Domenick hid in a fifty-gallon barrel. His father was out, so the agents hauled Domenick's twenty-two-year-old brother to jail, where he spent thirty days.[33]

Sam Catalano's dad spent eight months at a Tucson prison farm for bootlegging. Sam still remembers his father's recipe: one-hundred pounds of sugar, three pounds of yeast, a bucket-and-a-half of cracked corn. Combine in a fifty-gallon barrel with water, ferment, then drain and put in a copper still.

The Italians got into it, Catalano said, because "if there was a buck to be made, the wop was right there. . . . It was to feed us kids. I'm not ashamed of my dad bootlegging. I admire the guy."[34]

What the families could not make themselves they could get on credit from one of the countless mom-and-pop grocery stores that flourished in the days before supermarkets. Charles Conatore had a grocery

Bessemer Mercantile, a small grocery store run by Joe and Marie Gagliano, ca. 1930s. The store was later passed on to the Gagliano's daughter Rose and her husband, Joe Cortese, who continue to run it. Left to right: Maria Gagliano, Carl Giarratano, Rose Mulay, Ben Vinci, Tony Pecoraro, and Joe Gagliano. Courtesy of Rose and Joe Cortese, IAW-RF-B030-11

store in Minnequa Heights, the neighborhood south of Northern Avenue. During the Depression and during strikes at the mill—the longest one lasted almost four months in 1959—he told the families not to worry. "Long as I had money left in the bank, and I could buy groceries, they could eat." When people paid their bills in full, Charles gave them bags of fruit and candy for the kids.

The Conatores closed their store in 1982—just before they would have been hurt by a major layoff at CF&I. "Our guardian angel was right there," Rose said.[35] Still hanging on, on Elm Street, is Bessemer Mercantile, run by Joe and Rose Cortese, son-in-law and daughter of original owner Joe Gagliano (many still call the store "Joe Gag's"). The Mercantile would probably be enjoying a revival if it were in a more fashionable neighborhood or a larger town. It has black-and-white checkerboard linoleum tile, wooden shelving, and a mostly

Italian inventory: pizzelle and pasta machines, cannoli shells, plastic bags of polenta, ceci and confetti (candy-coated almonds), jars of black Moroccan and green California olives, of lupini beans and fave verde (green broad beans), of roasted peppers, and of corks and lids for those who still put up garden vegetables themselves. The deli case features capocola, hard salami, Genoa, mortadella, ricotta, open eye, mozzarella, provolone, goat cheese, romano, pepperoni and Italian sausage. Still, the shelves are half-empty.

Joe Cortese makes the sausage himself. Nowadays the demand is great only at Christmas. The meat comes from Denver in the form of pork butts that Joe bones and cuts up. The recipe is from Carmela Gagliano, who was born in 1895 and is still living in the back of the store. It hasn't changed since Joe Gagliano started the business in 1923. "We couldn't tell you a cup or a tablespoon," says Rose Cortese. "We had to watch her: a fistful of that and a pinch of this and a pinch of that."[36]

Just up the street from the Mercantile is Gus' Place. Freddy Masciotra said if his father had not added a beer joint to his grocery business after Prohibition he never would have gotten back all the money he went through carrying guys during the Depression.

Agostino Masciotra was from Agnone, a farming town about twenty miles from Naples. As a young married man he worked on the railroad in the daytime and at his father-in-law's downtown bar in the evening. When the county went dry in 1916 Gus stored the bar in the upstairs of what is now his brother Mike's house at Elm and Northern. In 1925 he opened his grocery store at the other end of the block, on Elm and Mesa. And when Prohibition ended in 1933, he wheeled his bar up Elm Street on roller skates and started selling beer.

ABOVE: **Joe Cortese (right) and Rich Harris slice pork they will use to make Italian sausages at Bessemer Mercantile. The recipe they will follow was passed down from Cortese's wife's parents, the previous owners of the store. Photograph by Ken Light, IAW-KL-B233-3**

LEFT: **Interior of Bessemer Mercantile as it appeared in 1990. Store owner Joe Cortese is behind the meat counter at the rear of the store. Photograph by Ken Light, IAW-KL-B232-18**

Mike Masciotra, know to all as Uncle Mike, tended bar until 1984, when, at age eighty-seven, he was hit by a car and broke his hip. A skinny, knobby-handed man, with a great nose, ears that stick out and brush-cut white hair, Uncle Mike leans on his cane and manages, every morning and evening, a slow, shuffling, skipping walk up Elm Street to the bar. "We set our clocks by Uncle Mike," says regular Domenick Bucciarelli. "Eleven o'clock and seven o'clock. Glass of beer and shot of Fernet."[37]

Gus' Place is a study in red: bar, bar stools, booths, chairs, tables, floor (red and white checkerboard) and ceiling. Photos and other memorabilia, mounted on wood panels with black, block-letter captions, line the walls. Over the back bar there is a large photo portrait of Gus himself in the white shirt he always wore, hoisting a schooner of beer in his left hand and a bottle of Old Quaker beer in his right. There's also a small oil painting of a "Dutch lunch."

Gus's owes much of its renown and longevity to its Dutch lunches. The portions are quite precise. A "large" costs $7.00 and consists of thirteen slices of ham, thirteen slices of provolone, and nine slices of salami, all arranged in a fan-shape on a nine-inch plate. "Smalls," which cost $5.50, are seven slices of ham, seven slices of cheese, and five slices of salami. Asked how those amounts were arrived at, Vera Gurovich, who has worked at Gus's for twenty years, says that is the way she was taught to make them, and, "they got to look nice."[38] She prepares about a dozen plates at a time, puts a square of wax paper on each, stacks the plates and carries the stack to the refrigerator in the kitchen behind the bar that used to be the deli. Dutch lunches evolved from a practice of Gus's grandmother, who served cheese and salami whenever anyone stopped by for a glass of wine. Gus started putting out trays of lunch meat—gratis—at the bar he ran downtown. He started calling them Dutch, as in Dutch treat, when he started charging for them.

Barry Masciotra, Gus's grandson, tends bar and tries to convince his father, Freddy, it is time to have a menu, maybe grill hamburgers. Freddy won't hear of it. "You can't change it," he says. "That's what it's known for."[39]

A *Denver Post* column, blown up and mounted on the wall, has a good description of what makes Gus's such an institution:

Gus' is not a cocktail lounge, nor a go-go club, nor anything but what it is and what it ought to be: a saloon where you can quaff a hefty schooner of beer, dip into a Dutch lunch, talk it up, or just let the rest of the world go by for an hour or two. No murky lights, no phony atmosphere, no scantily clad waitresses, no piano bar. Just a nice, old-fashioned saloon, with red linoleum on the table tops [and] straight-back wooden booths for the ladies.

The heartbeat of the town is the steel mill, and it is the men who work in the mill who keep Gus' going. When the whistle blows to end a shift, many of them head first for Gus' and then home. They troop in, wearing

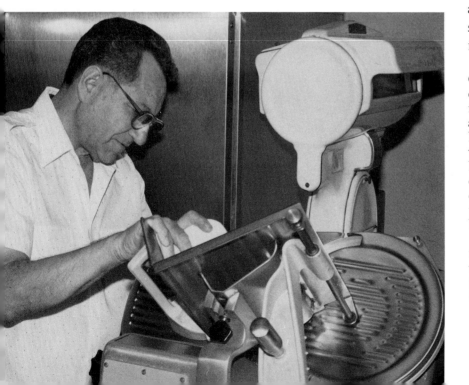

Second-generation tavern owner Freddy Masciotra slices provolone cheese that will be used to make up "Dutch lunches," build-it-yourself sandwiches, consisting of ham, salami, cheese, and bread, invented by Freddy's father Gus. Photograph by Russell Frank, IAW-RF-B021-30

LEFT: Gus' Place, a long-time gathering place for steelworkers and residents of the Bessemer neighborhood. Tavern regular and former bartender "Uncle Mike" Masciotra, who lives down the street, is about to enter. According to one patron, "We can set our clocks by Uncle Mike. Eleven o'clock and seven o'clock. Glass of beer and shot of Fernet."

BELOW: A few of the regulars at the bar at Gus' Place. The wall behind them is festooned with photos that commemorate people and events important in the history of the tavern and the Bessemer neighborhood. Photographs by Ken Light, IAW-KL-B223-10, B250-13

working clothes and carrying battered lunch buckets, and they are not ashamed of the dirt under their fingernails. They sit around and have a beer and talk, while the jukebox grinds out a polka or one of the old songs; somehow rock'n'roll would seem sacrilegious in Gus'.

If anything is changing about Gus' it is the average age of the customers. They are older now, and many of them have sons who have gone to college, and off to work and live in other towns.[40]

Not much has changed since the column was written in 1965. Rock'n'roll is now the music of choice for the younger crowd that frequents the place on Friday and Saturday nights, though polkas, Frank Sinatra, and other Italian crooners still entertain the daytime crowd. The big difference is that most of the regulars now are retirees who drive over from outlying neighborhoods. "I don't know anybody on this block anymore," Freddy Masciotra says.[41]

Thus was the immigrant ethic carried out. Domenick Bucciarelli's father told him, "Leave your family better off than I left you. . . . If you have an opportunity, grab it. Do better than I did."[42]

Implicit in the directive to "do better" was the need to "Americanize." In some households it was forbidden to speak Italian. "You're in America now," Joe Genova's mother would say. "You speak American."[43] Proud as they profess to be of their Italian heritage, Pueblo's Italians had little good to say about the impoverished place they left behind. Aside from the men who went back to Italy to see their families until they had enough money to bring their families to the states—and the inevitable stories about fathering children on every visit—most of the immigrants neither went back to visit nor had a desire to do so. "I didn't have anything over there, I didn't leave anything over there, and there's nothing for me to go back

for either," is what Genova remembers his father saying.[44] Ralph and Pete Montera remember their grandfather threatening to send them back to Bellafranga—his home village—when they misbehaved.

Anyone who worked at the mill did better there than they would have in the old country. The war years in particular were a bonanza for CF&I. Mill jobs were plentiful and they were good-paying. With money in their pockets, husbands could buy modern appliances for their wives and automobiles for themselves. Sons who had seen something of the world during their time in the service could move out of the house, out of the neighborhood, perhaps even out of town. "After the war and these guys came back, America just changed, just like that," said Gary DeCesaro. "Everybody was trying to progress, they did not look back. . . . That's why the heritage here is lost."[45]

As neighborhoods became more heterogeneous and the veterans returned from living in close proximity to people from other ethnic backgrounds, the commandment to marry an Italian seemed less binding. "In them days"—meaning before the war— "you didn't dare say you were going to marry outside the nationality," claimed Ralph Montera.[46] Before that, according to Paul Palermo, it was unacceptable even to marry outside your own home region. In the old country, of course, marriages were arranged. "My mother probably never saw my dad 'til she met him at the altar," Freddy Masciotra said.[47] Today there are many Italian-Bojon marriages in Pueblo—the children of which call themselves "Bo-wops"—and many Bojon wives who are skilled in the cookery of their Italian mothers-in-law.

Intermarriage and the passing of the immigrant generation, combined with modern conveniences like gas ovens, freezers, cars and televisions, loosened peoples' dependence on each other and their attachment to their old ways. The Genovas bought a gas oven and tore down their *forno,* "which was a big mistake," Joe says now.[48] Today there is but one derelict *forno* in Bessemer. They were outlawed by the city as an air quality control measure. Rose Conatore says people stopped making wine when they put furnaces in their basements—or when their fathers died.

What furnaces did to wine-making, freezers did to home canning. The demise of backyard food-making activities—and of the local mom-and-pop grocery stores that provided the foods that could not be made at home—was also hastened by the rise of supermarkets. "Today it's 7-Eleven and Loaf'n'Jug," said Sam Catalano.[49] Or as Pete Montera put it, "It's easier to buy your bread today than to bake it. And that's the same with canning."[50]

Bessemer Mercantile is one of three Italian grocery stores remaining, down from 125 (Freddy Masciotra closed his in 1979), and it, according to owner Joe Cortese, "has been going downhill since the freeway was built."[51] The construction, in 1955, of I-25, obliterated El Dorado Street and parts of Currie and Box Elder. The streets that remained were paved—no more bocce in the street—and their connection to the mill was severed. Not that it matters. The neighborhood is more Hispanic than Italian now. So is the Mount Carmel Church, though some of the older Italian ladies still attend and make Italian cookies and meatballs for the annual church festival in July. Gary DeCesaro says the Italian contingent at CF&I, of which he is a member, comprises only 5 percent of the workforce.

Working at the mill may have been the best job an immigrant or a child of the Depression could get, but high school and college graduates, educated because their

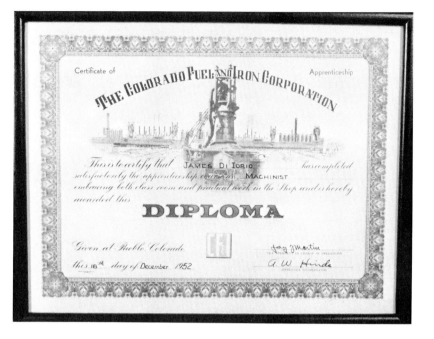

ABOVE: **Colorado Fuel and Iron Corporation certificate of apprenticeship (with blast furnace in the center) awarded to James DiIorio, December 18, 1952. Courtesy of Jim DiIorio, IAW-RF-B031-14**

LEFT: **Steelworker Vic Alfonso on the job at CF & I Steel Corporation. His father and four of his five uncles also worked at the plant. Photograph by Ken Light, IAW-KL-B299-11**

Ralph Montera points out the different vegetables he grows in his large garden, which includes squash, peppers, beans, garlic, tomatoes, eggplant, and many others. Photograph by Ken Light, IAW-KL-B246-22

millworker fathers could afford for them to stay in school, knew they could do better, if not in Pueblo, then in Denver or California. The fathers were proud to have worked there but did not want their sons to follow them in. All four of Pete Carleo's brothers worked with him at the mill. None of their sons did. Pete's son, a graphic artist in Denver, once took a tour of the mill and came away saying, "Pop, I don't know how you worked in a place like that."[52] "There are still a few Italian guys at the mill," said Ralph Montera, "but most either got educated or went into business."[53]

To a great extent, this is the standard American immigrant story: Grandad comes over from the old country, keeps his jug of wine under his chair at dinnertime, plays bocce with the boys on Sunday afternoon, and busts his butt in the mill all week long.

Dad, growing up during the Depression, has no choice but to follow his dad into the mill, understands more Italian than he speaks, plays golf instead of bocce, and drinks beer instead of wine. And the son leaves Pueblo, goes to college, and neither speaks nor understands Italian (though he wishes he could). But if he still lives in Pueblo, or if he comes back to visit, he still goes to mom and dad's on Sunday for spaghetti—the one great and near-universal holdover from the pre-war days. As Paul Palermo said, "It's not Sunday unless I have my spaghetti and my wine."[54]

Bessemer's heyday was short-lived. It flourished during the Depression, when the lack of cash reinforced the immigrants' conservative tendency to make food from scratch, raise their own vegetables, chickens, and rabbits, house the extended family

under one roof, and help each other with seasonal tasks like wine-making and hog-butchering. And the community began to disperse and disintegrate after World War II. So much was cast aside so fast that remembrances of Bessemer childhoods are invariably accompanied by expressions of regret at having let go of traditions that should have been maintained. Tony Martellaro acknowledged that his childrens' lives are easier than his was, "but I don't think they know how to enjoy themselves as much as we did then."[55] Charles Conatore said this even more forcefully. "Let me tell you something," he said. "People were more happy in them days than they are today."[56]

The Italians' misty vision of "them days" blinds them to the traditions that remain, namely vegetable gardening and spaghetti dinners on Sunday. Ralph Montera's garden covers an entire lot. He leaves its bounty in a wheelbarrow for the neighbors to share. His wife, Nettie, still cooks a pot of porridge and brings it around to the neighbors on

St. Lucia Day (December 13). Sam Catalano says he still raises "all the seasonings that they were used to using in their sauces in Italy": parsley, oregano, basil, and mint.[57] Getting together as a family on Sundays and holidays is still the supreme value. "The main thing is family," said Rose Conatore. "When you've got family, you've got hordes of things to talk about, to remember, to cherish."[58] Many families still eat baccala (codfish), home-made ravioli, lupini beans, and pizzelle on Christmas Eve. Many have hung on to their mother's rolling pin, or their father's wine press or lunch bucket. Lil Sciortino still serves fried bread and sausage. In some families the first-generation American parents would just as soon quit canning or making their own pasta, but their kids will not let them. "I don't want to lose my traditions and I don't want my children to lose the traditions," said Lil Sciortino. "I don't want another fifty years from now that we're not doing anything Italian."[59]

Italian-American steelworkers in the "pipe mill" at CF & I Steel Corporation. Left to right: Daniel Fabrizio, Dale Spinuzzi, Mike Venuto, John Granato, and Tony Costanza. Photograph by Ken Light, IAW-KL-B293-19

SHAPING TRADITION

The Saint Joseph's Day Table Ritual

PAULA M. MANINI

When Josephine Martellaro and Gen Archuletta wanted to make a Saint Joseph's Day table they asked Bessie Ingo for assistance. Ingo's grandparents had brought the ritual to Pueblo from Lucca Sicula, the small town in Sicily from which they migrated in 1890. Today Ingo and her sisters, Rose Dazzio and Ann Massarotti, are recognized bearers of the tradition in Pueblo's Sicilian community.[1] Martellaro, who is Slovenian, learned about Bessie Ingo and the tradition from her Sicilian husband and his family. Archuletta, who is Hispanic, heard about Ingo from a Sicilian acquaintance.

The adoption and adaptation of the Sicilian ritual by other ethnic Catholics is one way in which the tradition has changed. Within the Sicilian community itself, however, altar makers shape the ritual performance in many ways. Yet many Sicilian Puebloans promote the idea of an "authentic" table, and strive to make a table in "the real way," replete with the components one "needs to have" for a Saint Joseph's Day table. These comments imply the ritual is comprised of a body of fixed components, and, indeed, the table does have a general structure. However, the Saint Joseph's Day table ritual is "not a bounded entity made up of constitute parts, but a process of interpretation" that allows altar givers to shape the tradition to make symbolic statements about themselves.[2]

According to Sicilians in Pueblo, the Saint Joseph's Day table tradition began centuries ago when famine plagued the Italian island. Sicilian peasants prayed to Joseph, the island's patron saint, to end the famine and suffering. When the saint answered their prayers, the poor filled altars in thanksgiving, offering their most prized possession—food.

Sicilian immigrants brought the tradition with them when they arrived in southern Colorado in the late 1800s to work in the mines and steel mills, on the railroad, and in ranching, agriculture, and other enterprises that supported the mining and steel industries. Slavs and Slovenians from Eastern Europe and other Italians also migrated to the area, at the time largely populated by Hispanics.[3] Catholicism was one thing the Italians, Eastern Europeans, and Hispanics had in common, and it is the most significant factor influencing the cross-ethnic transference of the Saint Joseph's Day table tradition.

In Pueblo, the tradition evolved into large open-house events that feature a table laden with food, intended to thank the saint for his assistance in difficult times. Families

Saint Joseph's table at the Shrine of St. Therese church, Pueblo, Colorado, March 19, 1990. A statue of Saint Joseph holding Baby Jesus is in the center of the highest tier, the customary position for images of Saint Joseph. Photograph by Myron Wood, IAW-MW-B002-23

RIGHT: **Italian prayer card showing Saint Joseph and the Baby Jesus, from the photo album of Josephine and Anthony Gagliano. Printed on the back of the card is the "Orazione a San Giuseppe" (prayer to Saint Joseph). Photograph by Paula Manini, IAW-PM-B006-7**

BELOW: **Saint Joseph's table recently given by Giuseppe "Giovanni" Pagano in his home in Lucca Sicula, Sicily. Left to right: Giuseppe "Giovanni" Pagano; his son, Antonio; his wife, Francesca; and his daughters Tiziana and Vita. Pagano is the brother of Josephine Gagliano, who immigrated to Pueblo, Colorado. Courtesy of Josephine Gagliano, IAW-PM-B006-26**

usually invite the public to view the altar beginning at noon, March 18. The main ritual takes place on March 19, the Feast of Saint Joseph on the Catholic calendar, when a priest blesses the table, people portraying the Holy Family and other saints consume a ritual meal, and hundreds of people admire the table and partake of a meatless meal.

The Saint Joseph's Day table tradition is not, however, a two-day event. Rather, it consists of a series of activities that occur months before the open-house. These activities allow altar makers to shape the ritual to tell particular stories about themselves, their families, and their community. In her study of the ritual in a Sicilian town, Pamela K. Quaggiotto explains that personal aesthetics, social attitudes, economic status, gender roles, and religious devotion influence the performance of the ritual.[4] These factors also affect the recreation of tables in Pueblo.[5]

Sicilian Puebloans shape the ritual's details to convey information about them-

selves and their families to the larger community, but they often focus on the tradition's required components, giving the impression that the ritual performance is static rather than dynamic.

A vow that initiates a ritual exchange between Saint Joseph and a petitioner is the first action required in the process of making an altar. A woman or man can petition the saint, but it is the female head of the household who supervises the construction of the table.[6] The petitioner promises to make an altar if the saint resolves or assists in the resolution of a crisis. While family problems, especially illness, usually motivate individuals to make vows, they may also make tables to thank Joseph for their family's general well-being and prosperity. Al and JoAnna Collette, for instance, have prepared altars to celebrate their family's good fortune as well as to thank Joseph for his help in combatting family illness.

After a vow has been made, the saint must respond to the request. When the petitioner perceives Joseph has answered her prayers, she (or he) is obligated to make a table (a male will ask a close female relative to supervise the task) to fulfill their part of the ritual exchange. When making a vow, the petitioner may make one or more requests at a time, promise to make an altar once or to have it for more than one year, choose to "beg" for donations, or decide not to accept any donations at all. Some Sicilian Puebloans remember people who chose to "go begging" from house to house, or to "beg barefoot" for donations as an act of sacrifice, but contemporary social attitudes now make this practice unacceptable.

T he concept of sacrifice, however, remains important in the ritual today. Altar givers spend substantial amounts of time, energy, and money to prepare for the observances. These expenditures are seen as a sacrifice undertaken as a labor of love and expression of gratitude. However, they may also be interpreted as a statement of wealth and class. Scholars have found that economics and social status play major roles in the performance of the ritual.[7] Josephine Gagliano believes the ritual is "more luxurious" in Pueblo than in her native Sicily. Bessie Ingo and her daughter Rose Roderick believe modern tables are larger than those given by Ingo's parents because the family is wealthier and they have conveniences that facilitate the preparation of more types and larger amounts of food.

There does seem to exist an unstated pressure towards a grandiose and exaggerated display of abundance.[8] This not only reflects the strength of the altar maker's devotion to Saint Joseph but also sends a message to the community that she (and her family) has the resources needed to create an "authentic" table. Some Puebloans criticize the abundant and fancy display as an inappropriate way to honor Joseph, the patron saint of the poor. Quaggiotto discusses this paradox in the context of a economically stratified town in rural Sicily and locates the ritual, which belongs to the working class, in the tension created by a classist society.[9]

Despite the intentions of an altar giver to finance a table herself, donations cannot be refused and contributions of money, labor, and goods are usually significant. Josephine Martellaro, who had her first table in 1990, was amazed at the number of people, including strangers, who contacted her about contributing to the table. Josephine Gagliano wanted to pay the full cost of her table in 1989, so she did not solicit donations. However, she reluctantly placed a collection bowl on the table to hold the money people had placed amidst the food.

Josephine Martellaro of Pueblo with the Saint Joseph's table she gave in her home in 1990. Photograph by Myron Wood, IAW-MW-B001-15

An altar giver usually opens her home for a public viewing of the table at noon on March 18, and all day on March 19. One to three months previously, however, she and her assistants, most of whom are female relatives or close friends, begin to purchase items for the event. They prepare and freeze some foods ahead of time, delegate tasks, and organize the many details required to construct an altar, host an open-house, and serve a meal to five hundred or more people. As mentioned, other people offer cash, goods, or time to ensure the table's success. Despite this assistance, the altar giver, her family, and her assistants invest considerable amounts of their own time and money.

The fruits of their labor begin to converge the week before March 19. Men assemble the table's wood foundation in the altar maker's living room. The altar often spans an entire wall, from side to side and floor to ceiling, and usually has three tiers against the wall. The women cover the base with linen, sheets, tablecloths, or other fabrics, some new and some of which may be heirlooms. Here the women can express their personal tastes through decorative details and the color scheme, although white or pastel shades are customary.

An image of Joseph is the first object placed on the covered altar, and it always stands in the center of the highest tier. This is one component of the tradition to which participants faithfully adhere. The image may be of Joseph alone, Joseph holding the Infant Jesus, or of Jesus, Mary, and Joseph together. Bessie Ingo uses a print of the Holy Family that belonged to her mother-in-law, and which now hangs in her bedroom. Josephine Martellaro painted a picture of Joseph holding the Infant Jesus for her table. The Holy Family is also often represented with symbols made from bread; the Sacred Heart of Jesus, the palm leaf associated with Mary, and Joseph's staff. They are also portrayed by people during the ritual.

Sicilian Puebloans also place on the altars photographs of the people who received Saint Joseph's assistance in overcoming illness or other problems. Because the tables are blessed, they are sacred space within the home and become the physical locus of the intersection of the sacred and the secular, "the heavenly family and the earthly family."[10] The tradition hinges on the belief that human beings and Joseph can communicate with each other, and that there is a personal relationship between saint and petitioner. The photographs placed on the table show the beneficiaries of this relationship, and highlight the central importance of the family in the ritual and in the culture by aligning it with the Holy Family.

Altar givers also often include secular

objects that have personal meaning for them. Bessie Ingo has used linens from her dowry on her tables. Her sister Ann Massarotti and their mother have used a crocheted table cloth that is a family heirloom. The use of such items stresses an intimate female and familial role in the tradition. On her altar, Josephine Gagliano included a pillow case from her dowry and sugar figures given to her and her children by her mother and brother, who live in Sicily. She also displayed an Italian flag and the flag of the United States to show she and her husband are proud of both their heritages.

After the image of Saint Joseph is placed on the table, the altar giver and her helpers arrange candles, flowers, breads, cakes, pastries, cookies, fruits, raw vegetables, and other unperishable foods in a colorful, symmetrical assemblage. They prepare fish, *frittate* (vegetable omelets), *cannoli,* and other perishable foods on March 18 or 19, and these are the last items placed on the table. The fish and *frittate* are elaborately decorated, allowing the women another opportunity to express personal aesthetics and creativity.

Sicilian Puebloans insist certain foods must be on the table, including Saint Joseph's Day breads, fried *carduni* (artichoke stalks), *frittate* (some people say, one for each saint represented in the ritual), at least one whole fish, cakes in the shape of a lamb, a cross, and the Bible. In general, these foods symbolize the tradition's Sicilian origin and the religious nature of the event.

ABOVE: Yvonne Baca places a loaf of Saint Joseph's Day bread on the Saint Joseph's table being prepared at the Holy Rosary Church, March 18, 1991. This Hispanic parish has hosted a St. Joseph's Day table since 1975. Photograph by Paula Manini, IAW-PM-B010-29

LEFT: Detail of Saint Joseph's table given by Josephine Martellaro. The photographs are of Josephine's husband, Tony, and her granddaughter Brittany Carleo. Each recovered from a serious illness and Josephine prepared this table to thank Saint Joseph for his assistance. Photograph by Myron Wood, IAW-MW-B001-17

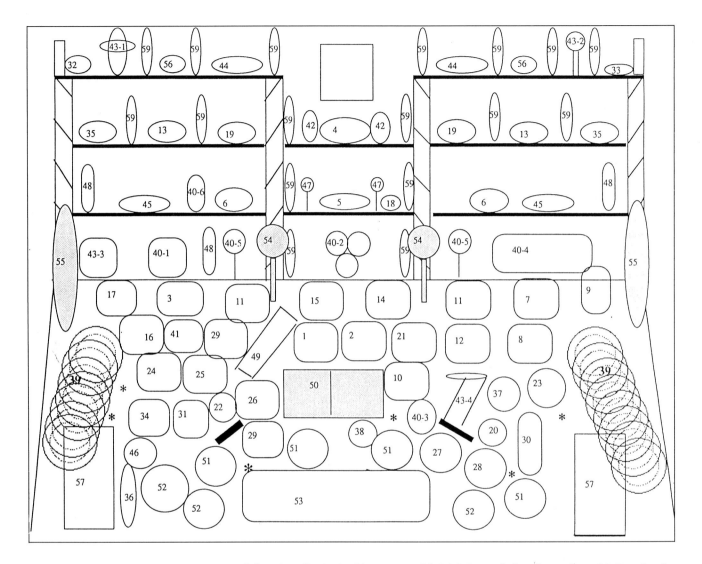

Computer-generated drawing of principal items on Josephine Martellaro's Saint Joseph's Day table. Courtesy of Josephine Martellaro

The numbers on the drawing relate to the following items: 1. Snickerdoodles and choco snaps. 2. Lady fingers. 3. Cherry winks. 4. Hostia. 5. Skeleton. 6. Ribbon roses. 7. Tarts. 8. Snarkles. 9. *Cannoli*. 10. Oatmeal with raisin. 11. *Pizzelle*. 12. Spritz. 13. Almond candy. 14. Wine cookies. 15. Peanut butter chip. 16. Almond crescents. 17. Honeyballs. 18. Pecan minis. 19. Rice Krispy treats. 20. Hay stack candy. 21. Round lady fingers. 22. Rocky road candy. 23. Fig cookies. 24. Peanut butter cookies. 25. Soft chocolate cookies. 26. Date whirl, Italian fruit, and chocolate drop cookies. 27. Krumkake and mini peanut butter cookies. 28. Pineapple upside down cake. 29. Easter bread. 30. Braided Easter bread. 31. Wheat bread shaped like a lamb. 32. Cream cheese cookies. 33. *Potiça*. 34. Wheat bread with design. 35. Spinges. 36. Jelly roll. 37. Rosettes.

38. Divinity and chocolate mints. 39. Breads of saints. 40. Designed breads from basic bread (40.1 is face of Jesus, 40.2 is Trinity, 40.3 is the moon, 40.4 is a fish, and 40.6 is a hand). 41. Poppyseed cookies. 42. Chocolate bunnies. 43. Designed fig breads (43.1 is a cross, 43.2 is a chalice, 43.3 is a heart, and 43.4 is a cane). 44. Popcorn lambs. 45. Lamb cakes. 46. Bowl for donations. 47. Goblets with Jordan almonds. 48. Wine. 49. Flowers made from dough. 50. Bible cake. 51. *Frittate* (omelets made with peas, asparagus, fava beans, and cauliflower). 52. Fried vegetables. 53. Baked salmon. 54. Lillies. 55. Palms. 56. Living wheat. 57. Bouquets. 58. Palm trees made from carrots, peas and bell peppers; flowers made from onions; swan made from apple, cucumber, fish, and artichokes (location of these items indicated by asterisks). 59. Saint Joseph's candles. 60. Tea rings, coffee cakes, raisin bread, banana nut bread, Easter bread.

Altar makers agree an abundant presentation should be created. Josephine Martellaro used fruit, colored popcorn balls, and Easter candies to fill up empty space and to create a bountiful appearance. Altar givers also use china, crystal, and silverware. Again, this display is rooted in social and economic issues, and there is a friendly competitiveness involved in the ritual's performance. People who view the tables often evaluate and compare tables.

Al Collette and Bessie Ingo say the table represents "new life," which is symbolized by such things as the plates filled with sprouted wheat, candy chicks, and flowers. Also, the feast day falls in the early spring during Lent and often close to Easter which, of course, commemorates the resurrection of Christ, the symbol of new life in Christianity. Sicilian Puebloans connect the ritual and Easter through the proximity of their occurrence, and with the use of Easter decorations and candies on the table. Also, participants exclude meat from the event, recalling an era when the Catholic Church prohibited the consumption of meat during Lent.

The table is ready for public viewing on March 18, although perishable foods will not be displayed until the actual feast day. On either day, anyone may admire the table. In the past, news of tables spread by word of mouth while today altar givers also place announcements in church bulletins, the diocese paper, and the local papers, and circulate memos at their places of employment. While the tables have always been open-house events, altar givers now try to reach a wider audience in an effort to share the experience with as many people as possible and to show the hostess' ability to serve hundreds of guests. This charitable component is also rooted in the tradition's class-based history. Saint Joseph has assisted the family, and now it is their turn to share with others. Altar givers sometimes send letters to the local paper listing the charities to which they have donated in the name of the patron saint of the poor.

On March 19, a priest blesses the table,

The "saints" seated at a table in Josephine Martellaro's living room on Saint Joseph's Day, 1990. Josephine Martellaro stands at the head of the table beside Charles Juinta, who represents Saint Joseph. Photograph by Myron Wood, IAW-MW-B001-30

and, immediately after the blessing, people chosen to represent the Holy Family and other saints are served a meal of the blessed food. Partaking of this ritual meal are the people on whose behalf assistance was sought from Saint Joseph. They sit at a table adorned with the finest table settings belonging to or borrowed by the hostess. They must taste everything displayed on the altar, and they receive boxes filled with pastries, cookies and cake to take home.

When the saints have finished eating, five hundred or more guests receive a spaghetti dinner with tomato sauce and breadballs or hard-boiled eggs. Although altar makers worry there might not be enough food, they feel that Saint Joseph will ensure that all the guests are fed. Male relatives often have the task of preparing the huge amounts of spaghetti and sauce needed for the public meal. Along with the construction and assemblage of the altar's frame, this is one of the primary tasks usually delegated to the men.

Sicilian Puebloans agree the Holy Family must be portrayed in the ritual. A woman may also invite people to represent other saints, as long as there is an odd number of them. John Amella believes the odd number is related to the thirteen participants at the Last Supper, and some people did compare the feast to that biblical event. Some of the most popular figures represented at the table are Saint Ann (Mary's mother), Saint Anthony of Padua (an Italian saint), and Saint Lucy (the patron saint of the eyes, whose feast day is also observed by many Sicilian Puebloans). Altar givers usually invite relatives or friends to portray the saints, and strive to select individuals who have a connection to a particular saint (such as a namesake) or people who have been ill.

The selection of saints allows a woman to convey messages about her relationships with particular people and saints. When JoAnna and Al Collette gave a table to thank Saint Joseph for their family's good fortune, they invited people who were their own and their children's godparents. Naich Cordo remembers that he and his siblings were often invited to portray saints when they were children. He believes this is because their neighbors wanted to help them and his widowed mother.

In 1992, Bessie Ingo and her family decided there would be no saints at their table, a component generally considered essential to an authentic table. They decided there had been so much illness in the family that many people should be involved as saints. In order to prevent disappointment, they decided to delete this element and make the table for everyone who had been ill. Thus, by changing the tradition they are maintaining one of its essential elements—the centrality of the family.

Tables are usually dismantled the evening of the nineteenth, or the following day. Leftover food and donated monies are distributed to charities supported by the altar maker and her assistants. Josephine Gagliano sent funds to her church in Lucca Sicula as

Josephine Martellaro passes a tray of cookies to a few of the many guests seated outside her home. While the tables have always been open-house events, altar givers now try to reach a wider audience in an effort to share the experience with as many people as possible. Photograph by Myron Wood, IAW-MW-B002-19

well as to organizations in Pueblo. Several people have donated leftover food to Pueblo's soup kitchen. This charitable aspect of the tradition is also an expression of the altar maker's economic resources. It shows the community that she is able to amass food and monies to distribute to others and further honors the patron of the poor.

Every recreation of a Saint Joseph's Day table is in some way shaped by the altar giver. Even the proscribed components convey information about such things as personal aesthetics and creativity, economic capabilities, cultural resources, social networks, the importance of the family, and the nature of their religious devotion. The table's many details allow altar givers the opportunity to shape the tradition, and even omit components previously deemed essential to an authentic event.

A central message contained in any table, however, is the altar maker's Catholicism and devotion to the saints, especially Joseph. A shared religious heritage that gives primary importance to the saints has greatly facilitated the ritual's movement from Sicilians to other Italians, Hispanics, and Slovenians in Pueblo. Similarly, David C. Estes found that members of an African-American Spiritualist Church in New Orleans adopted the ritual from the city's Sicilian community because it fit well with the church's observances of saints' days.[11]

Obviously, an essential element of the tradition is the devotion Sicilian Puebloans have to Saint Joseph, the Patriarch, husband to Mary, step-father of Jesus, Protector of the Family, and Patron of Workers, the Poor, the Universal Church, and of Sicily. A personal allegiance to this holy personage also prompted Josephine Martellaro to ask for his assistance in healing her husband and grand-daughter. And her love for the

saint motivated Gen Archuletta to use the tradition as a vehicle to encourage others to dedicate themselves to Saint Joseph.

Thus Catholicism in general and a devotion to Saint Joseph specifically (rather than a Sicilian heritage) provided the social base for the ethnic transference of the tradition. But why did Martellaro and Archuletta choose to express their devotion with a Sicilian ritual?

The tradition's cross-ethnic movement is rooted in Pueblo's history as a steel-making center for the area's mining industry. The Anglo-dominated mining and steel industries, led by the Colorado Fuel and Iron Company, used Hispanic, Italian, and Slovenian workers in various capacities beginning in the late nineteenth century.[12] According to historian John Williams, Pueblo's ethnic populations were generally segregated by occupation, area of residence, and churches. With the introduction of unions in the mills, the participation of men from many ethnic groups in World War II, and the Civil Rights movement, Italians, Slovenians, and Hispanics were able to overcome many racist barriers, while still maintaining a great sense of ethnic identity.

While Hispanic neighborhoods still exist today, the Italian and Slovenian neighborhoods have largely disappeared—except in nostalgic sense. The Italian and Slovenian churches have also disappeared, except in popular memory, but Holy Rosary Church is still identified with Hispanics. Popular opinion and census data indicate that Hispanics are at a lower socio-economic level than many other ethnic groups in Pueblo, while European ethnics have attained a relatively higher status.

Italians, Slovenians, and Hispanics still maintain a strong sense of ethnic identity in Pueblo. Fieldworker Russell Frank found joking behavior based on ethnicity at Gus'

Bessie Musso Ingo holds a tinted photograph of her late husband's parents, Salvatore and Rosa Ingo. An expert cook as well as a keeper of traditional knowledge concerning how to produce a Saint Joseph's table, Bessie's advice is often sought by other women in the Pueblo area who wish to "give" a table. Photograph by Ken Light, IAW-KL-B253-28

Place, a popular restaurant and tavern. There is a monument to Christopher Columbus in Pueblo, and Columbus Day is celebrated with an annual banquet. There is a predominance of Mexican and Italian fare in Pueblo's restaurants. Many Hispanics in Pueblo trace their roots to New Mexico, and distinguish between New Mexico and Old Mexico. There are special observances at Pueblo's Cathedral on December 12, the Feast Day of Our Lady of Guadalupe, the patron saint of Mexico and the Americas. And there is a local term for Slovenians—*Bojon.* During the Saint Joseph's Day ritual meal at the Martellaro home in 1990, Tony Martellaro teases his Slovenian mother-in-law, Josephine Croshal, when she doesn't recognize food served to her because "it's not Bojon."

Josephine Martellaro has a special devotion to Saint Joseph (her own and her mother's namesake), to whom she frequently prays and to whom she turned for assistance when her husband, Tony, had severe arthritis, and when Brittany Carleo, their grand-daughter, suffered from allergies and eczema. In return for his help, Josephine promised the saint she would make a Saint Joseph's Day table. Because Tony's arthritis abated and Brittany was successfully treated, Josephine had her first table in 1990.

Although the table tradition belongs to her husband's Sicilian heritage and not to her Slovenian culture, and even though she knew little about the ritual, Josephine wanted to recreate an "authentic" table. Her appreciation of tradition in general, commitment to its preservation, the notability of the tradition in Pueblo's Italian and Catholic communities, and the ritual's devotional aspects influenced her decision to follow a typical model of a table.

She relied on the expertise of Bessie Ingo and other tradition bearers to assist her. The Ingo and Martellaro families have known each other for years, and both live east of Pueblo in an agricultural area known as the Saint Charles Mesa. Her husband's background gave her access to experts on the tradition with the resources Martellaro needed to achieve the authenticity she so desired. Conversely, Bessie Ingo became centrally involved with the table because of her friendship with the family and because of Martellaro's commitment to do a table "the real way."

Martellaro soon realized an enormous amount of work was required to produce a table. Her daughter, Debbie Carleo, and sister-in-law, Jennie Rodasta, became her principle assistants but her other children, relatives, and friends also helped. They were amazed at the myriad of details involved in the ritual: a particular brand of flour needed for the special breads, the shapes and decorations of the Trinity and Moon breads, the procedure to select and serve people who represent saints, the essential foods for the altar and the saints, the appropriate meal for the public, the arrangement of items on the table, and the timing of the event's various components.

The altar makers gave a lot of attention to the preparation of food: where to get *carduni* and how to prepare it; and how to make *sfinghi* (cinnamon cookies), *pignolati* (honey balls), *frittate* (vegetable omelets), and many other Sicilian foods. They also learned it was acceptable to include popular American sweets such as peanut butter cookies, jelly rolls, Rice Krispies treats, and ethnic recipes such as *potiça,* a Slovenian nut roll.

Because of the number of details, their commitment to the preservation of the tradition, and their fear that the ritual might disappear with Bessie Ingo and her generation, Martellaro and her assistants are compiling a "how-to" notebook and photo album to assist future generations interested in the tradition. Adopting the Sicilian tradition and reconstructing an authentic table, Martellaro used the ritual to represent her devotion to Saint Joseph, her concern and love for her family, and her willingness to assume a large undertaking on their behalf. The table further symbolized her respect for her husband's heritage, her dedication to the preservation of tradition, and her esteem for the recognized bearers of the Saint Joseph's Day altar and feast tradition.

L ike Ingo and Martellaro, Gen Archuletta has a special fondness for Saint Joseph. She likens him to her father and to all fathers who protect and provide for their families. Archuletta remembers her mother telling her father to teach their sons whatever task he was doing, "Just like Joseph did with Jesus." Her mother would tell the children, "Help your father, like Jesus helped Joseph." Her father and brother both have Joseph as their middle names, and Archuletta often prays to an image of the saint she has on a home altar. It is easy to understand why Archuletta would want to honor the saint on his feast day. But why did she, a Hispanic woman, decide to use a Sicilian tradition to express her devotion? Unlike Josephine Martellaro, Gen Archuletta had no personal connection to Pueblo's Sicilian community.

When she first heard about the tradition

With greased pans arrayed on a table, five experienced cooks prepare to mix dough they will use to bake special bread that will be part of the Saint Joseph's table given by their friend Josephine Martellaro. At this moment, in order to ensure that nothing will be left out, they are examining a photo of a Saint Joseph's table given the previous year by Bessie Ingo. Left to right: Bessie Ingo, Annabelle DiIorio, Rose Dazzio, Jenny Rodasta, and Rose Roderick. Photograph by Myron Wood, IAW-MW-B001-8

Researcher Paula Manini (left) tape-records an interview with Gen Archuletta at her home in Pueblo. Archuletta's creation of a Saint Joseph's table represents the adoption of a Sicilian tradition by members of Pueblo's Hispanic community. Photograph by Ken Light, IAW-KL-B193-11

eighteen years ago, she thought it a wonderful way not only to honor the saint but to "spread the word" about him. Uncertain about what to do, she asked a Sicilian acquaintance for advice. He referred her to his mother-in-law, Bessie Ingo, who shared her expertise with Archuletta. However, concerned about the success of the table, Archuletta made a vow to Saint Joseph: if everything went well, she would make an altar in his honor every year as long as she was able. Thirty or forty people attended the first table held at Archuletta's home. Because of its success, the pastor at the Holy Rosary Church asked if she would move the event to the church. Archuletta believes he sensed the ritual was going to grow among Holy Rosary's parishioners, who she describes as "99 percent Hispanic."

There are many reasons to assume the tradition would take hold at Holy Rosary. Hispanic and Sicilians share several practices based in a Mediterranean religious complex.[13] This religious heritage is characterized by a special devotion to Jesus, Mary, and Joseph. According to William Doll, the current pastor at Holy Rosary, many Hispanics in Pueblo and in southern Colorado have images of the Holy Family on their

home altars similar to the ones in the homes of Sicilians and other Italians in Pueblo. Both ethnic groups also favor Saint Anthony of Padua, who is often represented holding the Infant Christ. Besides sharing a special devotion to those saints and a home altar tradition, there are other folk religious expressions associated with Hispanics and southern Italians. Processionals on holy days, the belief that saints can participate in earthly affairs, and the custom of making promises and vows to the saints are popular folk practices found in cultures influenced by Mediterranean Catholicism. Gen Archuletta, Lillian Flores, Theresa Spiccola, and two priests, William Doll and Norman Bouchard, commented on the similar religious practices of Hispanics and Italians.

Also, Doll believes one reason his parishioners adopted the table tradition so readily is that they can identify with Saint Joseph. In the sermon he gave for the Saint Joseph's Day mass in 1991, Doll stressed Joseph's poverty, hard work, persistence, and dedication to the family. The annual parish event, in fact, does reflect the cultural values and economic realities of the area where Holy Rosary Church is located. Residents in the West End as well as other Puebloans describe the church and neighborhood as poor. In comparison to the abundantly laden and lavishly adorned Sicilian tables, Archuletta and women from the church's Altar Society have less food on the altar and use paper plates and cups instead of china and crystal. Some people at the parish event believe the table was a more appropriate representation of Joseph's life as a poor and humble man.

Quaggiotto discusses this same issue, the tension between wealth and poverty, in the tradition in Sicily, where the working-class ritual is rooted in the area's class system and referenced to Saint Joseph's poverty.[14] Through the decades, and despite a formerly low economic status in Pueblo, Sicilians have been able to meet the ritual's requirement of abundance through access to a social and cultural network of people committed to the tradition. The less lavish parish table is due not only to a lower economic base but to limited access to the ethnic network which provides Sicilians with the cultural capital need to create an "authentic" table.

Although Archuletta asked Bessie Ingo for advice, accumulated extensive files on the tradition, and welcomed the contributions of Sicilians and other Italians, she never intended to replicate the Sicilian model. Her motivation to adopt the tradition was to "spread the word" about Saint Joseph. Many Italian Puebloans applaud her efforts, visit her table, make donations, and offer friendly advice. In the spirit of Joseph, patron of the Universal Church, some Sicilians in Pueblo have distributed flyers that invite other ethnic Catholics to adopt the tradition.

Archuletta and the women in the Altar Society at Holy Rosary Church who organize the event, maintain the tradition's basic elements. The table is adorned with a central image of Saint Joseph, lilies and candles, Saint Joseph's Day breads, fruit, and cookies and other sweets. There are cakes in the shape of the Bible, Cross, Sacred Heart, Lamb of Jesus, and the Chalice. William Doll blesses the altar and the food it holds, and the women donate leftovers and collected monies to charity. They create a symmetrical and colorful presentation, and dedicate the table to specially selected people. Numerous people work together to ensure a successful event. In 1990, approximately one hundred people admired the table over the two days it was open to the public. Some Italian visitors suggested the table needed sardines and oranges, and Theresa Spiccola offered to make the *frittate* the next year. She believes Hispanics have adopted the tradition because "they really have the

faith." On the evening of March 19, Doll conducted mass at the church and then blessed the table at the parish hall.

After the blessing, about one hundred shared a potluck buffet with Mexican, Italian, and more generically American foods. Although Archuletta does not allow meat dishes on the altar, they are part of the potluck dinner. The table was dedicated to people with loved ones stationed in the Persian Gulf and at other military posts, and families placed photographs of soldiers on the altar. The parish center was decorated with yellow ribbons and the American flag. Family members sat at a special table draped in red, white, and blue, and were the first served the blessed Saint Joseph's Day bread. Everyone in attendance received cookies from the altar, and leftover food was donated to Pueblo's soup kitchen.

Unlike Josephine Martellaro, Gen Archuletta and the people who organize the parish table, do not want to create an "authentic" Sicilian table, although they appreciate the tradition's history and complexity, and every year they strive to create a bigger event. But their goals are to create something special for the parish community, increase devotion to Saint Joseph, and portray the saint as a model to be followed by people today: Joseph was a hard worker; he provided for and protected his family; and he never gave up during hard times.

Whether they are Sicilian, Hispanic, or Slovenian, altar makers in Pueblo share a devotion to Saint Joseph and honor him through the table tradition. Each maker also shapes the tradition and uses it to convey information to others. Their messages may concern their family histories, personal aesthetics, economic resources, social status, ethnic affiliations, or their social relationships. However, each and every table, whether created by a Sicilian, Hispanic, or Slovenian woman is an expression of faith and devotion to Saint Joseph.

CALIFORNIA FIELDNOTES

San Pedro and Gilroy
PAOLA TAVARELLI

EDITORS' NOTE: Paola Tavarelli grew up in Carrara, Italy, home of the celebrated white marble that has attracted sculptors and builders since ancient times. Her family is, in fact, in the marble business, and she was exposed at an early age to a setting in which the lines between art and artisanship are blurred and the importance of tradition is manifested daily in the work of craftsmen who give shape to classic forms of decorative and funerary marble as well as to the designs of contemporary architects and artists. She pursued her interest in folklife at the University of Florence and at UCLA, where David Taylor recruited her for the Italian-Americans in the West Project in 1989. A veteran of fieldwork in rural Tuscany, she brought to her work with immigrant families in California the perspective of someone who herself was poised at that moment between Italy and America. (She has since returned to Italy and the family business, but this decision lay in the future in 1989.) Her situation helps to explain the special sensitivity she displayed to Italy-born Californians, especially young people who struggle to create in contemporary circumstances an Italian-American identity.

For most Californians of Italian descent, the issue of Italian-American identity was solved long ago, for the great majority of this population is entering its fourth and fifth generation. Yet immigration still continues, though it is a trickle compared to former years or to the flood of newcomers entering the state from Mexico or Asia today. Paola Tavarelli's fieldnotes, edited here by John Alexander Williams from originals housed in the American Folklife Center's project archive, reveal contemporary versions of classic immigrant dilemmas, along with glimpses of modern problems as European immigrant families confront a culturally diverse society very different from the one faced by earlier Italian immigrants. The

notes also reveal much about the processes of ethnographic research in circumstances where the lines between "them" and "us" are never clearly defined.

The notes are presented verbatim as Ms. Tavarelli transcribed them shortly after the interview in question took place. Passages of paragraph length or longer omitted by the editor are indicated by bullets (■ ■ ■). Brief omissions are noted by elisions (. . .) The archival address for each original is given at the end of the selection.

July 21, 1989.
San Pedro [Los Angeles], California.

[Interview in Italian at the restaurant La Piccola Trattoria, owned by Franco Doardi; others present include Franco's wife, Roberta, his daughters Lara and Silvia, all of whom work at the restaurant, and a friend, Toni, who has recently been hired to work there also.]

Franco Doardi with his wife, Roberta, and daughter Lara standing outside their restaurant, *La Piccola Trattoria*, in San Pedro, California. The Doardis immigrated to the United States from Venice in the early 1980s. Photograph by Ken Light, IAW-KL-B092-12

Franco talks about his passion for paintings. He says it is a "malattia di famiglia," a family passion: his father attended art school, his brother paints, he himself paints and his little daughter is good at drawing too. He never went to school to learn about painting. He says of himself, "I have a lot of fantasy." The restaurant's walls are covered with his paintings depicting Venice, Italy, his home town in "a catastrophic way." He painted all the pictures of this decaying or dying Venice since he moved to the States: "It must be being far away, because before I never painted Venice . . . before I painted still life, landscapes, the sea."

Franco came alone to the States almost nine years ago. He started to paint from the beginning, because he had a lot of spare time without his family. He came to work as a cook in the restaurant that two Italian-Americans (originally from Ischia) and two more recent immigrants from Ischia were going to open in San Pedro. He met one of the people from Ischia while working in Sicily as a cook.

In Italy Franco worked as a seasonal worker, in ski resorts during the winter and sea resorts in the summer. His wife says that it was his choice to work outside of Venice. She says: "We have been married for twenty-five years, but I had to come to America to be with him!" Franco also worked in Germany for three years. His wife tried to live in Germany with him when their first daughter was little, but did not like it and returned to Italy where she had her own job. She worked as "capo-zona" (area manager) for a cleaning contractor, a job that she liked because it allowed her to travel and meet a lot of people. Coming to America meant for her to give up her job, and at the beginning it was difficult for her to adjust to her new job as bus girl.

Franco has worked as a cook for twenty-seven years. He learned, as he says, "alla scuola dei vecchi," (the old timers' school), which means that he learned by working since he was young. He learned different regional cooking styles by working all over the country. In his restaurant now he cooks northern food, and many Venetian specialties.

They comment on the differences be-

Chef Franco Doardi prepares a dish in the kitchen of his restaurant. Photograph by Ken Light, IAW-KL-B094-1

tween Italian food and Italian-American food. His wife says: "Most of the people who came here and opened restaurants did not know anything about cooking. They started here." Franco comments that people cooked what they had been eating at home, what their mothers used to cook. I ask if they know how the famous spaghetti and meatballs came to be identified as the typical Italian food: "In Italy, in some families, especially in the south, many years ago, they had to put food together: they made the polpette (meatballs), the sauce, and pasta and put everything together. Of course you don't find this in the restaurants in Italy, these were things that they used to eat at home." I ask what she says to people who order spaghetti and meatballs at the restaurant: "Look, this is an Italian restaurant, we don't eat spaghetti with meatballs in Italy; and then I suggest spaghetti with our meat sauce, which is very rich."

[Franco's work history is discussed, and earlier unsuccessful attempts by the family to own their own restaurant are recounted. The Doardis describe how they acquired ownership of La Piccola Trattoria.]

Since they bought the restaurant, they have changed its decor. The previous owner had pictures of Ischia hanging on the walls; they substituted those with Franco's paintings of Venezia. The color of the walls and the tablecloths changed too. They would have liked to change the name of the restaurant too, but it cost too much and they decided to keep La Piccola Trattoria. The wife wanted to call it "Bella Venezia," or "La Gondola." Lara, the daughter, would like to call it "Il Romantico." She explains: "People want to be romantic when they go to a restaurant . . . and there is too much about Venice anyway: everybody says they are Venetians, wherever you go, Bella Venezia,

Venezia here, Venezia there, and nobody is Venetian!"

Lara (twenty years old) tells me about her work in the restaurant. She has worked as waitress during busy nights, and as bus girl to substitute for her mother. She has always been in charge of the bookkeeping, payrolls, and monthly taxes. I ask where she learned, and she says that she taught herself. Silvia (sixteen years old), the other daughter, has worked in the restaurant from the beginning as bus girl. The girls do not receive salaries; they are expected to help the family and receive money when they need it. Now Lara is planning to teach her sister the bookkeeping, since in nine months she is going to graduate from school and plans to go on with her career as a paralegal. Lara says that the restaurant business fascinates her, but she does not think she has inherited the courage that her parents have: "I like to work for them, with them, I like to see the work done, but if it were mine, I don't know if I could make it."

The wife tells how difficult it has been for her to make the decision to leave Italy and move to the States. She says that she did it because of Lara, who was really suffering the absence of her father. Lara recalls: "My school mates had told me that there were sharks in California, and my dad told me on the phone that he had been swimming in the ocean in December. I thought I was going to die!" The wife and the two daughters left with a tourist visa after having sold all their belongings and left with the intention of settling permanently in America.

Lara was eleven years old when they came to America and, as [was the case with] everybody else in the family, she did not know any English. Lara says that she learned English quickly thanks to two teachers in the town of Benin, who taught her intensively. "They told me, 'In six months you will speak English,' . . . and they kept their promise. They were really good. People tell me that I was good, but I know that I would not have learned so well if it were not for them."

Franco and his wife do not speak English well. Franco learned more Spanish than English since he works in the kitchen with Mexican helpers. His wife relies a lot on her daughter when she is around and seems to speak English well only when she is angry, Lara says. The parents admit that they depend on Lara for most of the work that requires speaking or writing in English and show their concern for the imminent future when Lara will not have much time to dedicate to the restaurant.

I ask if they would return to Italy if they had a good job opportunity there. Lara says definitely that she would not go back. She says: "My life is here now. I have my school here, my friends, my boyfriend . . . on vacation, for sure. I already told my boyfriend that our honeymoon must be in Italy!"

Silvia, the youngest daughter, likes the work at the restaurant, but says that it is not what she wants to do forever! Her passion is for music. She is now putting together a band with her friends (she plays the keyboard) and wants to go to school to become a paralegal like her sister: "To have a secure job." Lara, like the whole family, likes opera. She listens to the music of the sixties and seventies, which all her friends refer to and that she does not know. She says: "Music is just part of society, so you just have to know it, and I don't. I know the things right now but most people don't even appreciate it, so you might as well go for the old stuff, and go for the safe things." I ask if Lara's boyfriend speaks Italian; she says that he is trying to learn it. She says that they want their children to speak both German and Italian (her boyfriend is of German descent and speaks German fluently).

■ ■ ■

I ask Lara if she is still in contact with Italian friends. She says " . . . all my old friends, all the friends that used to be my pals, you can write to them the first year, but that's it, there is no way. You don't know what to say anymore in letters, you got nothing to relate to. . . . I went to see my best friend, and it was the biggest disappointment in my life. She changed, she wasn't the person I used to remember. . . . "

Lara met her boyfriend two years ago in school. She talks about a plan they have to go for a year to Detroit where he could get a degree in mechanics. The mother reacts right away and speaking in Venetian dialect says that she did not know about this! Lara says it is only one of the many plans they make and they don't know yet what they will end up doing. The mother says: "It's logical that she is going to get married but I was hoping that we would remain all together!" Lara replies: "If you don't take one year of sacrifice, you can have a life of sacrifice. You'd better take one year of sacrifice and sacrifice everything and then have the best!" Lara is very close to her boyfriend and cannot stand the idea of a separation, not even for a few weeks. Joking, her mother says that she will go with them on their honeymoon!

I ask the girls if they know how to cook Italian food. They have favorite dishes but do not enjoy cooking much. Lara says her favorite food is Italian food, naturally, "there is not a single thing I don't like. I don't go crazy for meat sauce . . . I love sea food, as long as it is cooked. I'm a pasta person. You just feed me, I eat everything!"

The mother says that her husband refuses to cook at home. I ask what they eat for the holidays. They make turkey for Thanksgiving, the traditional lamb for Easter, tortellini in brodo for Christmas, "as I did in Italy, I keep the traditions."

■ ■ ■

Lara and her mother describe for me all the woodwork in the restaurant that Franco worked on. He usually collects junk in the streets and accumulates it in his garage until he finds a use for it. For instance, he found the "skeleton" of a big guitar that he cleaned up and painted and then hanged at the entrance of the restaurant. The counter that separates the restaurant room from the kitchen looks like a brick counter, but it is woodwork painted to resemble bricks. Lara is very proud of her father's paintings. She explains the fact that he portrays Venice as decaying and dying as his way of showing that he misses his hometown: "He says he does not miss Italy, but if I know my father, and I think I know him well, he misses Venice, he is fanatical about Venice, you can ask him anything about Venice, and he can tell you the entire history of Venice." I ask why she thinks he wanted to leave Venice and live in America and she says: "He liked the life-style here, he likes the freedom. He liked the fact that me and my sister could have a future, opportunities, choices. . . . In Italy you can go to school, you can go to school all your life, but then, unless you know somebody . . . but even if you know somebody . . . it's difficult." The mother adds that he likes America for himself too, he likes the opportunity to try and work as much as you want.

I ask the mother if she is buying the trousseau for her daughters. She says that when she was in Italy the daughters were too little to be thinking about it, and now, in America, it does not make much sense to think about it. She knows that when they finish school and have their jobs they are going to have money to buy what they like and what they want. As a mother, she will

help financially for the wedding itself. "My mother bought the *corredo* for me: all these sheets that I had for twenty years and I got tired of them. I would have preferred something different."

■ ■ ■

[Lara relates some of the problems she encounters in business because she speaks with an accent. She describes her dealings with a black person over the telephone, who addresses her in what she perceives to be ungrammatical English.] I ask if she does not think that "Is you the owner" is a dialect, and she says: "Yes it is their dialect . . . but you are not supposed to speak dialect to start with when you are having a business relation on the telephone. . . . It is like if I were in Italy and I started to speak my Venetian dialect to some kind of office management! What? That's very ignorant, I think. It's your dialect, whatever, it's wonderful. Unless you are in your own town, and you do that, that's fine. But don't come out to me and speak to me something I'll never understand or I refuse to understand! I'm Italian, I speak the Italian language. My dialect is something completely different. I'm in America, I speak the American language, their dialect is their own business!"

She switches to Italian and tells me that when she went to Italy when she was seventeen she felt totally respected. People offered her espresso coffee, or a glass of wine, addressed her in the third person, and she felt honored. Something that you have to learn in this country, she says, is that you are considered a teenager, they don't respect you, and this is why in her opinion there are so many problems with teenagers in America.

■ ■ ■

Toni and Franco come at the table and start telling a series of jokes. The first one plays on the phonetic resemblance between the English expression "five cents" and the Italian expression *fai sens(o),* which means: "you make me sick." A guy goes to a store to buy something. When the seller asks for "five cents," the Italian replies: "e tu fai shifo," which means: "you disgust me!" The juxtaposition of the innocent English sentence with the offensive Italian sentence provokes the humor.

Toni goes on to tell another joke that can be understood only if one knows the "funny" accent with which people from the city of Bari, in the southern region of Puglia, speak. One robber goes into a tobacconist's shop in New York owned by a Barese, a guy from Bari. He aims the gun at the guy and says, "Kent" (a brand of cigarettes). The Barese replies, "Io nun saccho cantare." (I don't know how to sing.) *Kent* sounds like the imperative form of cantare, to sing, in the Barese dialect.

Toni is definitely a good joke teller. Everybody laughs, even if they have heard the jokes from him before. Encouraged by our laughter, he goes on to tell a dirty joke, again in Italian: "There is a press conference in Hamburg. There is an American, a Frenchman, an Italian, and an Englishman, and they are talking about tall grandfathers. The Frenchman starts talking about his grandfather: he was so tall that he could go to get coffee from Paris to London with one step! The Englishman says, "But this is nothing! My grandfather was so tall that when he had to sign a check for his petroleum in Saudi Arabia, he would just reach out with one hand! The American says that his grandfather was the tallest: he had to walk all curved because he was holding the moon and Mars on his back! The Italian asks, Was it heavy? I know it must have been heavy, those were the balls of my grandfather!"

Big laughs! He goes on to tell another

joke: "There are American tourists touring Rome on a carriage. They arrive at the Altare della Patria and tell the Roman guide, This is nothing, in America we could build this in a week! The guide does not say anything. Then they arrive at the Foro Romano. They say, In America we could build this in five or six days! Then get to San Pietro and they say, This is a very small church, in America we would need two or three days at the most! The roman guide was already tired of this. They arrive at the Colosseo, and they ask him, Excuse us, what is that? And the guide says, What? That one? I don't know, I passed by here this morning and it wasn't here!"

Lara goes on to tell another joke, on a similar theme: "There is an American who goes to a vegetable store in Italy and asks, What is this? And the greengrocer answers, These are oranges. The American says, Ah, in America oranges are this big (she makes a large gesture with her arms). What are these? These are potatoes. Ah, in America potatoes are this big! And he goes on, carrots in America are this big. Then he points to a watermelon and asks, What is this? And the Italian says, peas!!! [IAW-PT-A005]

July 21, 1989. San Pedro.

After my long interview with the members of the Doardi family at their restaurant La Piccola Trattoria, I decide to stop at the San Pedro library. I arrive there around three o'clock. I ask for Giovanna, an Italian-American librarian whose name was given to me by a librarian friend of mine in Los Angeles. I explain to her and to another librarian of Italian descent the reason for my visit, and they immediately locate for me the "Italian-American file," which is a folder containing newspaper clippings. I also ask them about the cookbook that was advertised in the local newspaper's special issue for the centenary. The cookbook is entitled *Around the World, Around Our Town: Recipes from San Pedro,* and is a collection of recipes from all the ethnic groups represented in San Pedro. I notice that the Italian recipes are simply identified as "Italian" and not by region!

▪ ▪ ▪

The two librarians who help me locate the material are very busy, and do not seem particularly interested in being interviewed. I ask the older librarian where her parents are from, and she tells me that her grand-parents came to the States from Genova, city of Colombo, and settled in Monterrey. Then they moved to San Pedro but "inte-grated" into the American community be-cause there were not many people from Genova in town. I leave the library around 4:00 P.M. [IAW-PT-F072189A]

Back from the Library, I call the house of Carmela Bottola, whose daughter Luisa is getting married tomorrow, Saturday, at

ABOVE: **Doves are re-leased in front of Mary Star of the Sea Church in San Pedro, following the wedding of Annal-isa Vottola and Edward Ogle. Photograph by Ken Light, IAW-KL-B011-21**

LEFT: **After her wedding ceremony, bride Anna-lisa Vottola Ogle is embraced by a well-wisher on the steps in front of Mary Star of the Sea Church. Photo-graph by Ken Light, IAW-KL-B012-7**

A group of Italian-American friends playing *bocce* in a public park in San Pedro. Photograph by Ken Light, IAW-KL-B014-2

twelve. . . . I talk with Luisa: she is very nice on the phone; she tells me to introduce myself tomorrow after the ceremony, but she does not feel comfortable inviting strangers to the reception. I tell her that we understand perfectly, and that we do not want to intrude. She tells me that although she is Italian she is very "Americanized," but "I'm proud of being Italian!" Her husband, Edward, is American, and they met in the church, both being very active at Mary Star.

She tells me there is going to be a release of doves outside the church after the ceremony. Two years ago, when the pope came to Los Angeles, she was in charge of the doves, and because of that, the owner of the doves decided to provide the doves as a wedding gift.

I ask her if she has the trousseau. She says she does, but she did not expose it as tradition requires. [IAW-PT-F072189B]

July 22, 1989. San Pedro.

Geralyn Ciaramitaro (born in 1971) was named after her maternal grandfather, Gerolamo; her sister Mary was named after her paternal grandmother, Maria; her brother Dominic was named after his paternal grandfather, Domenico. Geralyn, called Jay by family and friends, came to the park to join her cousins and friends who are presently playing bocce. . . . They are between eighteen and twenty-two years old. The parents come to the park to play bocce every Sunday. Jay's brother often comes to play with the adults. The younger group does not play regularly, they come when they have time, usually on Saturdays. The adult men and women play separately: "They usually don't play with the guys, because the guys think they are wimpy, so the girls have their own game, the guys have their own game. . . . The younger people—see there are not as many of us—so we all play together."

Jay learned when she was little. "Sometimes in the backyard . . . I'd see my dad play and I wanted to play, that's about it." She explains the game: "I never take score, because I get confused, but it's like, you play in groups of four, four people get the red, four people get the black, and you have to get close to the little ball . . . and then, I don't know how we do but I think we count how many fingers space between the ball from each person. Whatever ball is closest, we count a point for that team. . . . Probably we play an hour and then we start over, depending on who is losing; if it is a big lose, we start over."

To measure the distance between balls they use their fingers or feet. They usually speak English while playing, but all the jokes, "anything that's funny, we say in Italian."

Ken [Light, the project photographer] is taking a picture of the group. Jay screams to wait for her. After the picture, they stop

Researcher Paola Tavarelli (right) interviews young Italian-American men and women after they have finished playing *bocce*. Photograph by Ken Light, IAW-KL-B016-21

Sports is one vehicle for reinforcing ethnic identity. In this image, the soccer players in the solid jerseys are competing for a team called "*Internazionale*," composed of Italian-Americans from San Pedro. Photograph by Ken Light, IAW-KL-B020-15

Matteo Accetta of San Pedro wearing a crucifix and a medallion in the shape of Sicily. Accetta was originally from Trappeto, Sicily. Photograph by Ken Light, IAW-KL-B012-30

playing and everybody comes under the trees where the picnic tables are.

I clip the lavaliere [microphone] to one of the boys, Salvatore, who was born in Palermo and grew up in the town of Porticello. He says that there is a lot in common between the towns of Terrasini and Porticello, one east and the other west of Palermo. In both towns, the fish industry is dominant. Salvatore came to San Pedro in 1973, when he was twelve years old. His family left Sicily for "family matters in the old country." "Actually we landed in New York, like Columbus did! (laughs). No, we stayed in New York for four months, but because the climate was different, we moved over here to San Pedro. San Pedro because, where we come from, Porticello, is very similar. The climate is the same, and it's a fishing village also." His father (Mariano Crivello) was a

fisherman in Sicily and in San Pedro continued to fish with his cousin.

I ask where he learned English. "I learned it in school basically, because that was the only choice I had. Because I came here, I came to find a lot of fellow Italians and so we hanged around together; we had a group, and everything we did, everywhere we went, we spoke Italian. So it was very difficult to learn by doing, it was all because of school. And then eventually it started fading out when we knew that we had to be good in English. . . . My parents' intention was to come here, try it out and go back. . . . We are a big family: five brothers and three sisters." At home they speak Sicilian. His parents speak always in Sicilian among themselves and with the children, while the brothers and sisters mostly speak English among themselves.

▪ ▪ ▪

I ask what else they do that feels like they are carrying on the tradition. Sal says, "We do quite a few things; we get together from time to time, we play bocce. Of course, we have the soccer team and we try to keep all Italians. It makes much more difference to play with other teams because we come on Sunday and we talk about what's going on in Italy in the soccer league over there. Everybody brings a little piece of news."

On friendship Sal says, "I think we all feel more comfortable being around each other, Italian-Americans, again because we can understand each other's culture, and if I have to say something to someone else . . . I know how to take it or they know how to take it because we know each other really well. We know our background while if you spoke with an American fellow, then you'd better be more clear."

Sal finished school two years ago. He works with computers. "I was the first one out of the family not to go into fishing. . . . He (his father) was proud of it actually because he did not want my two oldest brothers to go either. . . . He knows how hard fishing is; he wanted us to have more decent jobs."

Sal introduces me to Paolo Di Gerolamo, who came to the States with his family when he was one year old. His family came by ship through Ellis Island and then took the train to San Pedro where his grandfather (Dominic Ciaramitaro) had been for the past ten years. His father, Gaetano di Gerolamo, married Rosalia Ciolino. Paolo is not going into fishing. He says that some of his friends went into the fishing industry and he would have gone too if his father had not been injured ten years ago and had to stop fishing. "I probably would have gone into fishing because by now he would probably have a fishing boat and all the combinations that everyone else has, and I probably would be stuck on a boat. You know, owner's son, has to be working on the fishing boat."

Another guy introduces himself. His name is Matteo, from the town of Trappeto, Sicily. He has a pendant hanging on his chest in the shape of Sicily, a gift from his parents.

I have two girls and two boys in front of me, and I ask if they feel that they were treated differently by their parents while growing up. Everybody answers affirmatively. Mary starts to talk, and I move the lavaliere [microphone] from Sal's to her shirt. Mary is fourteen. She says that her mom lets her go out, but she says that they would like to have the women home with mom all the time. Her parents are more interested in her having a career. "My mom, she would be happier if I had a career instead of being a housewife right away, I know that." She helps her mother in the house a lot, and she is learning how to

cook. Last summer her parents went to Italy and she took care of her smaller brothers at home. She tells me a couple of recipes for tomato sauce and eggplant parmigiana.

Another guy comments on the difference in strength between men and women and tries to defend the attitude of parents toward the daughters: "You worry when they are out, you worry about things that might happen. Plus they (the parents) were young once too, and they know how guys and girls . . . guys try to do something with girls."

Jay comments that her parents will not send her away to college. "They say they don't want me to be away from them because they want to watch me." Her brother, who went to college, chose to stay near the family, but Jay is sure that if he wanted to go away the parents would have paid for his school, while she knows that they would not pay for her. "Sometimes all of us regret being Italian, but then there are certain times, you know, like family gatherings, like Christmas, you say 'it's fun being Italian!' You know! (other people talk) . . . a lot of times we just hate it, especially if you are a girl. Guys sure love it! . . . American guys, they don't have traditions, they don't have family. . . . American families are not as warm as Italian families."

Mary compares her life with her friend's life. . . . "She can go out all night, it doesn't matter what time . . . she can have a boyfriend, I think, but compared to my mom! She wouldn't dare let me have a boyfriend, probably not even when I'm sixteen. . . . I call my friend's house, and she is probably never home and she is not close to her parents. I always think about leaving my mom home, like before I go, I think, 'oh oh, my mom would be home alone! Maybe I should think about that, maybe I'll stay home this time.' But my friend, she'd just leave, because she is not that close."

Jay tells me that they spend all their holidays with family, which could mean from ten to forty people. When they go on trips, they don't just go with family members, but with the "extended" family: "My mom would call her sisters and brothers and friends, and . . . like we went to Las Vegas last weekend, we went with eighteen people, all Italians; we just don't go in little groups, never! . . . It's just fun, I don't know, that's when you like being Italian!"

On Sundays, most families have their "Sunday pasta," when they have pasta con salsa: "You have to be home on Sundays at twelve o'clock." "Sunday tradition is always the same, we always have tomato sauce with pasta." They don't eat breakfast or dinner, but only the big Italian lunch. Sal adds: "Sunday here, you cannot tell the difference between a Sunday and a Tuesday. We try to maintain that a Sunday is a holiday."

I ask if their families are religious: "They say they are," is one comment. "I think it's changed big time," is another. Jay says, "We like to go to church, and my parents don't." Another man says, "It's funny when they first came here, my parents, my dad especially, he went religiously every Sunday, but then, as we grew up and everything, . . . I guess as they got Americanized, they did not do it anymore." Everyone present has been baptized and confirmed. Somebody says, "You have to have that before you get married. . . . I think it's all the same but it's more liberal." Everybody goes to church, or tries to go every Sunday. They don't go to the Italian Mass but to the American Mass, because they don't like the priest, they say. But tomorrow everybody is going to be at the Italian Mass at 5:15 (a special Mass officiated by an Italian priest visiting San Pedro).

∎ ∎ ∎

Some of these youths are going to be at the Italian-American club Monday evening for the weekly meeting. They tell me it is scheduled for 6:00 but "don't come until 7:30, everybody comes late." [IAW-PT-A008]

July 25, 1989. San Pedro. Interview conducted in Italian.

Grace Ciaramitaro and I are in the dining room, looking at the pictures of the exposition of her daughter's trousseau. In Palermo the custom is that before a girl gets married the mother gives the dowry or trousseau (she uses the words synonymously). In Sicily on the invitation that you send to the guests you also write the days during which the trousseau will be exposed. Usually it is exposed one or two weeks before the wedding ceremony for two or three days. The guests go visit and bring a present, either a gift or money. Grace goes through the pictures explaining what she exposed: there are tablecloths, towels, nightgowns, and negligees. The new dresses, hats, purses, and shoes that Grace bought for her daughter were exposed on life-size dummies. Grace's husband made some wood stools that Grace covered with colored tissue-paper: on top of these are arranged hand-embroidered tablecloths and sheets in a fashion that gives prominence to the embroidery. Most of the trousseau was bought in Italy by Grace during her last trip ten years ago, in 1979. She bought the *biancheria* (table, kitchen, and bed linen), not only for Mary, her oldest daughter, but also for the other two daughters, for whom she is planning to do the exposition too. She did not buy the same amount of trousseau for her son, but she has linen for him too. In fact she has already sent a bedspread to his fiancée.

The trousseau was exposed in the living room. From the curtains hang blankets (ten of them) and bedspreads. This exposition did not replace the shower party. Grace invited relatives and friends. American friends were astonished because they had never seen something similar before. Nobody else in San Pedro had done a trousseau exposition before. Grace says that she wanted to do it because she does not want to lose the Italian tradition. After she did it, one of her sisters-in-law decided to do the same for her daughter and borrowed the stools that Grace used. Grace hopes to be able to do it again for her daughters when they get married. She says that it is a lot of work but it is worth it: her mother and her relatives cried and said that it was like being back home, in Sicily.

Grace was born in Sicily and came to America when she was fifteen years old. She based the exposition for her daughter on the memory of the expositions she witnessed back in Sicily.

The trousseau was composed of twenty-five pairs of sheets, including the "good sheets" (*lenzuola buone*) and the everyday ones, or as she says, the American ones. Among the good ones there were some that belonged to Mary's grandmother, there were some with a Neapolitan embroidery, some made at the *tombolo* (lace-pillow), and some with Venetian embroidery. I see some rugs in the pictures Grace shows me, and she says that she even bought the rugs for the bathroom. Aprons, pot holders, and kitchen towels were included. She also exposed the silverware sets in silver and gold that she bought for her daughter. She also paid for the bedroom furniture, as a present for her daughter's shower, while the mother-in-law paid for the living-room furniture. Her daughter basically got everything she needed to start her own household. She worked as a dental assistant until she had her second baby. Now she is not working

Grace Ciaramitaro (right) and her daughter Mary with linens, blankets, and other items from Mary's trousseau on display in their home. Courtesy of Grace Ciaramitaro, IAW-PT-B001-3

but plans to go back to work soon since they are building their new house and they need the money. Grace says that the house they are building is going to be Italian style: bricks, marble, balcony.

For the trousseau, Grace and her husband spent twenty thousand dollars. Then Grace paid for her daughter's shower: five thousand dollars to rent a hall and provide a dinner (*pranzo*). For the dinner, Grace wanted to add something Italian, so she cooked lasagna and cannoli for everybody and asked the waiters to serve it together with the regular dinner. For her shower, her daughter received many presents that she chose in local stores (Grace Italianizes the word *store* and says *storo*). The Sicilian tradition is to give money on the day of the wedding. Her daughter received fifteen thousand dollars as wedding gifts.

"I Siciliani qua, i soldi vanno assai. Americani! sentono queste cose e si ritirano. Voi siete ricchi allora!" (Sicilians here spend a lot of money for weddings. Americans comment that Sicilians are rich!) Even Italians from other regions of Italy who participated in the wedding commented that not even rich Americans could afford what Sicilians spend for a wedding. I ask Grace if they run into debt for this wedding. She says that they did not have to because they saved money in advance.

While the American tradition requires the bride to pay for the wedding, the Sicilian tradition requires the bride and groom's families to share the expenses. The bride and groom pay only for the photographer, all the rest is taken care of by the families. Now that Grace's only son is going to get married in Canada, Grace is already thinking of a party in San Pedro for all the relatives and friends (*commari*) who are not going to be at the wedding in Canada. In addition to her share of the wedding expenses, she is willing to pay for another "small wedding" in San Pedro.

The family is getting ready to go to Canada this summer for the engagement party. For the engagement they have green-colored confetti (the sugared almonds). The color green symbolizes hope (hope to get married). The bride-to-be is going to be dressed in green too. People bring small presents, but most presents consist of money. For her daughter's engagement she says that she limited the invitations to the close family and a few *commari* (friends): only two hundred people! Her daughter received five thousand dollars in money plus the gifts.

The girl that Grace's son is going to marry was born in Canada, near Toronto, to a family of Sicilian immigrants. Her mother was born in Terrasini, like Grace, and they lived only two blocks apart. The boy and girl met in San Pedro when the girl was visiting her aunts and uncles. She came recently to San Pedro to choose her engagement ring.

The wedding of Grace's daughter ended up costing thirty-five thousand dollars. The two families split the costs. The bride and groom received thirty thousand dollars in presents. With that money, they bought their first house. Now they have resold the house, made money on it, bought some land, and are building a new house.

■ ■ ■

She talks more about the exposition of the trousseau. She says that she kept the trousseau exposed for a week because she was waiting for one of her cousins from Detroit and wanted her to see it. It was an occasion that Grace likes to remember and talk about. She says, "It was a joy; every evening people came, and I offered coffee, cannoli. First, I explained everything, and then they would come to the table . . . people came and went. It was like an open house." I ask if it was Mary who asked for the exposition. She says that she wanted to do it herself and that Mary let her do what she liked. "People told me, here you have stuff to marry three daughters, not one!" When she came back from Italy with the items of the trousseau she stored it in several chests. When it was time to give Mary her share, she called her three daughters, and in front of them she divided the items evenly.

■ ■ ■

Grace came to San Pedro in November 1957. She says that her father came here two years before the family because of the opportunities that America offered. He was a fisherman and boat owner in Sicily, and he was doing fine, but his brothers here in San Pedro convinced him to come. Grace's husband is from her same town, Terrasini. She says that they would love to go back to Italy to visit more often, but it is too expensive. The last time she went back was in 1979 for "la festa dei morti," All Souls' Day.

She tells me the story of her large family: her grandfather sent two of his children to Detroit when they were young, and this is why part of her family is still in Detroit today. One of her uncles came to San Pedro to fish, and since then other members of the family from Terrasini have come to work as fishermen. Her father was the youngest of the family. During his first two years in San Pedro, he stayed with his brother and fished with him. Then he bought a house in San Pedro in the early sixties for eighteen thousand dollars. When his family arrived from Italy they found the house already furnished (she says *fornitura* for *furniture*). Grace was sent to school for three months, but she wanted to get a job because she was engaged to an Italian boy back in Sicily and wanted to put together enough money to go back to Sicily and marry him. Instead she met her present husband, and changed her plans.

Grace's son comes in. I ask if he is happy to marry an Italian-American girl. He says, "My mother is happier than me!" Grace says, "It's nice because in this way you never end the Italian tradition." [IAW-PT-A0013]

July 27, 1989. San Pedro.

Around 6:30 P.M., [project fieldworkers] David Taylor, Doug DeNatale, and I drive to the neighborhood gardens to meet Goffredo, an Italian man who cultivates one of the plots. With him we find another man, Pasquale D'Ambrosio, friend of Goffredo, who worked as a bricklayer in Goffredo's company since he moved to San Pedro from Connecticut many years ago. Pasquale is seventy-nine years old and retired, but he still works, building stone walls and other small bricklayer works if people call him. He spends much of his time helping Goffredo in the garden. We walk together in the beautiful garden, where every kind of

vegetables is cultivated. Recently the two men built a fence around it to protect it from people who steal their produce. While Doug draws the layout of the garden and David takes pictures, I talk in Italian with Pasquale. He is a very charming man who looks younger than he is. His English is very poor, and he enjoys speaking in Italian with me. He tells me about his life. He even shows me a letter he recently received from his brother back in Frosinone, Italy, where he was born, which he carries in his wallet. Pasquale lived in Connecticut with his first wife, who was also Italian. He came to San Pedro on vacation and decided to stay when Goffredo offered him a job. His wife died several years ago, and he is now living with a Mexican woman much younger than he is, who is sick and in need of constant medical care. Because of this he did not marry her;

Researcher Doug De-Natale (right) interviews Goffredo Momi about the arrangement of his garden plot in San Pedro's public garden. Photograph by David A. Taylor, IAW-DT-B007-18

for he would have to pay for her medical expenses, which he cannot afford.

The two men offer me red and white carnations, which they grow in the garden. I pick a little bunch of basil, and I end up walking around with the colors of the Italian flag in my hands! We sit under the "Casa dell'amore" (house of love), a small hut that Pasquale built with cheap wood and recycled material just outside the garden. Under the hut there is a table and a bench, a telephone, a mirror, and a wooden colored figure of a boy sitting on a barrel drinking wine. Pasquale is proud of his creation; he shows me around pretending to call somebody on the telephone (which obviously doesn't work), combing his hair in front of the mirror, showing that nothing is missing from his Casa dell'Amore. The two men use the hut to rest in the shade when the sun is too hot or to eat their lunch. Coming into the garden we noticed also a street sign that says: "via delle palme" (palms street). Pasquale built the wooden sign and named the path that leads to the Italian garden "via delle palme" because there is a palm tree on the path. He tells me more about his family: he has a son who lives on the East Coast and a mentally retarded daughter who lives in a nursing home near San Pedro. From what he tells me, I gather that his life must have been very hard, but his attitude is admirable and his spirit lively. We smoke a few cigarettes and enjoy this lovely place while the sun sets. [IAW-PT-f072789]

September 11, 1989. Gilroy, California.

We arrive at the Bertolone's house around 5:45 P.M., after a stop at a flower shop where we buy twelve red roses for them.

We were invited for dinner the first time we met the family at their restaurant on

10th Street (Joe's restaurant). Since they opened the restaurant in 1980, they have always worked seven days a week. Only recently (a month ago), they decided to keep the restaurant closed on Mondays and take a day off. It seems to me that they are so used to working all the time that they have not figured out a better way to spend their day off than by inviting friends to their home for dinner.

Joe comes to the door followed by Sonia, the oldest daughter (nineteen) to whom my colleague Russell Frank gives the roses. We enter the kitchen, where we meet the mother, Elvira, and Mona, a woman who helps them at the restaurant. Sonia and Joe take us into the parlor/living room (in Italian, I would call it "il salotto buono") a room that is evidently used by the family only on special occasions. The situation is very familiar to me. When I was doing field-work among Tuscan farmers, they often opened up the "salotto buono" just to offer me a glass of wine or something to drink. It was evident that they spent most of their time in the big kitchen.

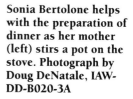

Sonia Bertolone helps with the preparation of dinner as her mother (left) stirs a pot on the stove. Photograph by Doug DeNatale, IAW-DD-B020-3A

Elvira Bertolone (left) prepares dinner in her home in Gilroy, California, as researcher Paola Tavarelli lends a hand. Photograph by Doug DeNatale, IAW-DD-B019-29

Joe and Sonia proudly show us Elvira's collection of porcelain dolls on display in the parlor. She started the collection only one year ago, but she has accumulated an incredible number of them already. The biggest one is Cinderella, followed by Sleeping Beauty. Sonia's favorite is a little doll made in Italy. Then they ask if we want to see the house. They show us the dining-room, evidently used also for special occasions. On the table a big gondola and the drawings for the town house that the family is planning to build in Los Banos in the near future. Then Sonia shows us the bedrooms; she opens the doors of the four bedrooms, and even of the bathroom. I know that David, Doug, and Russell are probably overwhelmed by this kind of behavior, but I recognize the typical Italian way: you show your friends the way you live, you open up your house for them as a way to show them your true friendship.

Sonia shares her room with her sister Mary (eleven years old, the only one born in the United States); Michael (seventeen years old) has his own room, and an exchange student from Spain has his own room. In the parents' room, Sonia opens the closet to show us her mother's sheets, which she brought from Italy. A big wooden rosary hangs on the wall on top of the bed, which is covered by an Italian bedspread.

Pictures of the children and of family weddings hang on the corridor's walls. Joe shows us a big poster of Sicily and points to the town in the center of the island (Province of Caltanissetta) where he was born. Sonia teases him about his Sicilian origins; he replies that he is proud of being a Sicilian, and even if he moved from Sicily to Liguria (town of Andora in the Province of Savona) when he was a boy, he still considers himself a Sicilian. He tells us that he worked in England and in other parts of Italy before coming to the States in 1978.

Sonia continues the tour of the house: she shows us the garage where the two Mercedes are parked (Joe gave Sonia a Mercedes when she graduated from high school), and then we go into the backyard. Elvira had a garden there the first year they bought the house. At the time, they were working with Joe's brother in a pizzeria. Then, when they opened their own restaurant, she did not find the time anymore to take care of the garden. We go back to the kitchen and sit around the table while Joe fills our glasses with red wine. Some antipasto (salami, prosciutto, mortadella, and cheese) is put on the table. The VCR is playing "Dangerous Liaisons," a movie loved by the whole family. Our hosts are very informally and comfortably dressed in their everyday clothes. Some children come in: Michael with the Spanish student, Mary with Mona's children. They will be in and out all evening. Later Mona's husband, Rick, will join us for dinner.

I leave the men around the table and go to Elvira, who is slicing potatoes and peppers and frying them in an electric fryer. She seems kind of uncomfortable in this kitchen, which she rarely uses. She tells me that she spends most of her time at the restaurant and that she never cooks at home, and in fact she misses basic ingredients for her cooking, such as salt, oregano, and coffee. During the evening she sends first Sonia, and then Michael, to the restaurant to get what she needs. I ask Elvira about her cooking. She worked in restaurants back in Italy, first as a waitress and then as a cook. She mentions a dish that she used to prepare in Italy but cannot make here because that particular cut of meat is not available on the American market (she referred to the "cima ripiena" or "stuffed pocket"). I ask her about the food she cooks at the restaurant, and she stresses the fact that the food she cooks is "really Italian." She shows me the

Val Filice, a noted cook in his hometown of Gilroy, California, prepares shrimp scampi on an outdoor grill beside the old tank house on his family's homestead. The tank house, a tower-like structure formerly used to store water for the Filice farm, is now used to store canned fruits and vegetables and other items. A symbol of the family's agricultural heritage, it also serves as a venue for outdoor dinners Val enjoys preparing for friends and family members. As the sign over the doorway indicates, he calls the place "The Tank House Ristorante." Photograph by Ken Light, IAW-KL-B169-13

tomato sauce she canned for the winter. I ask if she makes jam or canned fruit, but she says that it is not worth it because fruit costs too much. She tells me that when they first came they worked with Joe's brother in his pizzeria and she had time for gardening. Then Joe's brother "changed." . . . Joe and his brother do not talk anymore to each other; she comments negatively on her brother-in-law's new wife, who is a young Mexican.

Elvira tells me that when they came to America they had money. "I was a signora in Italy." They had two apartments and a vegetable store that they sold when they came to the States. Elvira calls Mona into the kitchen, and we start preparing dinner. I offer my help and start to peel garlic for the sauce; then I help Mona with the salad, while Elvira starts the sauce for pasta. Mona tells me that she began to work at the restaurant one year ago, and that she is the only person who lasted more than a week there! Apparently the Bertolone are very "direct" people, but Mona says she understands their rude way of asking for something. Mona's father was Italian, but he left the family when Mona was a child, so her Italian heritage is basically nonexistent, as

she says. She tells me that the big difference between Italian-Americans and Italians is that Italians will give you everything they can, but if you "spit on them once, that's it." She says that a lot of Americans do not understand this, but she does and accepts it. She continues saying that now the Bertolone family has become her family. When she went to visit her mom in another state, Elvira called her at least once a day, a fact that made her own mother jealous!

We set the table in a very informal way. Elvira cooks pasta (shells) with her tomato sauce, to which she adds garlic, onion, bay leaf and basil. Parmesan cheese is on the table. Sonia prepares the dressing for the salad with olive oil, vinegar, pepper, and salt (she looks for oregano, but they do not have any in the house). Sliced fried potatoes and peppers are ready. We sit around the table and are encouraged to eat and finish everything ("Mangia, Mangia!").

Sonia made some creme caramel (which tastes like the creme caramel my mother makes!); somebody puts ice cream on it, somebody else puts the "amarene fabbri," imported cherries very popular in Italy. We have Italian coffee and grappa Julia. Joe insists we finish the wine.

■ ■ ■

After dinner Elvira starts to clean up. David asks Joe what he wants for his children. Joe's answer shows his concern for his old age: he wants his children to take care of him when he is old; he does not want to end up in a home for old people and die alone.

We leave with the promise that we'll see each other soon. Sonia and Joe want to take all of us to San Francisco next Monday. The VCR is still on while we kiss good-bye. [IAW-PT-F091189A]

September 18, 1989.
Gilroy, San Francisco.

Sonia Bertolone asked me several times if I would go with her to San Francisco. Her family has been really nice with all of us from the first day in Gilroy, and I feel that Sonia is going to be really disappointed if I turn down her offer. She does not have many opportunities to spend time with a "real" Italian, and I feel I don't want to disappoint her as a friend! I plan to interview her while she drives and share with her the things she likes to do when she goes to the Italian section of San Francisco, North Beach. She comes to pick me up at the hotel with her brother Michael and the Spanish student who is staying at their house this year, and we drive to San Francisco under a torrential rain.

[Sonia] was born in Albenga, Province of Savona (Liguria) in 1971. Her family moved to Gilroy in 1977 when she was six years old. She remembers vividly when they left from the airport of Milan, and she was playing with her brother in the snow until the last minute before leaving. Her mother had somebody make two matching outfits for the kids to wear for the trip. She feels strongly that she is Italian, and swears that she will never give up her Italian citizen-

ship. She is planning to spend next year studying in Florence, and eventually to go to the university there. Her spoken Italian is very good, but she never writes or reads in Italian and fears her Italian is not good enough for university work. I encourage her to feel confident, and I promise to suggest some Italian literature that she can buy at the Italian bookstore in North Beach.

■ ■ ■

When we get to North Beach we first stop at Cavalli bookstore, where Sonia buys a couple of music tapes of Italian singers and a set of espresso cups for her mother. Then I offer them cappuccino and pastries at the Caffe Trieste, where Sonia usually stops for coffee. Then she shows me around all the stores where she buys things that she cannot find in Gilroy, like the Molinari grocery store that carries good prosciutto and bufalo mozzarella. We stop at a photographic exhibition of "Italian-Americans in North Beach," and both Sonia and her brother show a lot of interest in it. Sonia shows her disappointment over the "invasion" of the Chinese in that area; she is afraid they are going to take over the entire Italian neighborhood. Then we stop at the Italian church, where Michael lights a candle. Looking for the posters of the Festa Italiana, we end up on Fishermen's Wharf, where we stop for lunch.

Sonia is definitely in between two cultures. When I first met her I thought of the similarities between her situation and the one of Lara Doardi, the girl from Venice whose parents own the restaurant in San Pedro. But Lara, who had to fight hard at the beginning to gain respect for her family and for herself, seems to have found her own identity in this country. She would never think to go back to Italy. Sonia, on the contrary, seems still looking for her own identity and is trying to go back to Italy to be able to decide for herself where she wants to live and who she wants to be. [IAW-PT-F091889A]

September 19, 1989. Gilroy.

Val Filice invited the whole group of IAW fieldworkers for lunch at his Tank House Ristorante, which Russell Frank and I had visited before. . . . Val is a big man in his sixties. After he suffered from a heart attack, he tried to take life slower and now he spends much of his time gardening and cooking for friends and family members. He is a perfect host and makes all of us feel welcome. His wife, Elsie, is also there and his cousin Joe Filice with his wife. When we arrive, food is almost ready, and we sit around the table outside the Tank House and help ourselves with big portions of fettuccine with shrimp, cooked with a lot of garlic and red chili pepper. Our hosts keep pushing us to eat more and keep pouring wine in our glasses. Time goes by pretty fast while we eat and talk of nothing in particular.

When I sat down to write my notes a day later and tried to remember the conversation we had, I felt as if I had forgotten everything. I realized that I had the same trouble remembering the conversations I had with people during the Italian Catholic Federation dinner we attended the night before. I realized that on both occasions I felt that what people were expecting from me (or from us) was to share their food and enjoy each other's company and that I could not act as a friend/guest and a folklorist at the same time! It is possible that I just felt tired, after two weeks of fieldwork, and just wanted to relax and enjoy the food and company. It is also possible that I felt less responsible because the whole IAW group was present, and I trusted they were doing their job as participant-observers properly! As an Italian participating in events that involve sharing Italian food, I always feel much closer to the people who are cooking and offering me the food than to the researchers documenting the event! Food sharing is so much part of my culture and of my everyday life that I probably take everything for granted, and I find it difficult to write about.

This situation was very familiar to me: it reminded me of the many lunches my family in Italy shared with old and new friends, and I felt comfortable and enjoyed it as one of those lunches. The only time I felt uncomfortable was when our hosts expressed their ideas about Mexicans and told us stories based on their personal experiences with Mexican workers as a way to justify their dislike for these people. According to them, Italian immigrants had solid values and were hard workers who saved their money and invested it properly, while Mexicans don't know how to save but instead spend all their money on new clothes and don't respect other people's property. I find ironic that sons and daughters of an immigrant generation did not learn how to respect other immigrants' values and problems in adapting to life in America. As Val commented, life must go in circles: every group needs to feel superior to another group. Once the Italians were treated badly, and today is the Mexicans' turn. [IAW-PT-F091989]

THE COLUMBUS COMPLEX
JOHN ALEXANDER WILLIAMS

Columbus Day originated in New England and New York at the time of the third Columbian centenary in 1792, but the observance assumed its modern form in the West a century later and it is being redefined in the West today for the fifth centenary in 1992. Consider Columbus Day in any recent year in Colorado, the state which first made October 12 a legal holiday back in 1907. A mobile visitor there could take in three contrasting observances. Suburban schoolchildren recite the Pledge of Allegiance, a ritual first developed in connection with the fourth centenary in 1892, and they read stories about the young Columbus, perhaps making models of the Nina, Pinta, and Santa Maria with crayons and styrofoam cups. In Pueblo, where the state's oldest Columbus monument is located, a wreath is laid and politicians gather for an annual banquet put on by the city's Italian-American community. In Denver, Native American activists gather at another Columbus monument, a modernistic sculpture erected in 1970, posing for cameras with props that dramatize their view of Columbus as a genocidal invader.

In California, a somewhat different but equally complex mix is present on Columbus Day these days. Schoolchildren there also recite the Pledge of Allegiance, but they establish a more direct link with the Yankee origins of the Columbian tradition when they pose in groups in front of the monument to Columbus and Queen Isabella in the rotunda of the old state capitol, a ritual that forms an essential part of any student trip to Sacramento. San Francisco's Columbus Day parade is not the country's oldest—New York had one earlier, and Baltimore's has had fewer interruptions. But it is certainly one of the more colorful, and it has spun off an array of companion rituals that collectively make San Francisco's Co-lumbus Day the most colorful and elaborate celebration in the nation. One such ritual is the annual mock landing of "Columbus" and some companions at Aquatic Park, where they are greeted by friendly Indians and a beauty queen titled "Queen Isabella." Under the threat of disruption by Native American militants, the organizers of this incongruous spectacle have stopped using white fraternalists dressed up in Indian garb as their welcoming natives. Instead Yaqui Indians are brought up from Mexico for the occasion. In place of the Sioux warbonnets that the Improved Order of Red Men used to put on, these "authentic" Indians dress up in a vaguely Hollywood-Aztec style.

The observances described above represent three distinct phases in the evolution of the Columbian tradition of the United States, a complex of public art and ritual that has inscribed on the historical figure of Christopher Columbus a set of contrasting meanings about the nature of American citizenship and the relationship of

John Vanderlyn's painting *The Landing of Columbus* (1839), which hangs in the U.S. Capitol Building. San Francisco's Columbus landing pageant and the costuming of Columbus impersonators may owe much to this painting. Courtesy of U.S. Capitol Collection

the nation's future to its past. The oldest part of this tradition was a Yankee invention, developed by nationalist poets and writers of the early republic. It was characterized by public art, oratory, and schoolbook history lessons that emphasized Columbus's personal virtues and achievements. This tradition paid little attention to Columbus's Italian background or his Spanish collaborators and sponsors (except for a romanticized version of Queen Isabella). Still less did it emphasize his Roman Catholic religion and medieval mysticism. The Columbus for whom nineteenth-century cities and streets were named was, for all practical purposes, 100 percent American: individualistic, idealistic, romantic, and fearless. Making him a national hero in effect staked a claim on the entire American continent, for Columbus was not just the "discoverer" of the United States but of the entire hemisphere. It was this Columbus who inspired a New England boys' magazine to publish the Pledge of Allegiance and to promote it through a mass recitation by schoolchildren on Columbus Day in 1892.

Most Italians discovered Columbus in America, and when they did so, they found a symbolic figure bearing a stripped down version of his European background and an expansive vision of the American future. During the past century, Columbus's Italian background and his Catholic piety have been restored, for equally symbolic reasons. Italian-Americans took the lead in this work, but they had important assistance from two other groups: an Irish Catholic fraternal organization founded in New England and renamed in 1882 as the Knights of Columbus; and the "Americanist" wing of the nation's Roman Catholic hierarchy, bishops who worked to reform the American church and to promote the church as an assimilating agency training immigrants for

democratic citizenship. Together the bishops and the Knights of Columbus vigorously advanced the proposition that good Catholics were good Americans. By recatholicizing a Columbus who was already established as an American hero, the Irish-American Columbians further enhanced the admiral's value to Italian-American community builders. The result was that the Italianization of Columbus became the dominant theme in the Columbian tradition during the early twentieth century.

Italians, as is well-known, brought regional rather than national identities to the new world, and it was the Ligurians among them who refashioned Columbian symbols in order both to rally Italian regional groups to each other and to express the identity of all with the patriotic traditions of their new country. Ligurians had access to their own sources of Columbian hagiography—the notarial documents in the archives of Genoa, witnesses to the youth and young manhood of Cristoforo Colombo in that city; the mature Columbus's letter and "testament" to the Bank of St. George, kept under velvet wrappings in municipal vault in the Palazzo Tursi; and the frescoes of the Palazzo Belimbau, where a triumphal Columbus is displayed against a ceiling full of Baroque Indians with Rubenesque cheeks and tummies and ostrich feather garb. First in New York (1866) and then in San Francisco (1869), Ligurian immigrants rallied their *connazionali* to the process of "Italianizing" the Yankee Columbus Day, turning it from an occasion of solemn assemblies and oratory into a festival of parades and banquets. Another Ligurian, Angelo Noce, is credited with making Columbus Day an official holiday, in 1907 in Colorado. While the great masses of Italian immigrants clustered in northeastern cities, the greater Ligurian influence probably helps explain why the Italianization of the U.S.'s Columbian tradition developed more rapidly in the West.[1]

The role of the Columbian tradition in community building was first developed and elaborated in San Francisco. Here Italian immigrants had arrived earlier, beginning with the California Gold Rush, and while their numbers were smaller, they were strategically concentrated in the region's developing agricultural, mining, and commercial economies. They also more fully reflected the regional diversity of the Italian peninsula, in contrast to the later immigrants to the East and Midwest who were overwhelmingly from southern Italy and Sicily. The Bay Area and the West generally were unique among the destinations of migrating Italians in that they attracted roughly equal proportions from northern and southern Italy.[2] The early *prominenti* or leaders of the community, however, were northerners, and it was under their auspices that early Columbus Day observances were held. As would be the case with most Italian-American communities, San Francisco's was rent by deep fissures, not only between northerners and southerners, but between Genovese, Lucchese, and Piemontese among the northerners, between Siciliani and Calabrese from the south, between supporters of the newly unified Kingdom of Italy and its opponents, who themselves were divided among secularist republicans who opposed the monarchy and good Catholics who were scandalized by the Kingdom's 1870 seizure of Rome and the Papal States.

These differences were reflected in community life in many ways. For example, Italian patriots celebrated the national holiday of September 20, the anniversary of the Kingdom's "liberation" of Rome, while pious

fishermen from Liguria or Sicily tended to observe traditional saint's day festivals associated with their home villages, such as the festivals of Santa Rosalia, Madonna della Guardia, and Santissima Maria del Lume, which also took place during late summer or early fall. There were also class differences within the community, reflecting different origins in Italy but also the swift emergence in California of an Italian-American business elite who founded the marketing, financial, and processing enterprises that would eventually come to make up a substantial component of what is now called "agri-business."[3]

Columbus Day proved an ideal mechanism for bridging some of these gaps. And there were numerous persons in the Italian community whose interest it was to bridge them. Angelo Noce, an Italian national who later as the Kingdom's consul in Denver led the movement for a Columbus Day holiday in Colorado, was an early organizer of Columbus Day festivities in San Francisco. So were A. D. Splivalo and John Fugazi, anticlerical nationalists who were also bankers and founders of enduring business and civic institutions in San Francisco.[4] But so, too, were the priests of the parish church of Saints Peter and Paul, the so-called "Italian cathedral" in the North Beach section of the city. The Irish-American leaders of the Catholic church in San Francisco, following the conservative "national" rather than the liberal Americanist policy, established the "Peter-Paul" church in 1882 as a national parish, staffed by Italian-speaking priests, embracing all of the communities that had been created by immigrants from different regions in Italy, and pointedly named in honor of the patron saints of the Vatican. The priests of Sts. Peter and Paul began participating in Columbus Day observances in 1892.[5] Later the Knights of Columbus

Columbus and his men approach the shore in a longboat during San Francisco's Columbus landing reenactment, September 30, 1989. Photograph by Ken Light, IAW-KL-B175-5

added their own contributions, with both Irish-American and Italian-American participants. During the early twentieth century, the Knights led the statewide movement that resulted in the designation of "Discovery Day" as an official state holiday in 1909, while during the 1920s they revived a practice that has since become a regular feature of San Francisco's Columbus Day complex—the staging of a waterfront reenactment of Columbus's landing on San Salvador.[6] Finally, as Italian-American politicians rose to a position of parity with their Irish, German and Yankee counterparts, they also got into the act. San Francisco mayors had begun showing up at Columbus Day ceremonies a generation earlier, but it was the city's first Italian-American mayor, Angelo J. Rossi (1931–43), who instituted direct municipal sponsorship of the festivities by staging the coronation of "Queen Isa-

bella" in the rotunda of San Francisco's ornate city hall, a custom that still prevails.[7]

Today San Francisco's Columbus Day has expanded over a two-week period, embracing no fewer than eight separate events, each one representing distinct elements and traditions within the Italian-American community, and coordinated by a volunteer committee that can trace its organizational genealogy back over a century. The mock landing follows a half-century-old script, with the impersonator of Columbus—a role now being handed down from father to son in the Cervetto family—being greeted by welcoming Indians and a mock Spanish queen, "Queen Isabella," who is actually a beauty queen chosen competitively from among young women who are required to be of at least one-quarter Italian descent. "Queen Isabella" and "Columbus" ride together in the parade, which is held on a different day—usually the Sunday before the federal Columbus Day holiday—and they also appear at the speechmaking in front of the Columbus statue on Telegraph Hill, which is held on the Saturday before the parade. Yet another component is the procession of the devotees of SS. Maria del Lume, who still march in their white capes from Peter-Paul church to the waterfront. A recently added component is a "Festa Italiana," a commercial food and street fair organized by the restaurant owners of the Fisherman's Wharf area, an event which organizers of the traditional Columbus Day activities regard as intrusive.[8] It has to be stated, however, that non-Italian observers have difficulty keeping track of the various events and their meanings and sponsors. The *San Francisco Chronicle*, for example—when it reports on the contemporary festival at all—regularly emphasizes the unusual rather than the traditional features, such

Christopher Columbus (played by Joseph Cervetto, Jr.) plants the flag of Castile and León in the New World. Photograph by Ken Light, IAW-KL-B173-21

Soon after landing, Christopher Columbus and members of his crew encounter "Native Americans" (played by Yaquis from Sonora). Photograph by Ken Light, IAW-KL-B175-26

Christopher Columbus (holding a proclamation) sits with Queen Isabella (left, played by Valerie Ann Jacobs) and her court. Photograph by Ken Light, IAW-KL-B176-36A

During the Columbus celebration, October 8, 1989, members of the *Societa de la Madonna del Lume* march down Columbus Street ahead of a float carrying an image of the saint. The Transameria Building, a San Francisco landmark, is in the background. Photograph by Ken Light, IAW-KL-B185-12

as the parade participation of Filipino- or Chinese-Americans, the San Francisco Gay Freedom Day Marching Band and Twirling Corps, the self-parodying behavior of Italian-American princesses, or special events such as a "Renaissance Football Game" sponsored by the importers of the Italian liqueur "Amaretto." One reporter called the 1984 celebration "as traditionally Italian as a guacamole pizza."[9]

So constituted, the San Francisco Columbus complex is indeed, as another reporter put it, a mix of "giddy spirit and happily garbled historical detail,"[10] yet beneath this heterogeneous and superficial surface, the contemporary form of the complex engages deeper levels of ethnopolitical conflict: with Hispanics, with Native Americans, and with the rapidly expanding Chinese-American population next door to the traditional Italian neighborhood of North Beach. So far the *prominenti* have succeeded in managing these conflicts. As for Native Americans, the seizure of Alcatraz Island by Indian militants for a short time in November 1969 put the organizers on notice. While the mock landing in nearby Aquatic Park was held in 1970 without disruption, Native American protesters and sympathizers from Stanford University disrupted the event in 1976.[11] Meanwhile the organizers of the pageant were concerned enough to abandon their traditional practice of welcoming Columbus with whites dressed up in Plains Indian garb. Instead of the Redmen and Order of Pocahontas fraternalists with whom "Columbus" smoked peace pipes and paraded during earlier ceremonies, real natives were imported—and paid—to participate, first from northern California and later from Mexico. The Indians who come to Aquatic Park each fall now are Yaquis from Sonora. They bring impressive-looking costumes of a vaguely Aztec design. Even so,

Native American protestors returned to the event in 1991.

The confrontation with Chinese-Americans concerned territory as well as symbols. North Beach is adjacent to Chinatown, but the population history of the two neighborhoods has diverged sharply in recent years. As they move into their fourth and fifth generations in California, Italian-Americans live everywhere in the Bay Area, which means that no part of the region can fairly be characterized as an "Italian neighborhood." Yet North Beach remains the ethnic community's symbolic core, with Peter-Paul church, old and famous Italian restaurants, delicatessens and food stores, book stores and travel agencies, the offices of Italian-American organizations, and the

North Beach Museum organized to display the historical collection of cultural impresario Alessandro Baccari. Yet the Italian-American proportion of the neighborhood population declined from 21 percent in 1960 to 11 percent in 1970. By the latter date, 55 percent of North Beach's residents were non-white, most of them Asian, and Chinese enterprises had become almost as common as Italian shops on Columbus Avenue, the district's main street. To head off "a helter skelter" extension of Chinatown that would deprive both communities of North Beach's considerable tourist appeal, Baccari convened a meeting of Italian-American and Chinese-American business leaders in 1978, who hammered out a private "treaty" governing the neighborhood's further development. In order to preserve the tourist draw, the Italian share of North Beach's business sector was stabilized by Chinese restraint and by a considerable infusion of cash from Italian-American investors—a new generation of Medici, as Baccari characterized them—into the district's venerable restaurants and shops. The Chinese-American share of the neighborhood's resident population continues to grow, without impediment from Italian property owners or politicians. The result was "an Italian boutique" in an Asian neighborhood. Peter-Paul retained its traditional Italian shrines and feast-days, but it added masses in Chinese and Chinese-American personnel. Chinese New Year became an occasion for parish festivities. In 1981, when a Chinese festival fell close to the federal Columbus Day holiday, North Beach residents were treated to back-to-back parades.[12]

On a less elaborate scale, Columbus and Columbus Day have come to serve similar bridge-building functions in the Italian-American communities of other western

Members of the *Societa de la Madonna del Lume* march in procession. Photograph by Ken Light, IAW-KL-B186-4

Dedication of Christopher Columbus statue at Walla Walla, Washington, October 12, 1911. Courtesy of Doug Breen Saturno, IAW-JL-BWW010-19

cities. In Walla Walla, Washington, whose Columbus statue was dedicated in 1911, the tradition helped to unite a community that was sharply divided between northerners and southerners and so helped pave the way for the community's considerable achievements in agribusiness and ethnic revival. Pueblo, Colorado, is another case in point. Here a simpler and more plebeian version of the Columbus complex provides a touchstone for Italian-American identity in a setting where fragmentation was a product of local geography and economics as well as of Italian regional origins.

Pueblo's original circulation system is defined by three distinct street grids, each one representing a different set of urban functions as conceived by rival town builders in the late nineteenth century. These grids are poorly and confusingly integrated,

and the city's surface geography is further complicated by the fact that the Arkansas River changed its course through the center of Pueblo during a devastating flood in 1921. The original Italian settlement was located near the pre-1921 riverbank, but afterwards Italians dispersed to small enclaves intermingled with other ethnic groups and to St. Charles Mesa, an agricultural district east of the city. By 1921 the Mesa could already boast of a significant number of Italian small landholders who combined family-operated truck gardening and produce peddling with wage work in the area's smelters and mills. An Italian national parish church and school, Our Lady of Mt. Carmel, had been built in 1920, but since it was stranded after the great flood on the north side of the new riverbed, it could not serve as a community center the way that Peter-Paul church did in North Beach.

Pueblo already had a Columbus monument by the time of the flood, thanks to *prominenti* inspired by the indefagitable Angelo Noce. The monument, a bust of the admiral mounted on a fifteen-foot granite plinth, was dedicated in 1905. It stands in the center of a large rectangular public space known as Mesa Junction, which in 1905 was a strategic streetcar interchange. Here the lines that went east across Salt Creek to the Mesa intersected the lines that ran north to the city's business and warehouse districts and south to Bessemer and the Colorado Fuel and Iron plant (CF&I). The main depot of the Denver & Rio Grande Western Railroad is only a few blocks away. The railroad linked Pueblo's mills, freight yards, and warehouses with the mining towns scattered south and northwest of the city, places like Brookside and Florence on the upper Arkansas or Ludlow, Cokedale, and Segundo south of Pueblo in the foothills of the Sangre de Cristo range. All of the mining towns had Italian populations; Brookside and Ludlow were nearly *all* Italian. Some five thousand Italians from these and other Colorado communities travelled by special train to the unveiling of the Columbus monument, as other delegations would each year thereafter to march in the Columbus Day parade.[13] The marchers formed in front of the statue and paraded down the bluffs and across the river to the business district and back, stopping for speeches and ceremonies at a labor union hall en route.[14]

A federation of three Italian-American fraternal organizations or lodges organized the parade and the ensuing banquet during most of the twentieth century. The Christopher Columbus Lodge drew its membership from Sicilians and was itself an amalgamation of older regional lodges of immigrants

Christopher Columbus statue on East Abriendo Street at Mesa Junction, in Pueblo, Colorado. Dedicated in 1905, this is the oldest Columbus statue in Colorado. Photograph by Ken Light, IAW-KL-B231-6

from villages on the island's north and south coasts. The Fidelity Lodge was "Agnonese," its members originating in Agnone, a mountain village on the border of the Campagna and Abruzzi. The Protective and Benevolent Lodge had a mixed membership, including northerners and Calabrians. Each of the lodges had a women's auxiliary; a fourth lodge, the Agricultural Lodge of truck gardeners out on the Mesa, was active in Columbus-related events during the 1920s and 1930s, but had become defunct by the time that the Pueblo Columbus complex assumed its modern form.

Asked to define the principle of difference that divided the sponsoring organizations, the current Columbus Lodge president Charlie Musso puts it succinctly: "dialects."[15] Thus the annual parade and banquet, like the monument's location at Mesa Junction, represented a tenuous drawing together of an ethnic group whose normal state was one of fragmentation. For in addition to the fragmentation imposed by

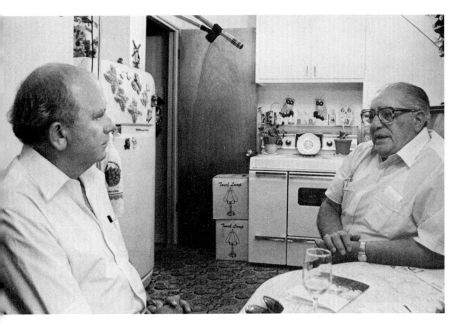

Researcher John Alexander Williams (left) interviews Charles Musso at his home in Pueblo, Colorado. President of the Columbus Lodge and long-time organizer of Pueblo's Columbus Day banquet, Musso is locally know as "Mr. Columbus." Photograph by David A. Taylor, IAW-DT-B035-1

the immigrants' regional differences, Pueblo's shattered geography, and the divide between the city and its mining-town hinterlands, there was further fragmentation imposed by the organization of work at Pueblo's largest employer, the Colorado Fuel & Iron (CF&I) Company mill. Notwithstanding the habitual use of the singular in everyday parlance, CF&I was not one mill but more than twenty, each one organized around a particular task of steel rail- and pipe-making processes, each with its own particular set of required skills, difficulties, and dangers, and each a bastion of one or another of Pueblo's welter of ethnic and occupational groups, who governed admission to the jobs in their sector on their own terms. Men whose names ended in a vowel were at a disadvantage, at least until union organization modified the system during the 1940s, for there were few foremen of Italian or "Spanish" (i.e., Mexican) descent. Italians were slightly better off than their Mexican-American neighbors, but both groups tended to be relegated to the sweatiest, lowest paying, or most dangerous jobs. They also shared

the worst neighborhoods. Mt. Carmel church held masses in Spanish as well as Italian and English, and when its members began their postwar moves to the suburbs, a mixed Italian-Mexican parish church, St. Joseph's, was established on the edge of the Mesa above a ravine settlement called Salt Creek, where the poorest refugees from the 1921 flood had created a squatter's barrio on CF&I land. Pious Mexican-American women adopted Italian religious practices, such as the *tavolata* or St. Joseph's Table tradition of the Sicilians, while men from both ethnic groups frequented some of the same Bessemer bars. Thus in blue-collar Pueblo—in contrast to San Francisco, where Italian- and Spanish-speaking communities started out intermingled but ended up far apart—the two communities have a good deal of interaction.[16] There was, however, no formal Hispanic participation in the elaboration of Pueblo's Columbus complex.

Charlie Musso is Pueblo's "Mr. Columbus" today. He joined Columbus Lodge in 1937, when he was twenty-five. Both of his parents were Sicilians, and he grew up on the Mesa, combining work on the family truck garden and produce wagon with occasional stints in the mill. Later he made a living as a salesman—of dry goods and gravestones, among other things—and he owned and operated a local bar. What he really sells best is Columbus, and this is because his true calling is politics. He won his first office at the age of twenty-four, upsetting a veteran Italian officeholder named Johnny Williams (Gugliermo). He got his first job at the mill through politics; "it was a question of who you knew." He started out as a Democrat, became a Republican, and is now a Democrat again, with no apologies to make.

Musso's father had been a member of the Columbus Lodge before him, but the son does not remember much about the Columbus Day parade, though he recalls marching in it before its demise during World War II.[17] About the transformation of the Columbus Day banquet from an ethnic to a political event, his memory is sharp and detailed. Vincent Massari deserves credit for this achievement, in Musso's opinion. A powerful Democratic state senator from the 1930s through the 1950s, Massari began running the Columbus Day banquet in 1942. Soon attendance was de rigueur for anyone in either party who aspired to hold local, regional, or statewide office. It still is.[18]

Massari financed the annual banquet through sales of tickets and of ads in the evening's printed program. Most people did not know that Massari and his daughter got a commission for each ad that they sold, but Musso did. Perhaps this had something to do with the expanded scope of the banquet. Musso continued the program of expansion after he took over the banquet, moving the venue from the relative confinement of the lodge's old hall on Northern Avenue to a capacious new art center in the middle of town. He tried taking it to an even larger venue at the University of Southern Colorado (whose sports arena is named for Vincent Massari), but the food was terrible. Now he is back at the Arts Center, feeding five hundred people each autumn. He used to hustle around the area selling tickets. Now he simply sits back and waits until the people at the court house or up in Denver call. The banquet always sells out.

Apart from keeping the venue and the caterer up to snuff, Musso's only real challenge is to keep the politicians coming back to Pueblo each October. A few years back, Colorado's hip young governor Richard Lamm staged a kind of rebellion, showing up at the Pueblo banquet only in election

years. Musso publicly took him to task for this, and Lamm returned to a regular schedule during the remainder of his term. Another famous Denver yuppie politico, whom Musso declines to identify by name, aroused his ire one year by starting a food fight. "They got half-loaded," Musso explains, and started using dinner rolls as projectiles. A threat of public expulsion from the banquet brought the offenders into line, and now everyone sits respectfully if not attentively during the evening's lengthy program of speeches, introductions, and toasts.

Musso also solved another problem recently that had been bothering him for years. This concerned the event's sponsorship. Many times in the past, Musso had moved in federation meetings that his lodge, the Columbus, take over the event exclusively. Since the dinner was held in their hall and they sold more tickets and did more work than the other two lodges, it seemed only right that the Columbus Lodge should get all the credit. He was always outvoted, perhaps because Massari was Agnonese, not Sicilian. But in 1986 Musso finally got his way. The Columbus Lodge is now exclusive sponsor and organizer of the Columbus Day banquet. The sponsorship also includes the wreath-laying and speeches at the Mesa Junction monument on Columbus Day morning. The only problem is that this triumph may turn out to be a phyrric victory. The lodge's membership is in steep decline, down from 250 when Musso assumed the presidency to 83 in 1990. Only two members were younger than forty in 1990; the rest ranged from sixty to ninety-five. Some of the smaller ethnic lodges in Pueblo have folded entirely. Musso wonders what will happen to the Columbus Day festivities in Pueblo after he is gone.

Activist accused in defacement of statue

Russell Means decries Columbus as murderer

By J. Sebastian Sinisi
Denver Post Staff Writer

Indian activist Russell Means was issued a police summons for defacing public property yesterday after he denounced Christopher Columbus as a mass murderer of Indians and poured blood over a statue of the explorer in Civic Center Park.

Means, who referred to Denver police officers as "Mayor Peña's conquistadores" during a noon protest, has 14 days to enter a plea in a Denver court. A guilty plea carries a possible fine of up to $999 for defacing public property.

Perhaps the most visible Indian activist in America today, Means drew a multi-ethnic crowd of about 200 people to the state Capitol and Civic Center Park yesterday as the nation observed Columbus Day.

Sponsored by the American Indian Movement and the Fourth World Center at the University of Colorado-Denver, the rally featured a number of speakers who called for the abolition of Columbus Day as a national holiday.

CU-Denver instructor and Fourth World Center director Glenn Morris also demanded that the city remove the Columbus statue and vowed "we'll be back every year" if the city fails to remove it. Means termed the statue "an abomination."

Other rally speakers included Indian

PROTEST: Russell Means prepares to pour blood on statue of Columbus.

The Denver Post / John Prieto

■ PUEBLO: Christopher Columbus Lodge event brings out politicians./2B

spokesman George Tinker of the Iliff School of Theology, Susan Johnson of the Colorado American Indian Movement and CU-Denver instructor Ward Churchill.

Means and Morris said Columbus

founded a Spanish land-distribution system in the New World that enslaved and killed 300,000 indigenous Indians on the island now known as Haiti and 20 million more in the Caribbean basin, Central and South America.

Morris read chronicles of atrocities

Please see PROTEST on 8B

Newspaper account of American Indian Movement (AIM) leader Russell Means pouring blood on statue of Columbus, Denver, Colorado, October 9, 1989. Photograph by John Prieto. From the *Denver Post*, October 10, 1989. Reprinted with permission.

As well he might. The Italianized Columbian tradition of the late twentieth century faces many challenges, one of them the mounting indifference of the rising generation of Italian-Americans. The reemergence of Italy as a center of contemporary art, fashion, and design has encouraged a tendency to redefine Italian-American ethnicity in terms of elite elements of Italian culture. To younger members of the community, Italian clothes, cars, and high-style cuisine attract more respect than old-fashioned Columbus Day rituals. Among those who seek a sense of personal connection with the authentic past of their grandparents, newly formed regional organizations for people of Sicilian descent (or Abruzzese, Calabrese, Genovese, and so on) exert a more powerful appeal than the long-established federations (such as the Sons of

Italy) that were formed out of the immigrants' original regional lodges. There is also a growing indifference among the general public to the Columbian tradition. San Francisco's heterogeneous parade still attracts crowds in the thousands, but attendance at the mock landing is down to a few hundred persons in good years. California Italian-American organizations had to fight hard for the return of the 1882 Columbus/Isabella monument in the old state capitol after preservationists had restored the building to its Gold Rush era elegance. Pueblo politicians in 1988 narrowly averted a legislative cost-cutting measure that would have repealed the legal status of the Columbus Day holiday in Colorado.[19]

But the most provocative challenge to the Italian Columbus Day complex comes from Native Americans. For the past two years, while Charlie Musso counts noses and has his picture taken with the politicians gathered in Pueblo, Columbus Day news in Colorado has been dominated by the American Indian Movement activist Russell Means, who gathers followers and reporters in front of the modernistic Columbus shrine in Denver's Civic Center, which he then proceeds to desecrate in some inventive way. In 1989 Means poured blood on the statue. In 1990, he framed it with a photo of Adolf Hitler and a skeleton clutching brown dolls to represent dead Indian babies. Columbus was a "mass murderer," in Means's opinion. He has pledged to abolish Columbus Day by 1992. In both demonstrations, Means made headlines. Charlie Musso's picture was inside on page 2. The politicians still came to Pueblo, and they included both Gov. Roy Roemer, whose state quincentenary commission was announced at the Pueblo banquet in 1989 (it spent the better part of its first year in angry squabbling before removing Columbus's name from its official title) and Rep. Ben Nighthorse Campbell, the nation's only Native American congressman, whose home district includes Pueblo. Means attracted only two hundred spectators to his 1990 performance, while Musso as usual packed the hall.

Still there are some reasons to believe that Means rather than Musso represents the future of the Columbian tradition in the United States.[20] The reputation of Indians and Columbus have been joined together since 1492, but in contrast to earlier Columbian celebrations, the Indian in 1992 will neither vanish nor keep silent. Native Americans understandably view the preparations for the observance with mixed feelings. They have no reason for celebration, yet many Indian spokesmen are reluctant to let pass such a singular opportunity to acquaint a larger public with Native American viewpoints about the last five hundred years, to win control once and for all of their own cultural representation, and to present to the American public an assertion of genuine pluralism, not simply of symbolic ethnicity but one which entails the acceptance and fostering of significant cultural differences within American society. While they represent less than one percent of the population of the United States, Native Americans bring to ethnopolitical conflict a moral—and a legal—force that few other ethnic groups can muster.

The demands of Indians and those of many Hispanics thus present ethnic claims of a different order than do groups of European origin who are in, as many sociologists see it, the "twilight" of their ethnicity.[21] These differences, and the ways in which quincentenary programs succeed or fail in recognizing competing symbolic claims, are

Untroubled by questions of ethnic identity, fourth-generation Italian-American Alexis Rose Zupancic celebrates Fourth of July at the home of her grandparents, Al and JoAnna Collette, in Pueblo, Colorado, 1990. Photograph by Ken Light, IAW-KL-B208-30

of more than casual interest in this period of world history. The liberalization of totalitarian regimes in Central and Eastern Europe has led to the resurgence of long-suppressed demands by ethnic and linguistic minorities, demands which are not only historic but also in many cases incompatible. These developments should remind us that the American experiment in cultural pluralism is as relevant to the transformations taking place today as are our national commitments to human rights and a market economy. The ethnic dimension of the quincentenary should provide an important reading on how that experiment is faring.

ITALIAN-AMERICANS IN THE WEST PROJECT

The concept for the Italian-Americans in the West Project was developed by American Folklife Center consultant John Alexander Williams. Field research was directed by Center folklife specialist David A. Taylor. The project's fieldworkers were: Susan Anderson, Bee Bergold, Douglas L. Banks, Thomas Carter, Douglas DeNatale, Russell Frank, Andrea Graham, Ken Light, Jens Lund, Paula Manini, Maria Notarianni, Philip Notarianni, Blanton Owen, Valerie Parks, Bea Roeder, Steve E. Simmons, Steve Siporin, Paola Tavarelli, and Myron Wood. Fundraising for the project was coordinated by Ray Dockstader, deputy director of the American Folklife Center, and Renée Kortum. During the planning phase of the project, helpful advice was provided by Dino Cinel, Archie Green, and Moyra Bryne-Severino. The exhibition curator was I. Sheldon Posen, the exhibition designer

was the Leone Design Group, and the project archivist was Stephanie Hall, archivist at the American Folklife Center. Consultants Marjorie Hunt and Barbara Kirshenblatt-Gimblett helped shape the exhibition and Camila Bryce-Laporte, program specialist at the Center, along with Anne Bowman, Victoria Brown, and Robin Fanslow, assisted with its development. James Hardin, the Folklife Center's editor, advised on and assisted with every stage of the editorial process for this book; and Johanna Craig, of the Library's Publishing Office, managed the production.

Many persons contributed to the work of the Italian-Americans in the West Project, welcoming field workers into their homes, discussing their lives and traditions, and providing encouragement and support in other ways. They are listed below:

San Pedro, California

Matteo Accetta
Isidoro Amalfitano
Fred Arduini
Anita Bacich
John Barbieri
Caterina Bologna
Andrea & Margherita Briguglio
John Calise‑
Joseph J. Canetti and family
Edmund Castagnola
Lucille Castagnola
Geralyn Ciaramitaro
Grace Ciaramitaro
Tonino Ciarrocchi
Salvatore Cigliano
Domenico & Grace Ciolino and family
Girolamo Ciolina and family
Pasquale Colaruotolo
Isidoro Colonna
D. J. Comparsi
Anthony P. "Phil" Cracchiolo
Antonia & Salvatore Cracchiolo
Joe Cracchiolo
Salvatore Crivello
Pasquale D'Ambrosio

Father Lorenzo DeDominici
Ferdinando DiBernardo
Libby DiBernardo
Paolo DiGerolamo
Lucy DiLeva
Neal DiLeva
Stan DiMeglio
Franco, Roberta, Lara, and Silvia Doardi
Stephano Finazzo
Gerrard Fiorentino
Fishermen & Allied Workers' Union Local 33, ILWU
Frank Iacono
Italian-American Club of San Pedro
Enez Rubino King
Antonette Lauro
Tony Marabella
Anthony Mattera
Frank Mattera
Philip Mazzella
Clint Miller
Goffredo Momi
Edward & Annalisa Ogle
Giovanni Palomba
Hector Patino
GianVittorio Perniciaro

Tony Pirozzi and family
Frank Pontillo
John Robinson
Louis A. Roupoli
Albina Royal
John J. Royal
San Pedro Bay Historical Society
San Pedro Peninsula Chamber of Commerce
Ben Scott
Leonard Taormina
Nino Terzoli
Vito Terzoli
Mike Vuoso

Gilroy, California

Joe, Elvira, and Sonia Bertolone
Louis & Judy Bonino
Jim, Jean, and Scott Burr
Chinto & Rose Conrotto
Richard A. Conrotto
Jennie M. Costa
Ernest Filice
Craig Filice
Joe & Judy Filice

John Filice
Teresa Filice
Timothy J. Filice
Val & Elsie Filice
Mario Fiorio
Mario Fortino and family
Ernest Fortino and family
Henry Frassetti
John Frassetti
Albert Gagliardi, Jr.
Frank & Alyceann Ginelli
The Guglielmo family
Italian-Catholic Federation of Gilroy
Ed & Phyllis Pedrizzetti
Bill & Mary Pirozzolli
Mike & Marie Pirozzolli
David Porcella
John & Rosanne Richardson
Gloria Rizzi
John Roffinella
Mimi Serafin
Eda Stimac
Carolyn Tognetti
Richard & Anita Venezia
Aldo & Aurora Viarengo

Pueblo, Colorado

Bob Abeyta
Vic Alfonso
Stella Nigro Allen
The Altar Society, Holy Rosary Church
Gary Amella
John Amella
Gen Archuletta
Joseph Bacino
Tony Bacino
Joe Benavidaz
Bruno Biggi
Blast Furnace Reunion Committee
Father Norman L. Bouchard
Bob Bragg
Domenick Bucciarelli, Jr.
Silvio & Rosalie Caputo
Debbie Carleo
Pete Carleo
Joe Carpine
Sam Catalano
CF&I Steel Corporation
Albert & JoAnna Collette and family
Charles & Rose Conatore
Naich Cordo
Sheriff Dan L. Corsentino

Joe & Rose Cortese
Tony Costanza
Sandi Cresswell
Annie P. Cuchiara
Charles & Carmella Cuchiara
Kenneth, Susan, & Anthony Cuchiara
Nell Cuchiara
Tony Cuchiara
Louis & Helen Daurio
Gary DeCesaro
Charles & Frances DeLuca
Tony DeSalvo
James & Annabelle DiIorio
Charles & Patricia Dionesio
Russell Dionesio, Jr.
Russell Dionesio, Sr.
Russell DiSalvo
Father William P. Doll
Laurie L. Drew
Marvin Drewes
Marianne & Spencer Everett
Marie Cuchiara Fabian
Daniel Frabrizio
Richard & Phyllis Fairchild
Joseph & Ann Ferraro
Anthony & Palma Ferraro
Joseph A. Fortino
Tony & Barbara Fortino
Stacey Fortino
Anthony, Josephine, & Vincent Gagliano
Maria Carmella Gagliano
Joe Genova, Jr.
Grace Giadone
Joyce Giadone
John Granato
Vera Gurovich
Sandy Holman
Peggy Thomas Hovet and family
Bessie P. Ingo
Pete Jimenez
Leo Jiron
Kerry Marie Kramer
Mike Kraska
Victoria Cristiano Marion
Frank & Emma Marascola
Tony & Josephine Martellaro
Fred A. Masciotra
Mike Masciotra
Ann Massarotti
Gene Mattarocci
Ralph & Nettie Montera
Pete J. Montera
Richard Moreschini

Mary Louise Morone
Charles V. Musso
Frank & Rose Nigro
Our Lady of Mt. Carmel Church
John Pagano
Frances Paglione
Louis Paglione
Paul L. Palermo
Rose Lee Pisciotta
Olga Potestio
Jim Prutch
Sollie Raso
Lou Riccillo
Jennie Rodasta
Angelo Rotondo
Joe Sandoval
Lou & Lil Sciortino
Theresa Spicola
Dale Spinuzzi
Stacy E. Spinuzzi
Pauline Steffy
John & Eve Taravella
Tony & Esther Thomas
Carolyn Cirullo Tollefson
John Tucci
Robert Van Alstyne
Charlie Vasile
Joseph Vasile
Luis Vasquez
Mike Venuto
Louise Williams
Dorothy Zanini

Nevada

Albert Biale
Arthur Biale
Benny Damele
Leo & Tony Damele
John & Roberta Damele
Jody & Pete Tony Delmue
Pete & Marlene Delmue
Bob, Pam, & Link Eddy
Susan Gallagher
Louis Gibellini
Camille & Victoria Pradere
Mike Rebaleati

Carbon County, Utah

Rochino and Margaret Ariotti
Dominick Besso
Ann Bonacci
Joe Bonacci
Vito & Filomena Bonacci
John & Yolanda Bruno
Richard Colombo
Lou Colosimo
Josephine Nick Copfer
Frank Dalpiaz
Matilda "Til" Davido
Dr. J. Eldon Dorman
Bertha Elegante
Kerry Nick Fister
Ross Gigliotti
Mary Nick Juliano
Stan Litizzette
LaVange McNeil
Bob Myer
Palmina Nick New
Teresa Fazio Ori
Lowell Pitts
Guido Rachiele
Edna Romano
Charlie Saccamano
Arvetta Satterfield
Rose Vea
Al Veltri

Walla Walla, Washington

Anthony Ambrose
Hubert & Ellen Anthony
Gregory Bossini
Louis Bossini
Bill Burk
Emilio & Carmela Destito Buttice

Mel Buttice
Richard Campanelli
Francis & Nadine Christiano
Lewis Colombo
Carrie Criscola
Virgil & Dorothy Criscola
Ben Daltoso
Maria Daltoso
David Deccio
Frank & Jennie Deccio
Jan Eaton
Ben & Bea Elia
Elveda Elia
Frank Fazzari
Robert Fazzari
Gary Figgins
Mary Elia Gunberg
Geraldine Hartley
Italian Heritage Association
Connie Johnson
Mary Kleyn
Cheryl Knotts
Horace Lazzari
Joe J. Locati
Nick & Connie Longo
Byron Magnaghi
Marilyn McCann
Becky Nesteby
Charles & Lillian Paietta
Bert & Rose Pesciallo
Elizabeth Destito Ponti
Rose Ponti
Walla Walla Gardeners' Association
Louis Rizzuti
St. Francis of Assisi Church
Douglas Breen Saturno
Victor A. Toppano
Father Adrian Van Der Heijden
David Venneri
James Vinti
Karen Weber

Others

Alessandro Baccari, San Francisco
Janice Bardo, Rodeo Drive Merchants'
   Association, Beverly Hills
Gerlando Butti, Italian Cultural Insti-
   tute, Los Angeles
Andrew Canepa, San Francisco
Jeff Capaccio, San Mateo, California
Joseph Cervetto, Sr., San Rafael,
   California
Richard A. Cuneo, Sonoma, California
Lena D'Aquanno, Monterey, California
Ronald J. Derenzi, San Francisco
Don Galleano, Mira Loma, California
Prof. Michael Owen Jones, Center for
   the Study of Comparative Folklore
   and Mythology, UCLA
Jerome Lucido, Monterey, California
A. D. Mastrogiuseppe, Western History
   Collection, Denver Public Library
Michael A. Merlino, Cañon City,
   Colorado
National Italian-American Federation,
   Washington, D.C.
Robert A. Pepi, Sr., Oakville, California
Joseph Perrelli, El Cerrito, California
Carmella Sauer, Florence, Colorado
George J. Silvestri, Jr., San Rafael,
   California
Eve Sodo, San Francisco
Frances Tarantino, San Francisco
Claire Zanger Tearse, San Jose,
   California
August Troiani, San Francisco
Peter C. Tubiolo, Covina, California
Elizabeth M. Varney, Colorado
   Springs, Colorado

NOTES

Introduction

1. Several general histories of the Italian-American experience are relevent to the themes treated in this volume. See especially Andrew Rolle, *The Immigrant Upraised. Italian Adventurers and Colonists in an Expanding America* (Norman: University of Oklahoma Press, 1968) and *The Italian Americans. Troubled Roots* (New York: The Free Press, 1980); Humbert Nelli, *From Immigrants to Ethnics: The Italian Americans* (New York: Oxford University Press, 1982); Luciano John Iorizzo, *Italian Immigration and the Impact of the Padrone System* (New York: Arno Press, 1980); and the essays in Lydio Tomasi and Madeline H. Engel, eds., *The Italian Experience in the United States* (New York: Center for Migration Studies, 1970).

2. Dino Cinel, *From Italy to San Francisco: The Immigrant Experience* (Stanford: Stanford University Press, 1982), 196–255.

3. Walt Whitman, "Italian Music in Dakota" ["The Seventeenth—the finest Regimental Band I ever heard"] in *Leaves of Grass: A Textual Variorum of the Printed Poems,* vol. III: Poems, 1870–1891, ed. by Sculley Bradley, Harold W. Blodgett, Arthur Golden, William White (New York: New York University Press, 1980), 687–88; Giovanni Ermenegildo Schiavo, *Italian-American History,* vol. I (New York: Arno Press, 1975), 149–55. Fiorello LaGuardia's father, Achille, was a military bandmaster, and so the future mayor of New York spent his childhood in Arizona; see Arthur Mann, *LaGuardia: A Fighter against His Times 1882– 1933* (Chicago: University of Chicago Press, 1959), 26–31.

4. Carla Bianco, *The Two Rosetos* (Bloomington: Indiana University Press, 1974), 31, 59.

5. Joanne Dodds, *Pueblo: A Pictorial History* (Norfolk, Va.: Donning, 1982), 109; and Morda C. Slawson, *A History of Renton from Coal to Jets* (Renton, Washington: Washington Historical Society, 1976).

6. "Comments by Sidney Robertson Cowell on Sicilian singers she recorded in northern California in March 1939," Tape AFS 3865 B 3; "List of Recordings made by Sidney Robertson Cowell in California, 1938–1940," 3851 26 M, both found in American Folklife Center, Archive of Folk Culture, Library of Congress; American Folklife Center, *Ethnic Recordings in America: A Neglected Heritage* (Washington: Library of Congress, 1982), especially Pekka Gornow, "Ethnic Recordings: An Introduction," and "Appendix: A Checklist of 78 Rpm Foreign-Language Records," pp. 1–50. Italian-language records were by far and away the largest category in foreign-language recordings included in this exhaustive checklist.

7. Giovanni Alfredo Di Simone (Johnny Desmond), "The Italian Contribution to American Popular Music," and Alessandro Baccari, "The Stage is Now Empty," both in *Columbus 1977* (San Francisco: Columbus Day Committee, 1977), 141–46, 157–59; University of California-Berkeley, Regional Office of Oral History, "Wine Making in the Napa Valley," (Louis M. Martini and Louis P. Martini, interviewed by Lois Stone and Ruth Teiser, October 31, November 21, 1967, April 2, June 19, 20, 1969, May 8, July 22, August 1, 1972), transcript pp. 44–48, 51–53.

8. Cinel, *From Italy to San Francisco,* 228–61, esp. 234–37; see also Iorizzo, *Italian Immigration and the Padrone System,* 156–57.

9. Bianco, *The Two Rosetos,* 134–37.

10. Tony E. Fratto, "Cooking in Red and White," *Pennsylvania Folklife* XIX:3 (Spring, 1970), 2–15.

11. Richard Raspa, "Exotic Foods among Italian-Americans in Mormon Utah: Food as Nostalgic Enactment of Identity," in Linda Keller and Kay Mussel, eds., *Ethnic and Regional Foodways in the United States: The Performance of Group Identity* (Knoxville: University of Tennessee Press, 1984), 185–94.

12. The evolution of the Italian restaurant as a cultural institution has received little scholarly attention. The "Italian-Americans in the West" project files include case-studies of family-owned restaurant businesses in California and Colorado. See interview with Franco, Roberta, and Lara Doardi at their restaurant, La Piccola Trattoria, in San Pedro, California, on July 21, 1989. Interview by Paola Tavarelli (IAW-PT-A005–7); interview with John Pagano at his Pass Key Restaurant, Pueblo, Colorado, June 27, 1990. Interview by David Taylor and John Alexander Williams (IAW-DT-A008); interview with Michael Merlino, Elizabeth Varney, and Carmella Saurer, at Merlino's Belvedere Restaurant, Cañon City, Colorado, June 27, 1990. Interview by David Taylor and John Alexander Williams (IAW-DT-R025–8). The University of California Berkeley Regional Office of Oral History project on the California wine industry contains information on such businesses as they related to the histories of winemaking families such as the Martinis and Mondavis (see Louis M. Martini interview, transcript pp. 1–30; and "Creativity in the California Wine Industry," Robert Mondavi, interviewed by Ruth Teiser, April 17, 19, 20 and October 15, 1984, transcript pp. 1–6.)

13. Angelo M. Pellegrini, *Lean Years, Happy Years* (Seattle: Madrona Publishers, 1983), 3–5, 13, 24–51, 61–67; and Martini and Mondavis interviews cited above, note 12.

14. Cinel, *From Italy to San Francisco*, 234–37; on the role of the Bank of America in financing and stabilizing the California wine industry after repeal of Prohibition, see University of California-Berkeley, Regional Office of Oral History, "The Petri Family in the Wine Industry," Louis A. Petri, interviewed by Ruth Teiser, September 4, 10, 1969, transcript pp. 43–46.

15. The best general history of the industry, based on the extensive interviews conducted by the University of California Regional Office of Oral History, is Ruth Teiser and Catherine Harroun, *Winemaking in California* (New York: McGraw-Hill Book Company, 1983.)

16. Humbert S. Nelli, *The Business of Crime: Italians and Syndicate Crime in the United States* (Chicago: University of Chicago Press, 1981).

17. On bootlegging in Italian-American communities during Prohibition, see University of California-Berkeley, Regional Office of Oral History, Frank Adams, interviewed by Ruth Teiser, April 11, 1969, transcript pp. 7–8, and Robert Mondavi interview, pp 1–2. See also IAW project interview with Jim and Scott Burr at the A. Conrotto Winery, Gilroy, California, September 17, 1989, by David Taylor, Douglas DeNatale, John Alexander Williams, and Paola Tavarelli (IAW-DT-A006–7). For references to underground buildings used for bootlegging, see fieldnotes dated May 8, 1981, by Howard W. Marshall, Paradise Valley (Nevada) Project, the American Folklife Center.

18. In this context it is relevant to note that Mario Puzo "confessed" that the idea for *The Godfather* came from his WASP publisher and that he acquired most of his knowledge of organized crime through library research (*The Godfather Papers and other Confessions* [New York: Putnam: 1972]).

19. David Taylor and John Alexander Williams, interviews with Eugene Guglielmo, Emilio Guglielmo Winery, Morgan Hill, California, March 15, 1989; Jack Stauch, Caparone Winery, Paso Robles, California (regarding the Caparone winery), March 16, 1989; and Robert Pepi, Sr., Robert Pepi Winery, Oakville, California, March 20, 1989, document these trends.

20. Micaela Di Leonardo, *The Varieties of Ethnic Experience: Kinship, Class, and Gender among California Italian-Americans* (Ithaca: Cornell University Press, 1984), 228.

21. Richard Alba, "The Twilight of Ethnicity among Americans of European Ancestry: The Case of Italians," *Ethnic and Racial Studies,* vol. 8, no. 1 (January 1985), p. 153.

22. Werner Sollors, *Beyond Ethnicity: Consent and Descent in American Culture* (New York: Oxford University Press, 1984).

The Royal Family of San Pedro

1. H. M. Gitelman, *Legacy of the Ludlow Massacre: A Chapter in American Industrial Relations* (Philadelphia: University of Pennsylvania Press, 1988), 18.

2. Barron B. Beshoar, *Out of the Depths: The Story of John R. Lawson, a Labor Leader* (Denver: Golden Bell Press, 1942), 361.

3. International Longshoremen's & Warehousemen's Union, *Program of the Twenty-Fifth Anniversary, Bloody Thursday, July 5, 1934–July 5, 1959* (Los Angeles: International Longshoremen's & Warehousemen's Union, 1959), 2.

4. *Ibid,* 6. According to Howard Kimeldorf, Tom Knudsen (not John Knudson) was fatally wounded. ("Sources of Working-Class Insurgency: Politics and Longshore Unionism During the 1930s," in *Insurgent Workers: Studies of the Origins of Industrial Unionism on the East and West Coast Docks And in the South During the 1930s,* edited by Maurice Zeitlin, pp. 7–70. Los Angeles: Institute of Industrial Relations, University of California, 1987).

5. Kimeldorf, 27.

The Melting Pot Works

1. Ron Reno, "research notes from the Roberts Mountain Archaeological Project" (Archaeological Research Services, Virginia City, Nev., n.d.).

2. Ron Reno, "The Charcoal Industry in the Roberts Mountains, Eureka County, Nevada" (Paper delivered at the Great Basin Anthropological Conference, Reno, Nev., 1990).

3. *Ibid.*

4. Benny Damele, interview with Andrea Graham, Dry Creek Ranch, Nev., 30 March 1990 (Archaeological Research Services, Virginia City, Nev.).

5. Albert Biale, interview with Andrea Graham, Eureka, Nev., 29 March 1990 (Archaeological Research Services, Virginia City, Nev.).

6. *Ibid.*

7. Phillip I. Earl, "Nevada's Italian War," *Nevada Historical Quarterly* III:2 (Summer 1969): 52.

8. Alan Balboni, "From Laborer to Entrepreneur: The Italian-American in Southern Nevada, 1905–1947," *Nevada Historical Quarterly* 34:1 (Spring 1991): 269. Balboni notes that in southern Nevada, Italians "applied their energies and talents to economic and social advancement, rather than to preserving remains of the past."

9. Franklin Grazeola, "The Charcoal Burners War of 1879: A Case Study of the Italian Immigration in Nevada" (M.A. thesis, University of Nevada, 1969), 19.

10. Biale interview, 29 March 1990.

11. Charles M. Russell, *Trails Plowed Under: Stories of the Old West* (New York: Doubleday, 1927), 2–3.

12. Benny Damele, interview with Andrea Graham, Dry Creek Ranch, Nev., 7 December 1989 (IAW-AG-A007).

13. *Ibid.*

14. Benny Damele died on November 12, 1991.

15. Louis Gibellini, interview with Andrea Graham and Blanton Owen, 4 November 1989 (IAW-BO-A002).

16. "A Rock Drilling Contest," *Mining and Scientific Press* 65 (August 6, 1892): 90.

17. See Archie Green, "Singlejack/Doublejack: Craft and Celebration" in *By Land and By Sea: Studies in the Folklore of Work and Leisure,* ed. Roger D. Abrahams, Kenneth S. Goldstein, and Wayland D. Hand (Hatboro, Pa.: Legacy Books, 1985), 95–111.

18. Grazeola, 15–17.

Places of Origin

1. Interview with Angela Scalzo, Rosina DeFazio, and Francesco Bonacci by Philip F. and Maria Notarianni, October 26, 1987, Decolattura, Italy.

2. This article is part of a larger study which began when the author traveled to the University of Calabria in Cosenza, Italy, on a Fulbright research grant during the 1987–88 academic year. The author wishes to thank the Commission for Educational and Cultural Exchange Between Italy and the United States, and Prof. Cesare Pitto of the University of Calabria, Department of Cultural Anthropology. For a basic discussion of Italians in Utah, see Philip F. Notarianni, "Italianità in Utah: The Immigrant Experience in Utah," in Helen Z. Papanikolas, ed., *The Peoples of Utah* (Salt Lake City: Utah State Historical Society, 1976), 303–31. In addition, for a review article of Calabresi in the United States, see Remigio Ugo Pane, "L'esperienza degli emigrati calabresi negli stati uniti," in Pietro Borzomati, ed., *L'emiarazione calabrese dall'unità ad oggi* (Roma: Centro Studi Emigrazione, 1982), 273–93.

3. Fortunata Piselli, "Gli emigranti, la famiglia, il paese: matrimoni, comparaggi, eredità," and Ilario Principe, "L'altra faccia dell'emigrazione," in Franco Guglielmelli, ed., *Alla scoperta delle identità reaionali. La Calabria* (Torino: EVENT, 1985), 69–72, 78.

4. Ilario Principe, "L'altra faccia dell'emigrazione," in Guglielmelli, ed., *Alla scoperta,* 15–18.

5. Franco Bartucci, "Quegli Emigrati Spaesati Alla Ricerca Della Memoria," *Calabria* 15 (Agosto 1987), 57–62.

6. State of Utah, *First Report of the State Bureau of Immigration Labor and Statistics* (Salt Lake City: The Arrow Press, 1913), 26. For 1911, 282 immigrants from the north and 248 from the south were admitted.

7. Silvagni moved to Las Vegas, Nevada, in 1929, where he became the owner of the Apache Hotel and the gaming casino Pache Club Garden. See, Alan Balboni, "From Banana Sellers to Successful Entrepreneurs: Italian-Americans in Southern Nevada, 1905–1907," unpublished paper in possession of the author.

8. See Philip F. Notarianni and Richard Raspa, "The Italian Community of Helper, Utah: Its Historic and Folkloric Past and Present," in Richard N. Juliani, ed., *The Family and Community Life of Italian Americans* (Staten Island, New York: American Italian Historical Association, 1983), 23–33.

9. Interview with Joe Bonacci by Philip F. Notarianni, Spring Glen, Utah, September 1, 1990.

10. Interview with Vito and Filomena Bonacci by Philip F. and Maria T. Notarianni and Steve Siporin, August 1, 1990, Spring Glen, Utah.

11. Faeta, "Il cammino," 207–8.

12. Interview with Marion Bonacci Lupo by Helen Z. Papanikolas, May 22, 1977, Helper, Utah. The interview is located at Special Collections, Marriott Library, University of Utah. See also Helen Z. Papanikolas, "Women in the Mining Communities of Carbon County," in Philip F. Notarianni, ed., *Carbon County: Eastern Utah's Industrialized Island* (Salt Lake City: Utah State Historical Society, 1981), 94–95. On Frank Bonacci, Philip F. Notarianni, "Rise to Legitimacy: Frank Bonacci as Union Organizer in Carbon County, Utah," *Rendezvous* (Idaho State University Journal of Arts and Letters) 19 (Fall 1983): 67–74; and Allan Kent Powell, *The Next Time We Strike. Labor in Utah's Coal Fields. 1900–1933* (Logan, Utah: Utah State University Press, 1985), 53–54, 65–67, 123–24.

13. Interview with Vito Bonacci by Philip F. Notarianni, September 1, 1990, Spring Glen, Utah; and interview with John and Yolanda Bruno by Steve Siporin, June 20, 1990, Helper, Utah.

14. Luigi M. Lombardi Satriani, "Tradizione e innovazione: le classi subalterne tra araicità e modernizzazione," in Giglielmelli, ed., *Alla Scoperta,* 94–96.

15. Faeta, *L'architettura popolare,* 192.

16. Interview with Mary Nick Juliano by Philip F. and Maria T. Notarianni, September 2, 1990, Price, Utah.

17. Subscription Lists and Correspondence Relevant to "Il Monumento Ai Caduti Grimaldesi." Copy in possession of the author. Also, Filippo Amantea Mannelli, *Inaugurandosi Il Monumento Ai Caduti Grimaldesi* (Cosenza: Tipi De "Il Giornale Di Calabria," 1927).

18. Richard Raspa, "Exotic Foods among Italian-Americans in Mormon Utah: Food as Nostalgic Enactment of Identity," in Linda Keller Brown and Kay Mussel, eds., *Ethnic and Regional Foodways in the United States. The Performance of Group Identity* (Knoxville: The University of Tennessee Press, 1984), 193.

19. On the Bruno experience, see interview with John and Yolanda Bruno by Steve Siporin, June 20, 1990, Helper, Utah. On sausage-making, see Philip F. Notarianni, "Italian Sausage Making Is a Family Affair," in *Beehive History* 4 (Salt Lake City: Utah State Historical Society, 1978): 10–13.

20. G. B. Maone, *Tradizioni Popolari della Sila* (Soveria Mannelli: Rubbettino Editore, 1979), 54.

21. Interview with Joe Bonacci by Philip F. Notarianni, September 1, 1990, Spring Glen, Utah; interview with John and Yolanda Bruno by Steve Siporin, June 20, 1990, Helper, Utah; and interview with Orlando and Clara Barber by Philip F. Notarianni, May 17, 1989, Magna, Utah.

22. A pertinent discussion on linguistic code switching, with reference to Calabrese, can be found in S. Chirico Raparo and J. Trumper, "Language Variation, Code Switching, and the Migrant Question," in Peter Auer and Aldo Di Luzio, eds., *Interpretive Sociolinguistics. Migrants–Children–Migrant Children* (Tubingen: Gunter Narr Verlag, 1984), 29–54.

23. Interview with Giuseppe Maletta, by Philip F. Notarianni, March 25, 1988, Rizzuti, Colosimi (CS), Italy.

24. Maone, *Tradizioni Popolari della Sila,* 26.

25. Interview with Raffaele Scalzo by Philip F. and Maria T. Notarianni, March 15, 1988, Decollatura, Italy.

26. *Deseret News* (Salt Lake City, Utah), August 31, 1977, 2C.

27. Commune Di Pedivigliano, "Programma Di Fabbricazione," 20 Dicembre 1978, Tecno. Deni, Cosenza. The original document is found in the Municipio of Pedivigliano (CS), Italy.

28. Interview with Prof. Bruno Coccimiglio by Philip F. and Maria T. Notarianni, November 23, 1987, Grimaldi, Italy.

Folklife and Survival

1. Edward Burnett Tylor, *Primitive Culture,* 2 vols. (London: John Murray, 1871), I:16, as quoted in Elliot Oring, "On the Concepts of Folklore," in Elliot Oring, ed., *Folk Groups and Folklore Genres : An Introduction* (Logan: Utah State University Press, 1986), 6.

2. Richard M. Dorson, "Introduction: Concepts of Folklore and Folklife Studies," in Richard M. Dorson, ed., *Folklore and Folklife: An Introduction* (Chicago: The University of Chicago Press, 1972), 44.

3. George List, "Folk Music," in Richard M. Dorson, ed., *Folklore and Folklife: An Introduction* (Chicago: The University of Chicago Press, 1972), 375.

4. *The Random House Dictionary of the English Language,* second edition, unabridged, 1987. S.v. "survival."

5. Tape-recorded interview with Mary Nick Juliano, Price, Utah, January 1983.

6. Tape-recorded interview with Til Davido, Price, Utah, June 21, 1990. IAW-SS-A006.

7. "Elizabeth Siletta Felice Marrelli," unpublished typescript, pp. 1–2.

8. Helen Papanikolas, "Ethnicity, Diversity, and Conflict," *Dialogue: A Journal of Mormon Thought* 24 (1991):85.

9. Papanikolas, p. 86; and C. H. Madsen, ed., "Carbon County: A History" (April 1947), typescript available in Special Collections, College of Eastern Utah Library, Price, Utah, p. 13.

10. Tape-recorded interview with Ann Bonacci, Helper, Utah, June 6, 1990. IAW-SS-A009.

11. Tape-recorded interview with Guido Rachiele, Price, Utah, June 19, 1990. IAW-SS-A001.

12. Tape-recorded interview with John and Yolanda Bruno, Helper, Utah, June 20, 1990. IAW-SS-A002.

13. Stephen S. Hall, "Italian-Americans: Coming Into Their Own," *New York Times Magazine,* May 15, 1983, p. 31.

14. Tape-recorded interview with Vito and Filomena Bonacci, Spring Glen, Utah, August 2, 1990. IAW-SS-A014.

15. Fieldnotes from interview with Mr. and Mrs. Ariotti, Spring Glen, Utah, August 3, 1990. IAW-SS-F080390.D.

16. Tape-recorded interview with Edna (Borla) Romano, Helper, Utah, June 21, 1990. IAW-SS-A004.

17. Papanikolas, p. 85.

18. Tape-recorded interview with Lou Colosimo, Price, Utah, June 22, 1990. IAW-SS-A007.

19. "Elizabeth Siletta Felice Marrelli," p. 1.

20. "Elizabeth Siletta Felice Marrelli," p. 2.

21. Philip F. Notarianni, "Helper—the Making of a Gentile Town in Zion," in Philip Notarianni, *Carbon County: Eastern Utah's Industrialized Island* (Salt Lake City: Utah State Historical Society, 1981), 159.

22. Tape-recorded interview with Charlie Saccomano and Richard Colombo, Spring Glen, Utah, August 6, 1990. IAW-SS-A015.

23. Tape-recorded interview with Dominick Besso, Price, Utah. October 7, 1990. IAW-SS-A018, -A019, -A020.

24. Tape-recorded interview with Ann Bonacci, Helper, Utah, August 6, 1990. IAW-SS-A010.

25. Tape-recorded interview with Ann Bonacci, Helper, Utah, August 6, 1990. IAW-SS-A010.

26. Tape-recorded interview with Til Davido, Price, Utah, June 21, 1990. IAW-SS-A006.

27. Tape-recorded interview with John and Yolanda Bruno, Helper, Utah, June 20, 1990. IAW-SS-A002.

28. Tape-recorded interview with Al Veltri, Helper, Utah, June 20, 1990. IAW-SS-R011. Tape-recorded interview with Edna Romano, Helper, Utah. IAW-SS-A005.

29. Tape recorded interview with Edna Romano, Helper, Utah, June 21, 1990. IAW-SS-A004.

30. Fieldnotes from interview with Kerry Nick Fister, Price, Utah, June 19, 1990.

31. Al Veltri, "Comments," in Philip Notarianni, *Carbon County: Eastern Utah's Industrialized Island* (Salt Lake City: Utah State Historical Society, 1981), 172–3.

32. Tape-recorded interview with Edna Romano, Helper, Utah, June 21, 1990. IAW-SS-A005.

33. Tape-recorded interview with Edna Romano, Helper, Utah, June 21, 1990. IAW-SS-A004.

34. *Ibid,* IAW-SS-A005.

35. For the contrast between "space" and "place," see Mary Hufford, *One Space, Many Places: Folklife and Land Use in New Jersey's Pinelands National Reserve* (Washington, D.C.: American Folklife Center/Library of Congress, 1986).

36. Allan Kent Powell, "Land of Three Heritages: Mormons, Immigrants, and Miners," in Philip F. Notarianni, ed., *Carbon County: Eastern Utah's Industrialized Island* (Salt Lake City: Utah State Historical Society, 1981), 9.

37. Tape-recorded interview with Al Veltri, Helper, Utah, June 20, 1990. IAW-SS-R009.

38. Tape-recorded interview with Stanley Litizette, Helper, Utah, October 8, 1990. IAW-SS-A023.

Walla Walla Sweets

The research was funded by the Library of Congress's American Folklife Center and conducted by the Washington State Folklife Council, who were funded by the Washington State Arts Commission and the National Endowment for the Arts—Folk Arts Program. Italian translations by Daniela Ghiselli Moats.

1. Ernesto Milani, *Lonate Pozzolo: storia, arte, societá* (Milan: Nicolini Editore, 1985), 364.

2. Ernesto Milani, "The Lonatese Experience in the Americas," in *Lonate Pozzolo—History, Art, Society.* Translated by Ernesto Milani and Lorenza Garzoli Ucchino. (Milan: Nicolini Editore, 1986), 24. (English translation of "L'Esperienza lonatese nelle Americhe," in Franco Bertolli, Elisa Bottini, and Rino Garatti, eds., *Lonate Pozzolo: storia, arte, societá.* (Milan: Nicolini Editore, 1985), 361–70.)

3. Joe J. Locati, *The Horticultural Heritage of Walla Walla County, 1818–1977: A Comprehensive Review of Fruit and Vegetable Growing, Shipping and Processing, Focused on Walla Walla County—With a Section on the Italian Heritage* (Walla Walla, Wash.: Privately printed, 1978), 50–55.

4. Locati, 16–17.

5. The history of the early Italian settlers appears in Locati, pp. 35–49; See also Mary Beth Lang, ed., *Washington's Centennial Farms: Yesterday and Today* (Olympia, Wash.: Washington State Department of Agriculture, 1989), 90.

6. Italian immigrant life in the valley is described in Locati, 93–119.

7. Quoted in Locati, 101.

8. David L. Nicandri, *Italians in Washington State: Emigration, 1853–1924* (Tacoma, Wash.: Washington State American Revolution Bicentennial Commission, 1978), 60.

9. Italian church history in Walla Walla is discussed in Locati, pp. 121–24.

10. The history of the onion crop is discussed in Locati, pp. 206–23.

11. Leading Italian dishes in the community, and their families and places of origin, are discussed in Gayle Cavalli, Marilyn McCann, and Connie Vinti, eds. *The Walla Walla Italian Heritage Association Cookbook: Featuring Authentic Italian Recipes and Family Treasures* (Walla Walla, Wash.: Italian Heritage Association, 1989).

12. Walla Walla *Union-Bulletin "76 Progress"* edition, February 22, 1976.

13. Anonymous, "An Artist's Place: Tom Moro Has Carved His Success as a Sculptor in Walla Walla," Walla Walla *Union-Bulletin,* August 11, 1983, p. 13.

Tradition in a Bottle

1. Eugene T. Sawyer, *History of Santa Clara County, California, with Biographical Sketches of the Leading Men and Women of the County who have been Identified with its Growth and Development from the Early Days to the Present* (Los Angeles: Historic Record Company, 1922), 1627.

2. Interview with Chinto Conrotto, Rose Conrotto, and Jean Conrotto Burr by David Taylor and Douglas DeNatale, September 12, 1989, at Gilroy, California. IAW-DT-R019.

3. Sawyer, *History of Santa Clara County, California,* 135.

4. [Santa Clara County Board of Supervisors], *Santa Clara County, California: Its Climate, Resources and Industries Officially Surveyed and Compiled by the California Development Board for the Board of Supervisors* (San Jose: Santa Clara Board of Supervisors, [1915]), 19.

5. According to the assessor's returns for 1914, in that year 9,150 acres were planted in wine grapes and 1,275 in table grapes. See [Santa Clara County Board of Supervisors], *Santa Clara County, California,* 15.

6. Ruth Teiser and Catherine Harroun, *Winemaking in California* (New York: McGraw-Hill Book Co., 1983), 2.

7. The early history of winemaking in Santa Clara Valley is sketched in Teiser and Harroun, *Winemaking in California,* 48–57. For an interesting contemporary account of winemaking in the Valley in the 1880s, see W. H. Bishop, "Southern California," *Harper's New Monthly Magazine* 65, no. 389 (October 1882), 713–28.

8. [Santa Clara County Board of Supervisors], *Santa Clara County, California,* 55.

9. Stephen M. Payne, *Santa Clara County: Harvest of Change* (Northridge, Cal.: Windsor Publications, Inc., 1987), 97.

10. Interview with Chinto Conrotto, Rose Conrotto, and Jean Conrotto Burr by David Taylor and Douglas DeNatale, September 12, 1989, at Gilroy, California. IAW-DT-R019.

11. Interview with Chinto Conrotto, Rose Conrotto, and Jean Conrotto Burr by David Taylor and Douglas DeNatale, September 12, 1989, at Gilroy, California. IAW–DT-R019.

12. Jack Voice, Jr., "Anselmo Conrotto," unpublished paper, ca. 1971, in the possession of Chinto and Rose Conrotto, p. 4.

13. Sawyer, History of Santa Clara County, California, 1627.

14. Voice, "Anselmo Conrotto," 4.

15. Interview with Chinto Conrotto, Rose Conrotto, and Jean Conrotto Burr by David Taylor and Douglas DeNatale, September 12, 1989, at Gilroy, California. IAW-DT-R019.

16. Prohibition lasted for more than fourteen years, from July 1, 1919, to December 5, 1933. Its effect on the California wine industry is discussed in Teiser and Harroun, Winemaking in California, 177–83. See also Ruth Teiser and Catherine Harroun, "The Volstead Act, Rebirth, and Boom," in Doris Muscante, Maynard A. Amerine, and Bob Thompson, eds., The University of California/Sotheby Book of California Wine (Berkeley: University of California Press, 1984), 50–81.

17. Grappa is made from distilled grape pomace, the pulp that remains after grapes have been crushed and the juice removed.

18. References to gravity-flow wineries in California are rare. However, one example was the Gallegos winery in Alameda County, which was completed in 1885 and destroyed by an earthquake in 1906. See Teiser and Harroun, Winemaking in California, 119.

19. In the production of white wines, the skins are separated from the juice as soon as possible.

20. Interview with Jim Burr and Scott Burr by David Taylor, Douglas DeNatale, John Alexander Williams, and Paola Tavarelli, September 17, 1989, at Gilroy, California (IAW-DT-A006). Anselmo also used to plant and prune according to phases of the moon, Jim Burr reported.

21. This is the basic winemaking process employed by Anselmo Conrotto, many smaller steps are also part of the process. For a concise description of winemaking practices in California, see Walter Schug, "The Vinification of Fine Wine," in Muscatine, Amerine, and Thompson, eds., The University of California/Sotheby Book of California Wine, 160–68. For a detailed discussion, see M. A. Amerine, H. W. Berg, R. E. Kunkee, C. S. Ough, V. L. Singleton, and A. D. Webb, The Technology of Wine Making, 4th ed. (Westport, Conn.: AVI Publishing Co., 1980).

22. In their report on grape-growing contained in the Santa Clara County Board of Supervisors' Santa Clara County, California: Its Climate, Resources and Industries (1915), Paul Masson and L. Woodard discuss the grape varieties grown in the county: "The grapes are all of the dry wine type. Two general grapes of wine are produced: Grenache, Mataro, and Carignane are the varieties used for making the standard wines. About two-thirds of the plantings are of the above varieties. The finer wines are made from Petite Sirah, Alicante Bouschet, and similar varieties. Some sparkling wines are produced. Pinot is a variety used for this purpose. The Zinfandel, on account of its heavy bearing, is grown extensively for red wine of the cheaper Claret type" (p. 15).

23. Interview with Chinto Conrotto, Rose Conrotto, and Jean Conrotto Burr by David Taylor and Douglas DeNatale, September 12, 1989, at Gilroy, California. IAW-DT-R020.

24. A short biography of Scagliotti appears in Sawyer, History of Santa Clara County, California, p. 1600.

25. The Emilio Guglielmo Winery is still being operated by members of the founding family. The Roffinella winery, dormant since 1946, was sold to Thomas Kruse in 1971 and it is now known as the Thomas Kruse Winery. The Scagliotti winery was sold in 1988 and is operated under the name Live Oak Winery. The Cassa brothers winery was purchased by Ernest Fortino in 1970 and it is operated as the Fortino Winery. The Marchetti winery changed hands in 1975 and is now operated as Sycamore Creek Vineyards. The Colombano winery was sold to the Pedrizzetti family in 1945 and they continue to operate it.

26. Voice, "Anselmo Conrotto," 8.

27. Interview with Jim Burr and Scott Burr by David Taylor, Douglas DeNatale, John Alexander Williams, and Paola Tavarelli, September 17, 1989, at Gilroy, California. IAW-DT-A007.

28. Interview with Jim Burr and Scott Burr by David Taylor, Douglas DeNatale, John Alexander Williams, and Paola Tavarelli, September 17, 1989, at Gilroy, California. IAW-DT-A007.

29. Interview with Chinto Conrotto, Rose Conrotto, and Jean Conrotto Burr by David Taylor and Douglas DeNatale, September 12, 1989, at Gilroy, California. IAW-DT-R020.

30. Interview with Chinto Conrotto, Rose Conrotto, and Jean Conrotto Burr by David Taylor and Douglas DeNatale, September 12, 1989, at Gilroy, California. IAW-DT-R020.

31. Interview with Chinto Conrotto, Rose Conrotto, and Jean Conrotto Burr by David Taylor and Douglas DeNatale, September 12, 1989, at Gilroy, California. IAW-DT-R020.

32. The A. Conrotto Winery also produces three fruit wines (apricot, cherry, and plum), cream sherry, and wine vinegar.

33. Interview with Chinto Conrotto, Rose Conrotto, and Jean Conrotto Burr by David Taylor and Douglas DeNatale, September 12, 1989, at Gilroy, California. IAW-DT-R021.

34. Interview with Chinto Conrotto, Rose Conrotto, and Jean Conrotto Burr by David Taylor and Douglas DeNatale, September 12, 1989, at Gilroy, California. IAW-DT-R020.

35. Interview with Jim Burr and Scott Burr by

David Taylor, Douglas DeNatale, John Alexander Williams, and Paola Tavarelli, September 17, 1989, at Gilroy, California. IAW-DT-A007.

36. The notion of curatorial responsibility is discussed by Grant McCracken in his book *Culture & Consumption: New Approaches to the Symbolic Character of Consumer Goods and Activities* (Bloomington: Indiana University Press, 1990), 44–53.

37. Interview with Chinto Conrotto, Rose Conrotto, and Jean Conrotto Burr by David Taylor and Douglas DeNatale, September 12, 1989, at Gilroy, California. IAW-DT-R021.

38. The marketing of kinship, and other aspects of family businesses, are discussed by James F. Abrams in his study *"It's Just Like Being at Home": The Structure and Style of Folklore in Philadelphia's Family Businesses,* Philadelphia Folklore Project Working Paper No. 3 (Philadelphia: Philadelphia Folklore Project, 1989).

39. Abrams, *"It's Just Like Being at Home,"* 11.

40. There are over seventy wineries in California that are operated by Italian-Americans.

"Get on One End of the Rope and Pull Together"

1. According to Russell DiSalvo, whose family came from Sicily, the workers were recruited in Italy, lived in company housing in Louisiana and worked to pay off their obligations to the company that had brought them over (IAW-RF-A051). This code and all others like it in these notes refer to fieldnotes or audiocassettes recorded in Pueblo in June-July 1990 and housed in the Library of Congress.

2. IAW-RF-A059.
3. IAW-RF-F070890.A.
4. IAW-RF-A035.
5. IAW-RF-A054.
6. IAW-RF-A042.
7. IAW-RF-A033.
8. IAW-RF-A032.
9. IAW-RF-A053.
10. IAW-RF-F062690.B.
11. IAW-RF-A039.
12. IAW-RF-A040.
13. IAW-RF-A050.
14. IAW-RF-A033.
15. IAW-RF-A033.
16. IAW-RF-A054.
17. IAW-RF-A039.
18. IAW-RF-A050.
19. IAW-RF-A032.
20. IAW-RF-A032. What the folks in town could not grow for themselves they could buy from their kin and countrymen who had ten- to twenty-acre vegetable farms just east of town on St. Charles Mesa. Further afield, in Vineland, Walsenburg, and Trinidad, were larger farms, including goat farms where Italian families bought their cheese and their Easter kids.

21. IAW-RF-A049.
22. IAW-RF-A044.
23. IAW-RF-A045.
24. IAW-RF-A041.
25. IAW-RF-A045.
26. IAW-RF-A041.
27. IAW-RF-A049.
28. IAW-RF-A037.
29. IAW-RF-A032.
30. IAW-RF-A035.
31. IAW-RF-A032.
32. IAW-RF-A039.
33. IAW-RF-A037.
34. IAW-RF-A049.
35. IAW-RF-A044.
36. IAW-RF-F062890.A.
37. IAW-RF-F062590.A.
38. IAW-RF-F062790.A.
39. IAW-RF-F062490.A.
40. IAW-RF-F062490.A.
41. IAW-RF-A035.
42. IAW-RF-A038.
43. IAW-RF-A033.
44. IAW-RF-A032. See Richard Alba, "The Twilight of Ethnicity Among Americans of European Ethnicity: The Case of Italians," *Ethnic and Racial Studies* 8 (1985), 136–37, for a description of the conditions in the rural villages of the south that led to the mass immigration of unskilled labor. Though the fathers and grandfathers of many of the people I interviewed sent money back to Italy, I did not hear of anyone who intended to return permanently to live.

45. IAW-RF-A057.
46. IAW-RF-A039. The rise in the intermarriage rate is charted in Alba, 149–53.
47. IAW-RF-A035.
48. IAW-RF-A032.
49. IAW-RF-A049.
50. IAW-RF-A039.
51. IAW-RF-F062890.A.
52. IAW-RF-A047.
53. IAW-RF-A040. In 1990, three of Pueblo's five city council members were Italian-Americans. As further proof, perhaps, of Italian assimilation in Pueblo, it is worth noting that while many of the town's Italians felt obliged to mention the presence of these men on the council, they were quick to distance themselves politically from these elected leaders.
54. IAW-RF-A032.
55. IAW-RF-A043.
56. IAW-RF-A046.
57. IAW-RF-A049.
58. IAW-RF-A046.
59. IAW-RF-A059. I would agree with Alba that these few, albeit important, vestiges of Italian family life constitute the "twilight of ethnicity" among Italian-Americans. Alba, 152–53.

Shaping Tradition

1. I use the terms *Sicilian, Italian,* and *Slovenian* to refer to American-born or naturalized Americans with those ethnic heritages. I use the term *Hispanic* to refer to Americans who trace their ancestry to Mexico, New Mexico, Spain, or a combination of the three locations.

2. Richard Handler and Jocelyn Linnekin, "Tradition, Genuine or Spurious," *Journal of American Folklore* 97:385 (1984): 273–90.

3. Sarah Deutsch, *No Separate Refuge: Culture, Class and Gender on an Anglo-Hispanic Frontier in the American Southwest, 1880–1940* (New York: Oxford University Press, 1987).

4. Pamela K. Quaggiotto, *Altars of Food to Saint Joseph: Women's Ritual in Sicily.* Ph.D. diss., Columbia University, 1988.

5. Most of the descriptions come from tables created in private homes. It should be noted, however, that two churches in Pueblo have annual tables. Louise Williams, Eve Taravella, and Dorothy Zanini began to make tables at the Shrine of Saint Therese about seven years ago. The other public table, at Holy Rosary Church, is discussed in the essay's last section.

6. The Saint Joseph's Day table is very much a family-based, women-centered event. Two works that explore the tradition in terms of gender and sexuality are by Quaggiotto, op. cit.; and *'Giving an Altar': The Ideology of Reproduction in a St. Joseph's Day Feast,* by Kay Turner and Suzanne Seriff in the *Journal of American Folklore* 100 (1987): 446–60. For a critique of Turner and Seriff's article, see Diane Christian, "No New Truths and All the Old Falsehoods," *Journal of American Folklore* 101 (1988): 53–55.

7. Quaggiotto, op. cit.; Suzanne Seriff, personal communication 1991.

8. Seriff and Turner, p. 448.

9. Quaggiotto, op. cit.

10. Turner and Seriff, p. 448.

11. Estes, David C., "Across Ethnic Boundaries: St. Joseph's Day in a New Orleans Afro-American Spiritual Church," in *Mississippi Folklore* 21: 1–2 (1987).

12. For information on the labor history of the region's mines and steel industry, see Sarah Deutsch, op. cit.; Philip F. Notarianni, "Italian Involvement in the 1903–04 Coal Miner's Strike in Southern Colorado and Utah," *Pane e Lavoro: The Italian American Working Class,* ed. George E. Pozzetta (Toronto: The Multicultural Historical Society of Ontario, 1980), 47–65; Bobbalee Shuler, "Scab Labor in the Colorado Coal Fields: A Statistical Study of Replacement Workers in the Columbine Strike of 1927–28," *Essays and Monographs in Colorado History,* no. 8 (Denver: The State Historical Society of Colorado, 1988); Barron B. Beshoar, *Out of the Depths: The Story of John R. Lawson, A Labor Leader* (Denver: The Colorado Labor Historical Committee of the Denver Area Labor Federation, 1980); and Zeese Papanikolas, *Buried Unsung: Louis Tikas and the Ludlow Massacre* (Lincoln: University of Nebraska, 1982).

13. Quaggiotto, op. cit.; Kay Turner, "Mexican American Home Altars: Towards Their Interpretation," *Aztlan,* vol. 13, 1982.

14. Quaggiotto, op. cit.

The Columbus Complex

1. On the role of Ligurians in early San Francisco, see Alessandro Baccari and Andrew Canepa, eds., Olga Richardson, trans., "The Italians of San Francisco in 1865: G. B. Cerruti's Report to the Ministry of Foreign Affairs," *California History,* vol. 60, no. 4 (winter 1981/82), 350–69. Four of the six founders of the nation's oldest Italian-American organization were natives of Genoa or its environs. (*La Societa Italiana di Mutua Beneficenza: The Early Years* [San Francisco: The Society, 1983], 52–57.) On Noce and Colorado, see B. R. Cassigoli and Ettore Chiarglione, *Libro d'Oro degli Italiani in American con Descrizioni e Biografi* (Pueblo: L'Unione [?], n.d. [1906?]), esp. 244–45 and International Publishing Company, *Attivita Italiane nella Intermountain West* (Salt Lake City: The Company, 1930).

2. Dino Cinel, *From Italy to San Francisco: The Immigrant Experience* (Stanford: Stanford University Press, 1982), 21, 29; U.S. Senate, 61st Congress; 2nd session, Document 633, *Reports of the Immigration [Dillingham] Commission: Immigrants in Industries. Part 25: Japanese and Other Immigrant Races in the Pacific Coast and Rocky Mountain States. Volume I: Diversified Industries,* 76, 116–17, 242–43, 267, 271, 309; *Volume II: Agriculture* (Washington: Government Printing Office, 1911; repr New York: Arno Press, 1970), 459–67, 549–54, 712, 758, 848–49.

3. Charles Speroni, "California Fishermen's Festivals," *Western Folklore Quarterly* XV:1 (January 1955), 77–83; Howard S. Becker, "Blessing the Fishing Fleet in San Francisco," *Society* 11:4 (May/June 1974), 83–85. On the matter of secular vs. clerical influences in public celebrations, I am indebted to Andrew Canepa, curator, Italian-American Collection, San Francisco Public Library, and August Troiani, secretary, Societa Italiana di Mutua Beneficenza, for their insights and suggestions for further research. See also *San Francisco Chronicle,* September 25, 1870, p. 3, and October 25, 1870, p. 3; and *San Francisco Daily Examiner,* October 24, 1870, p. 3. For Italian roots of California banking and agribusiness, see *Reports of the Immigration Commission, Part 25: Volume II,* 465–67; Cinel, *From Italy to San Francisco,* 134–61, 228–55, and Andrew Rolle, *The Immigrant Upraised. Italian Adventurers and Colonists in an Expanding America* (Norman: University of Oklahoma Press, 1968), 272–75.

4. Giovanni Perilli, *Colorado and the Italians in*

Colorado (Denver, 1910); John B. Molinari, "The History of San Francisco's Columbus Day Celebration," in 1977 Columbus Day Committee, *Program* (San Francisco, 1977), 29–30; *San Francisco Chronicle,* October 12, 1885, p. 1, October 14, 1889, p. 8.

5. Alessandro Baccari et al, *Saints Peter & Paul Church: The Chronicles of "the Italian cathedral" of the West, 1884–1984* (San Francisco: Alessandro Baccari, Jr., for Saints Peter and Paul Church, 1985); *San Francisco Examiner,* October 22, 1892, p. 3.

6. *San Francisco Chronicle,* October 17, 1904, p. 12, October 13, 1909, p. 9, October 13, 1910, p. 9, October 12, 1913, p. 12, October 13, 1913, p. 8; *San Francisco Examiner,* October 12, 1909, pp. 3, 5, October 18, 1910, p. 4, October 13, 1921, p. 6, October 17, 1921, p. 11; *Los Angeles Herald,* October 13, 1910, p. 13. The first mock landing was held in 1885 (*Chronicle,* October 12, 1885, p. 1; *Examiner,* October 17, 1885, p. 8).

7. Charles Speroni, "The Development of the Columbus Day Pageant of San Francisco," *Western Folklore Quarterly* VII:4 (October 1948), 325–35; Molinari, "History of San Francisco's Columbus Day Celebration," 29–33; Steven M. Blau, "The History of the Columbus Day Celebration in San Francisco," (mss., Italian-American Collection, San Francisco Public Library).

8. I am grateful to Andrew Canepa, August Troiani, and Alessandro Baccari for explaining the organizational structure of past celebrations and to Ronald J. Derenzi, president, and Eve Sodo, secretary, of the 1989 Columbus Day Celebration, Incorporated, for information on the latest celebration and for written materials, such as "1989 Columbus Day Schedule of Events" (copy in possession of the author). For the role of Joseph Cervetto and his son as Columbus impersonators, see *San Francisco Chronicle,* October 3, 1987, p. 5. For earlier Columbus impersonators, see Speroni, "The Development of the Columbus Day Pageant," p. 334. For a similar negative assessment by community leaders of a commercial food and street fair, see Anthony T. Rauche, "Festa Italiana in Hartford, Connecticut: The Pastries, the Pizza, and the People who 'Parlo Italiano,'" in Theodore C. Humphrey and Lin T. Humphrey, eds., *We Gather Together: Food and Festival in American Life* (Ann Arbor: UMI Research Press, 1988), 205–17.

9. *San Francisco Chronicle,* October 12, 1981, p. 2, October 8, 1984, p. 10, October 14, 1985, p. A3, October 5, 1986, p. B4.

10. Quoted in Blau, "A History of the Columbus Day Celebrations in San Francisco," p. 52ff.

11. *Ibid.,* p. 49.

12. Phyllis Cancilla Martinelli, "From Ethnic Enclave to Ethnic Dispersion: Residence Patterns of Italian Immigrants," paper presented to the Pacific Sociological Association Annual Conference, March 27, 1976; interview with Alessandro Baccari, May 22,

1989; *San Francisco Chronicle,* January 26, 1978, p. 6, October 4, 1981, p. 4, September 5, 1988, p. A8.

13. Victoria Cristiano Marion, "Pueblo Mosaic," *Pueblo Chieftain,* undated clipping [1970s?], Columbus Day clipping file, McClelland Library.

14. Jenny Pingatore, interviewed by Victoria Cristiano Marion, June 21, 1978 (transcript in "Pueblo Mosaic Project" file, McClelland Library), p. 9.

15. Unless otherwise noted, my account of Charles Musso's activities is based on an interview with Musso, June 25, 1990. Interview notes have been transcribed and deposited as IAW-JW-F062590.A, American Folklife Center, Library of Congress.

16. Russell Frank's interviews with Joe Genova and Paul Palermo (IAW-RF-A032, A033); Ralph, Pete, and Nettie Montera (IAW-RF-A039), Tony Martellaro (IAW-RF-A042), Pete Carleo (IAW-RF-A047), and Sam Catalano (IAW-RF-A049) document the ethnic factor in job distribution and promotion at CF&I (American Folklife Center, Library of Congress). See also "WICHE project" interview with Mr. and Mrs. Lee Martinez of Salt Creek, McClelland Public Library. (Martinez changed his name first to Martini, then to Martin, to aid in job-seeking, which gives practical force to Pueblo's ethnic pecking order.) Social interaction among Italian- and Mexican-American families is documented in the "Pueblo Mosaic" interviews with Josephine Carnelli and Victoria Cristiano Marion (McClelland Public Library) and in the fieldwork of Paula Manini, Bea Roeder, and Paola Tavarelli in the Library of Congress IAW project.

17. Interview with Charles Musso, June 25, 1990, transcript p. 2.

18. A Columbus Day clipping file in McClelland Public Library documents the growth and elaboration of Columbus Day activities since 1927. See especially *Pueblo Chieftain* clippings from October 10, 1947, October 10, 1978, October 11, 1988, October 10, 1989.

19. *Denver Post,* April 12, 1988, p. A1.

20. *Denver Post,* October 10, 1989, 1B, 2B, October 9, 1990, 1B, 3B, Colorado Quincentenary Commission, undated announcement, 1991.

21. Richard D. Alba, "The Twilight of Ethnicity among Americans of European Ancestry: the Case of the Italians," *Ethnic and Racial Studies* 8:1 (January 1985), 134–54; Alba and Mitchell Chamlin, *Italian-Americans: Into the Twilight of Ethnicity* (Englewood Cliffs, N.J.: Prentice Hall, 1985). Cf. Micaela di Leonardo, *The Varieties of Ethnic Experience: Kinship, Class, and Gender among California Italian-Americans* (Ithaca: Cornell University Press, 1984) and Phyllis Cancilla Martinelli, *Ethnicity in the Sunbelt. Italian American Migrants in Scottsdale, Arizona* (New York: AMS Press, 1989).

Thomas Carter records details of Louie Gibellini's blacksmith shop, Eureka, Nevada. Photograph by Valerie Parks, IAW-VP-B003-4

Doug DeNatale tries his hand at *bocce* on a court used by a group of Italian-American men in Gilroy, California. Photograph by David A. Taylor, IAW-DT-B019-31A

Russell Frank interviews Italian-American women preparing meatballs in the kitchen of Our Lady of Mt. Carmel Church, Pueblo, Colorado. The meatballs and other foods were sold the next day at the annual Our Lady of Mt. Carmel Festival. Photograph by David A. Taylor, IAW-DT-B003-9

CONTRIBUTORS

Thomas Carter is a folklorist teaching in the University of Utah's Graduate School of Architecture. His research has focused on the vernacular architecture of the western United States, and particularly on the early architecture associated with the Mormon settlement of the Great Basin. He has been a coeditor of *Perspectives in Vernacular Architecture* and wrote, with Carl Fleischhauer, *The Grouse Creek Cultural Survey* (1988).

Douglas DeNatale is the director of the Center for Folklife and Oral History at the University of South Carolina. In 1987, he served as project coordinator for the American Folklife Center's Lowell Folklife Project. Dr. DeNatale has contributed articles on folklife and cultural conservation to many publications.

Russell Frank is a folklorist and journalist who lives in Sonora, California. He spends half his time writing for *The Modesto Bee* and half engaged in field research for cultural institutions throughout the country. Dr. Frank wrote a doctoral dissertation on the traditional narratives of California's "Gold Country," and it includes many stories told by and about Italian ranchers and miners.

Jens Lund teaches in the Liberal Studies Program at the University of Washington, Tacoma. He has been the director of the Washington State Folklore Council and is the author of *Folk Arts of Washington State* (1989). He has organized logger poetry gatherings in the timber communities of the Pacific Northwest and managed a Samoan "street doo-wop" group from Seattle's inner city. Dr. Lund lives in Olympia, Washington.

Paula Manini is regional property administrator for the Colorado Historical Society at the Baca House, Bloom House, and Pioneer Museum in Trinidad, Colorado. An anthropology and folklore student at the University of Texas at

Austin, she is writing a master's report, "'Saint Joseph Isn't Just for Italians': A Hispanic Recreation of a Sicilian Home Altar Tradition," based on data from Pueblo, Colorado, collected during the Italian-Americans in the West Project. She has been a curatorial assistant in the Anthropology and History Department at the Texas Memorial Museum and program coordinator at Texas Folklife Resources in Austin.

Philip F. Notarianni is the coordinator of public programs for the Utah State Historical Society and an adjunct professor in the Ethnic Studies and Liberal Education programs at the University of Utah. A resident of Magna, Utah, Dr. Notarianni is the son of Italian immigrant parents and is married to Maria Teresa Maletta, an immigrant from Calabria. During the 1987–88 academic year, he researched the places of origin of Calabresi in Utah under a Fulbright Research Grant. He has served as a member of the temporary faculty in cultural anthropology for the University of Calabria in Cosenza, Italy.

Blanton Owen is a folklorist and commercial pilot who has worked for the Bureau of Florida Folklife Programs; the Blue Ridge Institute, Ferrum, Virginia; and the American Folklife Center. He started the folklife program at the Mountain Heritage Center, Western Carolina University, Cullowhee, North Carolina; was senior folklorist for the Stokely Folklife Festival at the 1982 World's Fair in Knoxville, Tennessee; and inaugurated the folklife program and archive for the Nevada State Council on the Arts, Reno. At work on two publications about the vernacular architecture of the West, he lives in Virginia City, Nevada.

Jens Lund changes tape reels during fieldwork for the American Folklife Center's Pinelands Folklife Project, 1983. Photograph by Joseph Czarnecki, 7-276899-36

Paula Manini (left) interviews Eve Taravella, Louise Williams, and Dorothy Zanini at Taravella's home in Pueblo, Colorado. Photograph by Ken Light, IAW-B195-35

Historian Philip F. Notarianni at the Spring Glen, Utah, home of Vito and Filomena Bonacci, during fieldwork in Carbon County. Photograph by Steve Siporin, IAW-SS-C012-2

Blanton Owen leans against the prop of the aircraft he used to visit the isolated eastern Nevada communities where he conducted field research. Photograph by Andrea Graham, IAW-AG-B005-15A

Steve Siporin doing "in-depth" *forno* documentation in Helper, Utah. Photograph by Thomas Carter, IAW-TC-B005-17A

Paola Tavarelli helps with the grape harvest at the A. Conrotto Winery, Gilroy, California. Photograph by David A. Taylor, IAW-DT-B020-5A

David Taylor (second from right) and Paola Tavarelli (third from right) interview members of an extended family at the home of Susan and Ken Cuchiara, Pueblo, Colorado. Photograph by Ken Light, IAW-KL-B264-5

John Alexander Williams prepares to sample a meatball sandwich at Collette's Catering and Take-Out, Pueblo, Colorado. Photograph by David A. Taylor, IAW-DT-B025-16A

Steve Siporin is associate professor of English and history in the Folklore Program at Utah State University, Logan. He has lived and studied in Italy and wrote his dissertation on Venetian Jews. Dr. Siporin is working on a translation of the memoirs of Augusto Segre, a Jewish-Italian author. He has curated an exhibition of Idaho folk art and edited the accompanying catalog, *"We Came to Where We Were Supposed To Be": Folk Art of Idaho.* He is the author of *American Folk Masters: The National Heritage Fellows* (1992).

Paola Tavarelli is a folklorist from Carrara, Italy, where her family is engaged in the marble business for which the region is noted. She has pursued her studies at the University of Florence and at the University of California, Los Angeles, where she was recruited by David Taylor for the Italian-Americans in the West Project.

David A. Taylor is a folklife specialist at the American Folklife Center in Washington, D.C., whose expertise is in the areas of material culture, occupational folklife, traditional design systems, and maritime culture. His books include *Boatbuilding in Winterton, Trinity Bay, Newfoundland* (1982) and *Documenting Maritime Folklife* (1992). In addition to fieldwork conducted in connection with the Italian-Americans in the West Project, Dr. Taylor has carried out extensive research in maritime communities in Maine, Florida, Newfoundland, and Norway.

John Alexander Williams is professor of history and director of the Center for Appalachian Studies at Appalachian State University, Boone, North Carolina. He was the director of the Christopher Columbus Quincentenary Jubillee Commission, 1986–88, and consultant to the American Folklife Center, 1989–91. He has taught at the universities of Notre Dame, Illinois (Chicago), and West Virginia, and served on the staff of the National Endowment for the Humanities. Dr. Williams is the author of two books and many articles on American regional, cultural, and social history.